The Shaping of the Celtic World

Also by Patrick Lavin

Thank You Ireland:
Some Phenomenal Success Stories of the Irish in North America

Celtic Ireland West of the River Shannon:
A Look Back at the Rich Heritage and Dynastic Structure of the Gaelic Clans

The Celtic World: An Illustrated History

Arizona: An Illustrated History

New Mexico: An Illustrated History

The Navajo Nation: A Visitor's Guide

Ancestral Quest: Tracing My Ancestors in Ireland

The Shaping of the Celtic World

And the Resurgence of the Celtic Consciousness in the 19th and 20th Centuries

Patrick Lavin

iUniverse, Inc.
Bloomington

The Shaping of the Celtic World
And the Resurgence of the Celtic Consciousness in the 19th and 20th Centuries

iUniverse books may be ordered through booksellers or by contacting:

iUniverse
1663 Liberty Drive
Bloomington, IN 47403
www.iuniverse.com
1-800-Authors (1-800-288-4677)

Cataloging-in-Publication Data available from the Library of Congress.

1. Europe—Celtic peoples—prehistory—Bronze Age—pre-Christian.
2. Celtic expansion—Gaul—Greece—Rome—Iberia—Caesar.
3. Roman Empire—Carthage—Po Valley—Etruscans—Celtic decline.
4. Rhine—Danube—Neckar—Thames—Galatia—Marseilles—Cadiz.
5. Britain—Ireland—Wales—Scotland—Cornwall—Mann—Brittany.
6. Indo-European—Hallstatt—Beaker Folk—Urnfielders—La Tène.
7. Druids—King Arthur—Picts—Saxons—Scots—Germans—Lugh.
8. Saint Patrick—monasticism—Britons—Welsh—Vikings—Normans.
9. Isle of Man—Celtic Christianity—Gaelic Order—Galacia—Britonia.

ISBN: 978-1-4620-6087-0 (sc)
ISBN: 978-1-4620-6088-7 (ebk)

Printed in the United States of America

iUniverse rev. date: 11/02/2011

For my children, Debbie, Frank and Edie;
my sisters, Anna and Freda; and
my cousins, Eileen, Nanette and Jim.

They feared nothing except that the sky would fall on their heads.

—Celtic chieftain comment to Alexander the Great (355 BC)

Acknowledgments

I am grateful to those who helped make this book possible. I am indebted, as always, to my wife for reading the book in manuscript format—her invaluable help and constructive ideas added a great deal to the enhancement and clarity of the text. I am also indebted to my daughter for her assistance in getting the book into artistic shape for publication. Thank you, Joan and Edie, for the inspiration and support you provided along the journey.

There are those, of course, who contributed in other ways and whose help I am thankful for: the many Wikipedia users (acknowledged in the List of Illustrations) who generously uploaded the photographs, maps, and images that were used herein; and the many historians and archeologists (acknowledged in the Bibliography) whose citations will be evident throughout the book.

TABLE OF CONTENTS

List of Illustrations

Illustration No. 9: Kingdoms of Great Britain
Map by Wikipedia User "Sakurambo"

Illustration No. 10: Battersea Shield
Photograph by Wikipedia User "QuartierLatin 1968"

Illustration No. 11: Desborough Mirror
Photograph by Wikipedia User "Fuzzypeg"

Illustration No. 12: Wandsworth Shield
Photograph by Wikipedia User "Johnbod"

Illustration No. 13: Waterloo Helmet
Photograph by Wikipedia User "Ealdgyth"

Illustration No. 14: Wales in the Roman Era
Map by Wikipedia User "Notuncurious"

Illustration No. 15: Aberlemno Cross
Photograph by Anne Burgess

Illustration No. 16: Hunterston Brooch
Photograph by Wikipedia User "Johnbod"

Illustration No. 17: Ancient Ireland
Image in the public domain—copyright has expired

Illustration No. 18: Glendalough Round Tower
Photograph by Wikipedia User "Superbass"

Illustration No. 19: Gallarus Oratory
Photograph by Wikipedia User "Ingo Mehling"

Illustration No. 20: Gundestrup Cauldron
Photograph by Malene Thyssen

Illustration No. 21: Ragstone Head
Photograph by Wikipedia User "CeStu"

Illustration No. 22: Tara Brooch
Image in the public domain—copyright has expired

Illustration No. 23: Ardagh Chalice
Photograph by Wikipedia User "Kglavin"

Illustration No. 24: Book of Kells
Image in the public domain—copyright has expired

Illustration No. 25: Kingdoms of Ireland
Map by Wikipedia User "Erigena"

Chapter I—

The Celtic People: An Introduction

During the last millennium B.C., to the northwest of the Alps, over a territory ranging from France, across southern Germany, as far as Bohemia, a remarkable people was evolving and taking on the form in which they became known to history.

—Jan Filip

The story of the Celtic people is one of the most remarkable in the history of ancient Europe. Their destiny carried them in a few short centuries over the greater part of the continent, which they conquered and colonized. They laid the foundation for western European civilization; before the rise of the Roman Empire, their influence was felt across Europe from Asia Minor to the Atlantic seaboard. A remarkable people endowed with artistic talent and technological skills, the Celts were among the finest metal craftsmen of the ancient world. From Celtic workshops have come some of the most magnificent treasures of early Europe—gold and bronze crafted into amazingly vibrant art. This art borrowed freely from Classical and Eastern sources and preserved a particular brand of Celtic distinctiveness. It was the Celts who invented chain armor, though they often preferred to fight naked. They were the first to shoe horses and to shape handsaws, chisels, and other tools. They invented seamless iron rims for their chariot wheels, as well as the iron plowshare. In fact, it would not be an overstatement to say that it was the Celts who created Europe's first major industrial revolution.

Their legacy includes a host of famous place-names. Many great rivers of northern and central Europe—the Rhine, Danube, Neckar, Thames, and numerous others—owe their names to remote Celtic antiquity. The great cities of London, Belgrade, and Paris preserve in their names the presence of otherwise forgotten Celts. In the many areas of Continental Europe inhabited by Celtic peoples, significant excavations and finds have brought their material culture to light and established, for future generations, instant contact with the realness of Celtic civilization. The most spectacular excavations have been those of the "princely" graves in Germany and France; the most notable, possibly, that of Dürrnberg near Salzburg in Austria. There, excavation of a prehistoric salt-mining settlement, consisting of a village and a cemetery with two thousand graves, yielded a vast collection of artifacts. (Hubert 1988, xiii)

Spread of Celtic Realms

The Celts originated in homelands at the headwaters of the Rhine and Danube rivers. It was there the first identifiable Celtic period (dating from around 700 BC) was named after *Hallstatt*, a town near Salzburg in the Salzkammergut area of Austria. From there they moved westward across what was later called Gaul, and southwards into the Iberian peninsula as far as present-day Cadiz, which they reached sometime before 450 BC. At about the same time, other Celtic tribes moved southwards over the Alps, occupying the Po River valley in northern Italy. It is believed some tribes may have reached as far as Rome, even as far south as Sicily. (King 1998, 21)

Other tribes would later follow an eastward course through Macedonia, invading Greece via Thrace and Thessaly. They attacked the Temple of Delphi in 279 BC. As many as twenty-five thousand Celts went even further eastwards into Asia Minor and settled the area that became Galatia (in present-day Turkey). On the Atlantic seaboard there were frequent movements between Armorica (present-day Brittany) and southwestern Britain and Ireland. The last great western migration in pre-classical times resulted from incursions of the *Belgae* tribes from northern Gaul into southern Britain and Ireland about 250 BC. (King 1998, 63)

The third century marked the climax of Celtic expansion, at which time Celtic peoples were occupying a vast area stretching from Ireland in the west to the Black Sea in the east. Some of those who had moved eastward mingled with the Hellenistic world, opening up their culture to more material comfort than that of their kinfolk who had moved westward. The Celts spread their dominion—both by conquest and by peaceful incursion—across Europe. They moved into areas formerly occupied by Paleolithic and Neolithic peoples, dolmen builders, and workers in bronze. They did not annihilate these indigenous inhabitants; instead they imposed on them an aristocratic ruling social order and their Celtic language, arts, and traditions. (Rolleston 1911, 20)

Gaul Killing Himself and His Wife, circa 200 AD
(National Museum of Rome, Italy).
Located in the Palazzo Altemps, this marble sculpture—also known as "Galatian Suicide"—is a copy of the Hellenistic original from 200 BC.

Roman Expansion

In 225 BC, after a century and a half of Celtic aggression, the Romans finally won a decisive victory over a huge Celtic army at the Battle of Telamon near Rome. This marked the turning point in the Celtic-Roman conflict. In the aftermath of the second Punic War (218-202 BC), Rome embarked on the first significant stage of its territorial expansion. On all fronts—in Iberia, southern Gaul, the Po valley, and Asia Minor—Rome confronted Celtic armies. By 192 BC, Celtic domination of the northern Italian peninsula had come to an end.

As Rome expanded from a city-state to a powerful Empire, the Celtic realms crumbled, one after the other, from the onslaught of Roman thirst for conquest and power. In 52 BC, the Romans overran Gaul (then the center of the Celtic world) and all but wiped out Celtic culture there. The Celts of Cisalpine Gaul were the first to surrender, followed in succession by the Celts of Iberia, Transalpine Gaul, and Gaul proper. After a century or more of fierce warfare on the Iberian peninsula, the Romans succeeded in subduing the Celtic tribes in the Celtiberian Wars of 29-19 BC.

The Romans went on to conquer the Celts in Britain in AD 47 and, thereafter, occupied the island for three hundred and fifty years. By the end of the first century AD, most of the land previously occupied by the Celtic peoples southwest of the Rhine-Danube line was under Roman occupation. To the north of the Danube, the Celtic territories of Bohemia and Moravia were in the hands of German tribes. Only the Celts of Ireland and northern Britain escaped Roman rule. The Romans conquered Europe in the same way the Celts had much earlier, the difference being the Romans did it with the backing of centralized political and military power, whereas the Celts relied on a loose alliance of tribal armies lacking unified leadership. It was only along the extreme northwestern periphery, in north and west Caledonia and in Ireland, that Celtic-speaking communities continued to exist outside the Roman system.

Decline of the Celts

Conquered by the Romans and overshadowed by Roman civilization, Celtic society began a steady decline throughout Europe. This decline accelerated in the late third century AD with the migration of German-Frankish tribes south into Gaul and beyond. By the early fifth century, much of Gaul and other areas had been brought under Frankish domination. In Britain, Anglo-Saxon settlement had advanced rapidly across most of the Romanized southeast of the island. The surviving Celtic tribes of Britain and Ireland were also on the move during this period. In the fourth century, Celtic tribes from southeast Ireland established permanent settlements in Cornwall and southwest Wales, while in the western region of present-day Scotland tribes from northeast Ireland took control of a large territory from the Picts. These Irish settlers brought with them their own distinct dialect of the Celtic language. Another movement took place from south Wales and southwestern England across the Channel to present-day Brittany. The reason for this migration, according to some sources, was pressure from the Saxon advance from the east. The Irish expansion into Wales is also believed to have played a part.

Celtic communities of the Atlantic area survived in different degrees of isolation throughout the early Middle Ages. The Viking attacks, which began in the eighth century, ravaged coastal areas of Scotland, Ireland, Cornwall and Brittany. In Scotland and parts of eastern Ireland settlement followed, introducing a strong Scandinavian element to local culture. Later, the westward advance of the Normans established a hold on Wales and in parts of Ireland. Subsequently, the remaining Celtic populations fell victim to the growing imperialism of England and France.

Wales fought off Anglo-Norman incursions, with some success at times, until she was compelled to surrender her sovereignty to the English crown in 1284. Six years later in 1290, the first step was undertaken to consolidate Scotland under the jurisdiction of the English crown. It was not until 1603, however, that Scotland also surrendered her self-determination. One hundred and four years later (1707), Scotland gave up its political independence and entered into complete union with England. In 1532, Brittany, which had flourished as a self-ruling duchy for centuries, finally merged with the developing nation of France to become the last of the continental European Celtic kingdoms to lose its independence. Only in Ireland, where Roman influence was never established, did the old style of Celtic culture and customs continue and flourish. Throughout the Middle Ages, Celtic Ireland was from time to time in retreat, but it was a slow and stubborn retreat until the seventeenth century when it, too, finally collapsed.

While Britain and France were imposing their values and rule of law on their Celtic subjects, they were inadvertently creating a new spirit of Celtic revivalism. The Celtic past, in all its manifestations, took on a renewed consciousness. This consciousness had five key dynamics. Firstly, the onset of the printed medium made the classical writings of Greek and Roman authors more widely available from the sixteenth century onward. This gave historians easier access to what early historians had to say about the early Celts. Secondly, in Britain, Ireland, and France, an increasing knowledge of prehistoric monuments and artifacts helped create a vision of the past. Thirdly, the heroic epics, law tracts, and folk tales of Ireland (and to a lesser extent Wales) offered an incredible source of information for historians to explore early Celtic society in all its details. Fourthly, archaeological advances in the nineteenth and twentieth centuries provided a new reality through the discovery, first of the weapons and artifacts used by Celtic peoples, and later of the settlements in which they had lived and the growth of the economies which had sustained them. Finally, in the first half of the twentieth century, the art of the Celts came to be recognized as a subject worthy of study, making it possible to bridge the gap between the classical vision, mythical tales, and archaeological reality.

The Celtic kingdoms of Ireland, Scotland, Wales, and Brittany, all but wiped out, were at the same time experiencing a rebirth of their Celtic heritage. Beneath the inspiration of eighteenth century Celtic revivalism was a strong undercurrent of nationalism. This was particularly true of Ireland where, in the nineteenth century, the Celtic legacy from the distant past took on a strong, stirring appeal as a symbol of unity. This led to the creation of the first independent Celtic state, the Irish Free State in 1922. More recently, Scotland and Wales were given a degree of self-rule within the United Kingdom. Brittany, however, remains a province of France.

Today, no national or ethnic group calls itself Celtic as its primary name, but in the view of many, "Celticness" is very much the cultural influence shared by several modern societies or peoples. In Scotland, Wales, Ireland, and Brittany, Celtic culture and political identity are still actively observed. In England, France, Spain, southern Germany, the Czech Republic, northern Italy, and the Balkans, traces of Celtic heritage still survive. And in the larger world—in the United States, Canada, Australia, and New Zealand—the legacy of Celtic culture, carried to those countries by Irish, Scot, Welsh, and Breton immigrants, flourishes.

Celtic culture and language have prevailed despite many setbacks throughout history. Gaelic is still spoken in the *Gaeltacht* along the western seaboard of Ireland. Welsh continues to be widely spoken throughout much of Wales, and the Welsh continue to honor their ancient Celtic bardic tradition each year at the National Eisteddfod. On the Isle of Man, Manx is still spoken by many of the islanders. Breton, the most widely spoken Celtic language in Europe, is the language of the people of Brittany. The Scottish Highlanders are proud of their Celtic language and heritage, as are their descendents who colonized the province of Nova Scotia in Canada. Although extinct since 1777 when the last native speaker died, Cornish is making a comeback.

One has only to imagine what the history of the Celts would have been had they left some written evidence of themselves compared to what we know of the Egyptians, the Greeks, the Romans, and even the Germans. Yet, Celtic traditions endured notwithstanding the challenges from the Goths, Huns, Vandals, Romans, and more recent spheres of influence. Celtic culture continued to flourish in many areas throughout the post-Roman era. After the Roman Empire collapsed, the Celts of Ireland (and to a lesser extent Wales and Scotland) enjoyed a cultural re-flowering that was to leave a legacy to the modern world. The greatest weakness of the Celts was their reliance on "natural superiority;" they never took it upon themselves to effectively organize their resources. Creating the *La Tène* culture seemed easy to them; organizing an empire evidently was a more challenging matter.

In material culture, the Celtic peoples heralded modern civilization. Their widespread use of iron enabled them to conquer vast tracts of land and to increase the amenities of life by felling forests and opening up new areas for agriculture. It revolutionized their method of warfare by making available in quantity the strong, iron slashing sword, and improved their economy by opening up hitherto undeveloped land, later to be controlled by their great hill-top towns or *oppida*. Yet they were separated by a great gulf from the greatest civilization of that world. They did not use the art of writing to any great extent and then not until near the end of their self-determination. They chose to record their past orally and communicated with other nations by word of mouth. Inescapably, we view the ancient Celtic peoples of continental Europe through Greek and Roman eyes, for they have left no written record of themselves. The Celtic peoples did not acquire the written word until the fifth century AD. (Chadwick 1971, 46)

What we know about the Celts comes from two sources: archaeological material and references from classical authors, mainly the Romans. As one might expect, the information available from classical historians is biased in one way or the other. Such is the nature of historical sources. The Celts themselves seem to have had an unyielding fixation against putting matters in writing. For writings from the Celtic-speaking peoples themselves, we had to wait until the eighth century AD, at which time the Irish (and to a lesser extent the Welsh and the Scots) began to record their traditions under the influence of the literate Christian-Latin culture.

Chapter II—

Origin and Characteristics of the Celts

Their aspect is terrifying . . . . They are very tall in stature, with rippling muscles under clear white skin. Their hair is blond, but not naturally so: they bleach it, to this day, artificially, washing it in lime and combing it back on their foreheads . . . . The way they dress is astonishing: they wear brightly colored and embroidered shirts, with trousers called bracae and cloaks fastened at the shoulder.

—Diodorus Sidulus (first century BC)

People we know today as Celts were one of several great prehistoric societies that flourished on the European continent during the first millennium BC. Along with the Dacians, Illyrians, and Thracians, they bordered on the northern frontiers of the more cultured societies that developed first in Greece and then in Rome. For a long time, little was known about these people until trade and commerce with their literate southern neighbors provided insight into their way of life and customs. Eventually, they acquired their place on the European stage as a powerful society, becoming one of the most advanced "barbarian" peoples of the then-known world. Their story begins in the prehistoric age, where archaeology and language are our only guides. They appear in the early Iron Age, beginning about the seventh century with a culture known as Hallstatt (named for a site in Upper Austria).

Who Were the Celts?

Historians agree that the Celts were a branch of the Indo-European speaking family from which most present-day Europeans originate. They were the first European people north of the Alps to merge into recorded history. Yet, the first references to them appear about the sixth century when the peoples of the Mediterranean cultures came face-to-face with them. Neither a race nor a nation, the Celts are best described as a broad ethnic group whose numerous tribes shared a common culture and spoke closely related dialects of a single language. Throughout their long history, they maintained their separateness, never developing to form a central government or anything resembling an empire. (Ellis 2001, 10)

Most archaeologists are in agreement that the Urnfield people were Celtic or, perhaps, proto-Celtic (meaning their language had not quite developed into a form which we would immediately recognize as Celtic today). Others argue that the Celts emerged in the Middle Bronze Age from a mixture of round-headed Beaker Folk from the south, descendant from Neolithic and ultimately Mesolithic stocks. The Urnfield cultural continuum is roughly dated from 1200 to 700 BC. These people were farming folk living in small communities who were skilled in working bronze and, towards the end of the period, working iron as well. In many places, they lived in hill-forts. They buried the cremated remains of their dead in urns of clay in flat cemeteries, accompanied by small personal items. It was this distinctive practice that identified them as Urnfielders. By 1100 BC, urn cremation had spread throughout the heart of Europe to present-day Italy, eastern France, Switzerland, Germany, and southern Poland. (Ellis 2001, 11)

Originally hunters, they evolved into semi-nomadic herders who began drifting away from the Steppes and into the lush valleys of central Europe where they settled in the Alpine region of present-day Austria. There among the indigenous tribes, they established a tripartite caste system of warrior-lord, farmer, and serf that matured into a Bronze Age culture known in archaeological terms as the Urnfield Culture of northern Europe. This culture is identified as having been centered in the Danube basin around eastern France and western Germany, later spreading into eastern Germany and south across the Alps into the Po Valley. It also extended southwest into southern France, across the Channel into Britain and Ireland, and is believed to have reached into the Iberian peninsula. It was at this juncture in history, about the late eighth century in the early Hallstatt period, from which the earliest definitive evidence distinguishing the Celtic people as a distinct and coherent society dates. The foremost technological characteristic that separated the Hallstatt tribes from their Urnfield predecessors was the substitution of iron for bronze in weapons and tools.

The foremost aspect of Celtic expansion, however, began circa 500 BC; over the next several centuries, Celtic tribes went on to conquer and colonize most of central and much of southwestern Europe. Archaeological evidence suggests that one of the primary reasons for this expansionism was the emergence of a new order of warrior clans that began to replace the late Hallstatt culture chieftain class from which a new culture was forged. This event may be looked upon as the time when the Celtic people moved out of the obscurity of barbarian Europe and into the civilized world of the Mediterranean, passing from prehistory to history.

They had arrived on the European stage as a warrior class and went on to become an amazing people that flourished before the Roman Empire spread its wings over Europe. As a group of peoples, they shared many bonds of social customs, art, religious practices, and of course language—which is spoken to this day in several European areas, particularly along the Atlantic seaboard in Ireland, Scotland, Wales, and western France.

Origin of Term "Celt"

The meaning of the term Celt is unclear. The Celts are said to have never called themselves "Celts" in sources known to historians before recent times. Henri Hubert writes that Medieval British and Irish sources, though they sometimes recognized the relationship between their languages, never expressed that relationship in ethnic terms and were probably unaware that their languages were any closer to one another than they were to Latin or Greek. The term is first found in Greek sources and may be a variant of the name given to the Anatolian branch of the family *Galatae*, which must itself be a variant of *Galli*, the name by which the Romans knew the Celts that occupied Gaul and Northern Italy. (Hubert 1988, xi)

When the Celts first emerge into recorded history, the few Greek records of them (before Alexander's time) speak only of a wild and uncivilized collection of tribes known as *Keltoi*, who dwelt in the distant lands of Italy, Spain, and beyond the Alps, all the way to the mysterious northern sea. (Freeman 2006, 5) The term "Galatae" would later become more widely used. The Romans consistently used "Galli" for all peoples of the Celtic language and culture. Whether this originally was the name of an individual tribe, or a description given by a wandering tribe or tribes to themselves, is not known nor has not been stated in the Classics. (Rankin 1996, 2) Diodorus Siculus (circa 60-30 BC) considered that the term "Celt" was the proper name for the people he was describing. Julius Caesar (100-44 BC) writes that the Gauls of his day referred to themselves as *Celtae*. (Ellis 2001, 9)

Celtic Language

The Celts spoke a language belonging to the great Indo-European family of languages, which included Teutonic, Balto-Slavonic, and the classical languages of Greek and Latin. In philological vernacular, it is known as Celtic and is recognizably akin to the surviving Celtic dialects of the present time. Much of what is known about the

Celtic language has come to us in the names of chieftains and tribes and, in particular, words and terms recorded as belonging to the Celtic people. There are other sources as well, including inscriptions incorporating Celtic words and names (but mainly written in Latin and more rarely in Greek) on altars and other monuments in the Celtic regions of the former Roman Empire, spanning from Britain to Asia Minor. Celtic place names have survived widely in France, Spain, and southern Italy, and to a lesser degree eastwards to Belgrade. In northwest Germany, they are common to the Rhine. The distributional evidence of Celtic place-names in western and central Europe conforms closely with the regions in which the Celts are known to have been the strongest, and in which their influence lasted the longest. (Herm 1976, 71)

The one essential element linking the tribes of the Hallstatt period was a common Celtic language. Celtic scholars believe this common Celtic was spoken before the start of the first millennium. Soon after, two distinct dialects of Celtic emerged, which are defined by their modern names—Goidelic and Brythonic, or the famous Q- and P-Celtic divisions. (Ellis 2001, 11)

Although Gallic (Brythonic) disappeared completely, the British linguistic group to which it belonged (P-Celtic) survived in the form of Cornish, Modern Welsh, and Breton and its four dialects, Tregorois, Leonard, Cornouaillais, and Vannetais. Goidelic developed into Modern Irish (*Erse*), Manx, and Scots Gaelic. When it comes to examining the evolution of the Celtic languages, we know more about Irish than any of the others. It is the closest of all Celtic languages to its early form, which we know as Indo-European Q-Celtic. (Markale 1993, 291-292)

The Celts were distinguished in various ways: by social organization, religion, dress, and methods of warfare. These are the characteristics on which the early historians particularly focused. However, the main distinction then, as now, was the language (which we previously mentioned was derived from Indo-European) sometimes referred to as the "Old-European language." Historians believe that around 1000 BC, Indo-European began to disintegrate into individual languages such as Italic (the early form of Latin), Germanic, Slavic, Baltic, and of course Celtic.

Professor Barry Cunliffe writes that the study of ancient European languages has shown that forms of Celtic were spoken over much of the Iberian peninsula, Britain, and Ireland, and yet there is no historical record of Celtic migrations into these areas. He writes that it was left to archaeologists and linguists to construct models of incursions from their two dissimilar viewpoints. In Iberia, classical sources indicated a Celtic presence by the sixth century BC; this was supported by linguistic arguments suggesting that the Celtic spoken on the peninsula was more ancient than that recorded in Gaul. Archaeologists then had to show evidence of Celtic migration from west central Europe through the Pyrenees during the material culture of the Late Bronze Age. With Britain and Ireland, historians had to rely on simple invasion theories such as those formulated by Christopher Hawkes in a paper entitled "Hillforts" published in the journal *Antiquity* in 1931. According to Barry Cunliffe, simple invasion theories of this kind were in common use until recent times and are still found, from time to time, in the more popular literature. (Cunliffe 1997, 16-17)

There continues to be disagreement among linguists about the origins of the Goidelic and Brittonic branches of the language: how and when they came to Ireland and Britain. According to one theory, the two languages diverged from the parent Celtic tongue at an early period after which Goidelic speakers are thought to have migrated to Ireland and Brittonic speakers to Britain. A second theory has it that the divergence of Brittonic from Goidelic took place after Goidelic-speaking people had occupied the British Isles for centuries. This was followed by colonization of P-Celtic speakers into Britain in the latter part of the first millennium. From then on, the Brittonic dialect developed and prevailed everywhere but in Ireland where Goidelic continued to be spoken. (Jiménez 2001, 145-146)

Early References to the Celts

The earliest references we have to the Celts occur in the writings of the Greek historians and ethnographers from the sixth and fifth centuries BC. Hecataeus of Miletus describes them as fierce warriors who fought with a seeming disregard for their own lives. He also mentions Narbonne as being a Celtic town and *Massalia* (Marseilles) as being located in Celtic territory. (Jiménez 1996, 27)

One of the earliest references, which may contain material going back to the sixth century BC, is provided in the rather obscure poem *Ora Marituim* written by Rifus Festus Avienus at the end of the fourth century AD. He references obscure authors, many of whose texts no longer exist. One was an early lost work, referred to as the *Massilliot Periplus* by Himilco the Carthaginian who explored the waters of Northern Europe at the end of the sixth century BC. Avienus credits Himilco with making one direct reference to the Celts from the *Oestrymnides* . . . "where the air is freezing, he comes to the Ligurian land, deserted by its people: for it has been emptied by the power of the Celts a long time since in many battles . . . ." No further mention is given except that Himilco referred to Britain as *Albion* and to Ireland as *Ierne* (hence, old Ireland *Erin* and modern *Eire*). Both names are widely accepted to be an early form of the Celtic language. (Cunliffe 1997, 3)

Herodotus of Halicarnassus writes about the Celts in his second book, *Histories*. The Celts, he wrote, live outside the pillars of Heracles (Strait of Gibraltar) and have common boundaries with the Cynesioi, who live to the west of all other inhabitants of Europe. This would appear to suggest that, in the time of Herodotus (fifth century BC), the Celts were settled on the Iberian peninsula. Herodotus also mentions the Danube valley as another place the Celts occupied. In a passage, he tells of Celts living near the upper reaches of the Danube, "the Danube rises amongst the Celts and the city of Pyrene." (Dillon & Chadwick 2003, 1)

The Athenian aristocrat Xenophon tells of Celts fighting as mercenaries in the army of the Sicilian king Dionysius in southern Greece in 369 BC. They were known to Plato who includes them in a list of barbarian peoples given to drunkenness, loving wine to an excessive degree. Plato's student, Aristotle, makes several interesting observations about Celts, such as they openly approve of sexual relations between men. But then again, we are told that homosexuality was common in the Greek world at the time. Later Classical authors, among them Posidonius, describe homosexuality among the Gauls in some detail. Aristotle's second observation tells of the Celts dipping their newborn babies in freezing water to toughen them for the life ahead. (Freeman 2006, 27-28)

Celtic Customs and Behavior

Classical writers, particularly the Romans, were profuse in describing the customs and behavior of the Celts. According to some, the Celts had a great craving for knowledge; they were generous to a degree, prompt in action, but not very capable of sustained effort. Others saw Celtic customs and behavior as strange and alien to Greco-Roman civilization. In their accounts, the Celts are described as a people of bizarre behavior, cruel, and prone to much savagery. Classical writers had many opportunities to observe Celtic armies in action. Their vision of the characteristics of a Celtic warrior depicts him as ferocious, impetuous, boastful, flamboyant, and mercurial—not a foe to be lightly tangled with.

One of the features of Celtic warfare which impressed itself upon the Classical mind was the fact that some warriors fought naked except for the sword belt and a gold neck torc. One of the key figures in the Roman historical tradition was Polybius, a citizen of the Greek town of Megalopolis. In his description of the battle of Telamon in 225 BC, he singles out the *Gaesatae* (spear men) tribe who fought in this manner. "Very terrifying, too, were the appearance and gestures of the naked warriors in front, all in the prime and finely built men, and all in the leading companies, richly adorned with gold torcs and armlets." (*Histories* 29.5-9, Cunliffe 1997, 93)

Strabo's oft-quoted description tells how:

> "The whole race . . . is madly fond of war, high spirited and quick to battle, but otherwise straightforward and not of evil character. And so when they are stirred up they assemble in their bands for battle, quite openly and without forethought, so that they are easily handled by those who desire to outwit them."

He says that when they are aroused:

> "They are ready to face danger even if they have nothing on their side but their own strength and courage . . . their strength depends on their mighty bodies, and on their numbers . . . . To the frankness and high-spiritedness of their temperament must be added the traits of childish boastfulness and love of decoration. They wear ornaments of gold torques on their necks, and bracelets on their arms and wrists, while people of high rank wear dyed garments besprinkled with gold. It is this vanity, which makes them unbearable in victory and so completely downcast in defeat." (Cunliffe 1997, 93)

Greek historian Diodorus Siculus (60-30 BC) describes them as follows:

> "Their aspect is terrifying . . . . They look like wood demons, their hair thick is shaggy like a horse's mane. Some are clean-shaven, but others—especially those of high rank, shave their cheeks but leave a moustache that covers the whole mouth and, when they eat and drink, acts like a sieve, trapping particles of food . . . . The way they dress is

> astonishing: they wear brightly colored and embroidered shirts, with trousers called breeches and cloaks fastened at the shoulder with a broach . . . . These cloaks are striped or checkered in design, with the separate checks close together and in various colors." (MacBain 1996, 56-57)

In another characteristic reference, Diodorus Siculus gives a revealing description of the Celts in battle:

> "When the armies are drawn-up in battle-array, they [the chiefs] are wont to advance before the battle line and to challenge the bravest of their opponents to single combat, at the same time brandishing before them their arms so as to terrify their foe. When someone accepts their challenge to battle, they loudly recite the deeds of valour of their ancestors and proclaim their own valorous quality, at the same time abusing and making little of their opponent and generally attempting to rob him before hand of his fighting spirit." (*Histories* 5.29, Cunliffe 1997, 101)

Greek historian Polybius mentions the Celtic tactic of noisemaking on the battlefield to frighten the enemy:

> "There were countless horns and trumpets being blown simultaneously in their ranks, and as the whole army was also shouting its war-cries, there arose such a babble of sound that it seemed to come not only from the trumpets and the soldiers but from the whole surrounding countryside at once." (Jiménez 1996, 29)

The vision of the naked Celt is a recurring theme in Graeco-Roman art. Another recurring theme in the literature and in art is the wearing of the torc in battle. The torc had a deep, religious significance; deities are usually shown wearing torcs. It gave the wearer the sense of being protected by the gods—it was a symbol of his life and being. When, in 361 BC, the Roman Manlius confronted a Celtic chieftain in single combat, the Celt fought naked but for his shield, two swords, and his torc and armlets. Manlius killed him and took his torc, in doing so acquiring the name "Torquatus." Again, in 191 BC, when the Roman army defeated the Celts at Bologna, the spoils included one thousand, five hundred gold torcs. In AD 60, when the British Queen Boudica led her troops into battle, she wore a cloak and a gold torc, and carried a spear. (Cunliffe 1997, 99)

Several writers have noted that the Celts, in preparing for battle, often coated their hair with clay and lime and combed it into stiff spikes to emphasize their fearsome looks. Off the battlefield, however, they were preoccupied with the idea of physical attractiveness and took great pains with their appearance. Both sexes were exceedingly conscious of their hair and wore it long and in plaits. (Jiménez 2001, 30)

The position of Celtic women in their society was of great interest to the Romans because they appeared to have equal status with men, which Roman women did not. Some tribes were led by women, the most noteworthy being Boudica who commanded her *Iceni* tribe in a bloody revolt against the Romans in Britain in AD 60. One writer claimed that Celtic women were the equal of their husbands in both size and strength. He added that ". . . although their wives are beautiful, they pay very little attention to them, but rather have a strange passion for the embraces of males." (Jiménez 1996, 32)

Julius Caesar had the unique opportunity of observing a variety of Celtic tribes from close at hand during his years of campaigning in Gaul. His *War Commentaries* are, by their very nature, biased as portrayed in the following comment. "While the Romans are steadfast, level-headed, well-led and achieve victory by dogged determination, the Celts are volatile and unpredictable and, though fierce in the initial onslaught, can easily lose heart and panic." It is their adversative qualities to those of the Romans to which he gives most attention. The Celts are presented as impulsive barbarians, lacking ability to plan rationally. In presenting the Celts as a ferocious and unreliable foe, historians believe that Caesar may have been exaggerating in order to enhance his own achievements and provide a justification for his action.

Celtic Feasting and Merriment

Classical historians describe how Celtic warriors were accustomed to great feasting, drinking, and listening to bards boastfully sing of the glories and deeds of their dead heroes and themselves. Even in their merriment they were prone to fight, sometimes with fatal results. Early in the first century BC, a Greek philosopher named Posidonius journeyed deep into the heart of the Celtic lands in Gaul. What particularly struck him about Celtic feasts was the violence always simmering beneath the surface, a violence that often erupted into bloodshed. He relates that, on one occasion, he watched two giant Gaulish warriors draw their swords in what was, at first, a friendly contest—a few half-hearted blows landed on shields, then thrusts and jabs began with increasing vigor:

> "Soon the repartee was replaced by grim determination to humiliate the opponent and avoid losing even a mock battle in front of friends. A quick stab drew blood from the rival's arm then a counterthrust had both men bleeding. A few in the crowd called for an end to the hostility but soon it was too late. The mixture of wine and pride was unstoppable as the warriors began to fight in earnest. The long Celtic swords cut through the air again and again, until one of the drunken warriors made the fatal mistake of lowering his shield for only a moment." (Freeman 2006, 135-136)

Posidonius tells of another occasion where he attended a Gaulish banquet. He was thrilled at the old-fashioned simplicity of his host and his guests, and amused at their Gallic frivolity:

> "They are just like the people in Homer's time . . . . They sat on a carpet of rushes or on the skins of animals in front of little tables. There was plenty of meat, roast and boiled, which they ate, after the fashion of lions, gnawing the joints, but they would at times use their small bronze knives, kept in a separate sheath by the side of the sword. Beer was their drink. One peculiar habit was the unusual way they drank their wine and thick beer deliberately drained through their bushy moustaches like water through a sieve." (MacBain 1996, 59-60)

Many of the Celtic tales from the La Tène era and from the later *Irish Heroic Tales* strangely reproduce the world of the Greek heroes and the war upon the plains of Troy.

Plato (429-347 BC), in his *Laws*, describes the Celts as warlike and hard-drinking. Aristotle (384-322 BC) refers to them as a hardy northern people that exposed their children to their harsh climate with little clothing to toughen them, and who punished excessive obesity among their men. He also describes them as warlike and ferocious, and fearless to the point of irrationality. Aristotle also made mention of the fact that they took little notice of their women, preferring male company instead. (Cunliffe 1997, 4)

But stories of "irrational behavior" by any others than Greeks were favorites in the Greek world of the time. Whenever the Celts held a feast, they sat in a circle with the most powerful man at the center, like the chorus leader in a Greek play. His power may be because of his bravery in war, noble birth, or simply his wealth. Next to him sits the host of the feast, followed in order on both sides by the other guests in descending rank. Behind each guest stands his shield bearer, while the lesser warriors sit apart in their own circle. As one historian describes it, feasting among the Celts was much more than eating—it was court ceremonial, social one-upmanship, and barroom brawl all rolled into one. (Freeman 2006, 130)

Many ancient writers remarked on the Celt's fondness for alcohol. In a passage in his *World History*, Diodorus Siculus writes:

> "The Gauls are exceedingly fond of wine and sate themselves with the unmixed wine imported by merchants; their desire makes them drink greedily and when they become drunk they fall into a stupor or madness. And therefore many Italian merchants, with their customary greed, look on the Gallic love of wine as their own godsend. They transport the wine by boat on navigable rivers and by wagon through the plains and receive in return for it an incredibly large price: for one amphora of wine they receive in return a slave, a servant in exchange for a drink." (Jiménez 1996, 31)

Chapter III—
Pre-Celtic Europe

The heavens and earth are divided into four parts—the Indians occupy the land of the east wind, the Ethiopians that of the south wind, the Celts the west, and the Sythians the north.

—Ephorus (400-330 BC) on Europe

Roughly ten to fifteen thousand years ago, Europe began to assume something resembling its present physical appearance. For eons previously, masses of ice had been slowly withdrawing northward as, century after century, the climate improved and with it the warming of the earth rapidly increased. With warmer weather, tundra gave way to forest and settlers from the east and the south quickly moved into the formerly cold terrain. Farming was still many centuries away, but these earliest Europeans hunted abundant animals and gathered plants that sustained a range of life from Ireland to Russia. It is acknowledged that, some fifteen thousand years ago in western France and parts of Spain, a large population survived by hunting. They lived in caves, and at Lacaux and other places painted on cave walls splendid pictures of the animals they hunted. Archaeologists refer to the middle Stone Age people of this period as Mesolithic hunter-gatherers. (Moody 1967, 31)

Mesolithic Age

The Mesolithic Era began about 10,000 BC and ended with the introduction of farming, a date which varied from one geographical region to another. The Mesolithic people who lived in Europe in the millennia after the retreat of the ice are known mainly from the remains of their more enduring tools, those of flint or stone. It is for the most part a scant record, from which little can be reconstructed except some information about their basic economy. They derived at least some of their food supply from what was available on the shores of rivers and lakes and from hunting. Early hunting populations were small, but the post-glacier environment provided sustenance for increasing numbers. Archaeologists can tell very little about the Mesolithic people. It is not known what their habitats were like, nor even their graves, for no human remains have survived. (de Paor 1986, 18)

Neolithic Age

The Neolithic Age, which began in the Levant about 8000 BC, is traditionally considered the last part of the Stone Age. Unlike the Mesolithic period where more than one human species existed, only one (*homosapiens*) reached the Neolithic stage. In the period after 7000 BC, people living in the great river valleys of Mesopotamia, Egypt, and eastern Asia developed farming and began domesticating animals. The dog appeared very early. Before long, Neolithic man had domesticated cattle, sheep, goats, and pigs. Originally a huntsman, he became herdsman of the animals he once hunted. Expanding populations in the Middle East forced these farming people to spread out in the never-ending search for new land. They pushed west along the Mediterranean to Spain and France and on into Ireland and Britain. (Moody 1967, 35)

Minoan and Mycenaean Cultures

Europe's first great civilization was the Minoan culture. It began its spectacular development on the island of Crete in the eastern Mediterranean about 2700 BC and flourished through much of the Bronze Age until 1450 BC. By this time, the island had become a center for a widely-flung exchange network linking the Aegean coasts of Asia Minor with the mainland of Greece. Afterwards, Mycenaean Greek culture became the dominant culture at Minoan sites in Crete.

Mycenaean culture developed to such an extent that, over time, its influence spread beyond the Minoan homeland of Crete to the Asia Minor coast and the island of Rhodes in the east, and to southern Italy and Sicily in the west. During this period, in the heart of Anatolia, the Hittites were reaching a peak of their development. One of their particular achievements was their knowledge of iron production, a skill at this stage unknown in the Mediterranean and Europe. Iron was, at first, a rare and highly valued commodity used principally for aristocratic gift exchanges. By the middle of the second millennium BC, the Mycenaean-Minoan civilization had become a centralizing focus in the Aegean, which lay at the core of a complex network of exchange contacts drawing merchandise from Egypt in the south and from central, western, and northern Europe.

Greek Dark Age

In the late second millennium, sometimes referred to as the "Greek Dark Ages," the stability of life in both the Mediterranean world and Europe was severely shaken and eventually fell apart in a series of upheavals. The great cities of the Mycenaean civilization were destroyed or abandoned. Many reasons are given for this complex and poorly understood event: mass incursions from the barbarian north, overpopulation, and plague are among the suggested underlying problems. Surviving texts refer to the raids of the "Sea

People" who impinged upon coastal Egypt. The Hittite civilization suffered serious disruption, and cities from Troy to Gaza were destroyed. This was a time of great relocation of peoples when much of the old order disappeared. Fewer and smaller settlements followed, suggesting famine and depopulation. The ripples of those devastating events were felt far and wide. Existing trading systems broke down or were transformed. Some communities, once part of the European-wide trading networks, found themselves cut off as new trading configurations emerged. (Cunliffe 1997, 39-40)

During the first two centuries of the first millennium (1000-800 BC), another crucial period in the configuration of Europe occurred. At this time, the principal social and economic groupings that were to dominate the region for the next millennium began to come together. In the Aegean, extensive movements of Greek-speaking communities led to a repopulation of some areas of Greece and the expansion of others. Some groups moved eastwards across the Aegean, settling the islands and eventually carving out for themselves a foothold on the peninsulas and sheltered havens of the Aegean coast of Asia Minor. This brought about three broad configurations: Aeolians in the north, Ionians in the center, and Dorians in the south. The Levantine coast (now Syria, Lebanon, and Israel) also developed a culturally distinctive maritime periphery, peopled by communities known as the Phoenicians whose cities—Byblos, Tyre, and Sidon—became famous in trading ventures reaching the Atlantic. (Cunliffe 1997, 41) Both the Greeks and the Phoenicians would eventually have a significant impact on "barbarian" Europe.

New Cultural Configurations

It was during this period, also, that new cultural configurations were developing on the Pontic Steppe along the northern shores of the Black Sea. The area had long been settled by communities that depended upon the horse and horse-drawn vehicles to enable them to maintain a degree of nomadic mobility over the huge tracts of the Steppe. In archaeological terms, these communities are known as the Catacomb culture (after their favorite burial mode). (Cunliffe 1997, 42) In the eastern hinterland, roughly centered on the middle stretches of the Volga River, another semi-nomadic group developed, adapting a different burial rite, a wooden cabin-like grave set in a pit beneath a barrow mound. These burials typified the Timber Grave culture. Archaeological evidence suggests that the Timber Grave culture expanded westwards during the early centuries of the first millennium, eventually taking over much of the Pontic Steppe region previously occupied by the Catacomb culture.

On the western fringe of Europe facing the Atlantic, in an arc stretching from northern Scotland to southwestern Iberia, progress was spawning significant and enduring social and political changes. An inter-tribal commercial system linking up a collection of tiny political units was actively engaged in trading activity. During the Bronze Age, metals were among the more important items of merchandise shipped: copper and gold from Ireland, Wales, and western Iberia; and tin from Cornwall, Brittany, and Galicia. (Cunliffe 1997, 42)

In the heart of Europe, stretching from eastern France to Hungary and from northern Italy to Poland, archaeologists point out that a considerable degree of progress was taking place in the period from about 1300 to 700 BC. About 1300 BC, a new type of burial rite spread across Europe; the cremated remains of the deceased were placed in cinerary urns and buried in well-organized cemeteries. This culture, which spread in the area just to the north and east of the Alps, is believed to belong to a branch of the Urnfield culture, and they were also believed to have resemblances to the later Hallstatt Celts. In addition, a strong linkage is found in areas such as metalwork, tools, and jewelry, connecting with the Hallstatt culture. (Freeman 2006, 20)

Many of the groupings which first appear at this period retained their individual characteristics throughout the Urnfield period and into the Hallstatt Celtic period which followed. Historian Jean

Markale writes that, toward the end of the Bronze Age, major physical upheavals in Northern Europe resulted in whole scale migrations of peoples. He maintains that this was the time when the Celts left their homeland in the Harz Mountains to spread westward throughout northern and western Germany along the Baltic and North Sea coasts, establishing trade relations with their neighbors around the Elbe and in the British Isles, particularly in Ireland. (Markale 1993, 25)

Greek Colonial Expansion

The eighth century BC was a formative period in the history of Europe: in the Mediterranean, it saw the beginnings of the Greek colonial expansion and the development of the far-flung Phoenician trading system. Continued infiltration of Pontic Steppe communities into the Great Hungarian Plain made the horse even more readily available to the merging Hallstatt aristocracy of central and western Europe.

At the same time, the two Ionian city states of Chalcis and Eretria—at first together and later separately—began to sail through the Straits of Messina to explore the resources of the Tyrrhenian Sea between the Italian peninsula and the islands of Corsica and Sardinia. The establishment of a Greek presence beyond the southern fringe of Etruscan territory provided a significant stimulus to the progress of Etruscan culture. Along with the Greek merchants, others arrived (including Phoenicians) bringing a range of exotic goods and ideas from the east Mediterranean in return for iron, copper, and silver from Elba and the Colline Metallifere just north of Populonia and Vetulonia. Parallel with the expansion of Greek influence in the western Mediterranean and the rising power of the Etruscans, the Phoenicians of the Levant were rapidly establishing their own trading enclaves as far west as the Atlantic. Phoenicians had already founded a port-of-trade on the Atlantic island of Cadiz in 1104 BC. Another intermediate port was established at Utica on the northern coast of Tunisia about the same time. (Cunliffe 1997, 45-46)

Colonists from the Greek city of Phocaea founded Massalia as a trading center about 600 BC. The Roman scholar Terentius Varro (116-27 BC) describes it as a trilingual center with Greek, Latin, and Gaulish heard on almost every corner, which would point to a strong Celtic influence in the second century BC. Positioned near the mouth of the Rhone River in southern Gaul, the town was ideally situated, both geographically and culturally, as a meeting place for the peoples of the western Mediterranean. To the south was Italy and Sicily with access to the vast commercial resources of the eastern Mediterranean and the Black Sea; to the west was Spain and the trade routes along the Atlantic coasts of Europe and Africa. (Freeman 2006, 81)

The trading routes extending north up the Rhone from Massalia would have enhanced the Celts' trading with the eastern merchants. From Massalia, Greeks were able to expand their trade routes into the Atlantic Ocean to the kingdom of *Tartessus* beyond the Strait of Gibraltar. The maritime communities of these trade routes, stretching from Scotland to southwestern Iberia, were linked in a complex of trade networks in some cases probably stretching back in time to the Neolithic period. Metals were among the more important commodities shipped: copper from Ireland, Wales, and western Iberia; tin from Cornwall, Brittany, and Galicia; and gold from Ireland, Wales, and northwestern Iberia. These metal-rich communities would have provided much of the bronze and gold circulating in western Europe at the time. (Freeman 2006, 21)

Posidonius Explores the "Mysterious Celts"

A Greek philosopher named Posidonius (145-82 BC) visited Massalia and journeyed deep into the heart of the Celtic lands in Gaul in the first century BC. He was interested in exploring the "mysterious Celts," reputed to be cannibals and savages. He traveled widely in the Alps, Gaul, and Spain observing for himself different Celtic societies. He discovered that the Celts were not barbarian but instead a sophisticated people who studied the stars, composed beautiful poetry, and venerated a priestly cast known as the druids. Posidonius was amazed at the Celtic women who, he discovered, enjoyed greater freedoms than the women of Rome, and was surprised to learn that women could even become druids. (Freeman 2006, 85)

According to Posidonius, Massalia survived a Celtic siege in the early fourth century BC, and continued to thrive as a major Greek outpost in the western Mediterranean. Posidonius gave credit to Celtic merchants of the time for inventing the wooden barrel for transporting wines instead of the easily breakable ceramic jugs used by the Greeks and Romans. Expeditions, like that undertaken by Posidonius and others, significantly broadened the classical knowledge base of the Celts. (Cunliffe 1997, 4)

Urnfield Culture

Historians attempting to untangle something of the origins of Celtic peoples have had to rely almost entirely upon archaeological evidence. Herodotus, whose *Histories* were composed in the mid-fifth century BC, suggests that an ethnically distinguishable entity known as the Celts existed a century or more before the historic European migrations when they were thought to occupy a swath of western Europe from Iberia to the Upper Danube. Strong support for such a view comes from the study of the Celtic language group and examining the question: When did Celtic or, better yet, "proto-Celtic" become distinguishable from other Indo-European languages? According to some linguists, this may have happened by the beginning of the Neolithic period. To other linguists, a date closer to the end of the second Millennium BC or even later is more acceptable. What is widely accepted, however, is that early forms of the Celtic language were spoken in Iberia, Ireland, and around the Italian Lakes as early as the sixth century BC. (Chadwick 1971, 21)

Archaeologists are now acknowledging that the Urnfield folk were Celtic or proto-Celtic. From the Urnfield Culture, the Celts emerge as an agricultural people—farmers cultivating their lands and living in a tribal society. The earliest Urnfielders, dating to the thirteenth century BC, were centered on the Middle Danube, occupying much of what is now Hungary and western Romania. By the twelfth century, urn cremation had spread to Italy, and to a broad zone of what may be called Middle Europe, including eastern France, Switzerland, Germany, the Czech Republic, and southern Poland. (Chadwick 1971, 24) In many places they lived in hill-forts and buried their dead in the distinctive manner that gives them their name—Urnfielders. We can conjecture that at some stage of their historical development, the Celts spoke a common Celtic language. Celtic scholars have speculated that this Common Celtic was spoken just before the start of the first millennium BC, and then, soon after, two distinct dialects of Celtic emerged which are identified by their modern names—Goidelic and Brythonic. (Ellis 2001, 11-12)

Many archaeologists now identify the emergence of the Celtic culture with the appearance of the Urnfield folk in south central Europe. There seems to be a cultural continuum from the time when they appear, at the close of the Bronze Age, through the Hallstatt period and down to La Tène. According to Dillon and Chadwick this is too late. In their opinion, the separation of Celtic as a distinct dialect can be dated to the early second millennium BC. (Dillon & Chadwick 1988, 2)

Chapter IV—

Hallstatt and La Tène Cultures

From the abundance of archaeological evidence unearthed in recent times in the form of exquisite jewelry and metal work, it is widely acknowledged that during the La Tène era Celtic civilization evolved and flourished throughout Europe for several hundred years before the rise of the Roman Empire. The Hallstatt era of Celtic history lasted until about 450 B.C., at which point there was a change in Celtic society that can be described only as a social and artistic revolution.

—Philip Freeman, *The Philosopher and the Druids*

The foremost technological characteristic that separated the Hallstatt Celts from their Urnfield predecessors was the substitution of iron for bronze in weapons and tools. The use of iron had a long history among prehistoric peoples, beginning with the discovery of smelting techniques in the Middle East about 2500 BC. Ironworking spread across the Mediterranean region into Europe, reaching Britain in the first millennium BC. To attain the high temperatures needed to break down iron ore, the Celts learned to make charcoal, a process demanding great skill and persistence.

Charcoal is produced when wood is burned in an atmosphere that is poor in oxygen. To achieve this, the Celts ignited a vertical stack of small logs, usually oak, by placing hot embers in the middle, and then covered them with leaves and dirt, leaving a hole at the top for the smoke. After a long period of smoldering, the fire consumed the wood's natural gases and reduced it to charcoal, a porous form of carbon that burns at a much higher temperature than wood. The hot charcoal was then laid on a bed of iron-bearing rocks, baked, and put in a smelting furnace: a shallow pit lined with clay. A primitive bellows was used to force air into the mixture to heat it sufficiently—a temperature of 1400° degrees F—to cause the rocks to soften. (Jiménez 2001, 140-141)

The Hallstatt Culture

It is generally acknowledged that the Urnfielders were the immediate ancestors to the Celts. As such, the earliest definitive archaeological evidence distinguishing the Celtic people as a distinct culture dates from the seventh century BC in what is identified as the Hallstatt period named after a village in the Salzkammergut in Austria. It was there in AD 1846 that mining engineer Johann Georg Ramsauer discovered an early cemetery close to substantial prehistoric salt and iron mines. Excavations revealed that it belonged to an aristocratic iron-using people who had flourished throughout the area from before 700 BC.

Excavations at Hallstatt continued until 1863, by which time approximately one thousand graves had been opened and recorded. The graves, both cremations and inhumations, were well furnished with artifacts, including an array of weapons, bronze and ceramic vessels, personal belongings, and jewelry. This enormous collection, together with well-preserved organic material, such as clothing and wooden tools recovered from the nearby salt mines, provided the archaeological world with a detailed insight into the material culture of central European early Iron Age. Most of the Hallstatt graves were recognized as belonging to the period spanning the seventh and sixth centuries BC with a few continuing into the early fifth. (Cunliffe 1997, 28)

Archaeologist Jan Filip writes that in the Hallstatt period it was possible to distinguish the peoples later known from European history: Scythians in the east, Illyrians in the southeast, Germanic tribes in the northwest, and of course the Celts. The region where the historical Celtic culture was centered was to the northwest of the Alps, and it covered an area from northwestern France, across southern Germany, and into Bohemia. While archaeological sources can even identify diversity in the social and cultural composition of the individual ethnic regions, common features and period characteristics, however, place them all clearly in the Hallstatt period. (O'Driscoll, ed. 1982, 35)

Jan Filip believes that it was during the Hallstatt period that social divisions emerged in different parts of the European mainland, particularly in the Celtic settlements of central Europe. This development led the way to a new form of social structure: the upper class, mostly hereditary chieftains, succeeded in detaching themselves from the rest of the tribe, which remained at a lower standard of living. This, he claims, can be clearly shown in the funeral rites of seventh and sixth centuries BC: members of the aristocratic class were buried in barrows, in spacious chamber graves surrounded by rich entombment possessions. Archaeologists often call these burials "Wägengraber" or even "Fürstengräber." Many have been excavated in Bohemia, and they have also been found in neighboring Bavaria and other parts of southern Germany, in Switzerland, and in France. Some date from the sixth century BC, and among the funeral furnishings are articles confirming increased contact with the Mediterranean area.

Salt and iron were the currency forms used by the Hallstatt Celts to measure their wealth and authority. While salt and iron provided the wealth, farming still provided the basis of the Celtic economy. With new metal tools, forests could be cleared quickly and crops harvested more efficiently. Farming became more productive and the population expanded. As a result, Hallstatt chiefs were growing prosperous from improved farming and from trading with a new and expanding marketplace.

The Greek world, emerging from its "dark" centuries, was expanding its territories and establishing outposts on the far limits of the Mediterranean. Greeks from Phocaea on the Adriatic were cultivating the first vineyards in the area. From this settlement there developed a riverboat trade along the Rhone to southwest Germany. By the sixth century BC, the center of Hallstatt power had moved from the upper Danube (upper Austria and Czechoslovakia) to the upper Rhine (southwest Germany, Switzerland, and Burgundy). During the same phase, these new areas began to benefit from the luxuries that the Greek traders had to offer. Richly painted Attic cups, bronze drinking vessels and wine to fill them, were transported north to garnish Celtic feasts in return for salt products, iron, and possibly slaves. (Laing 1979, 3-4)

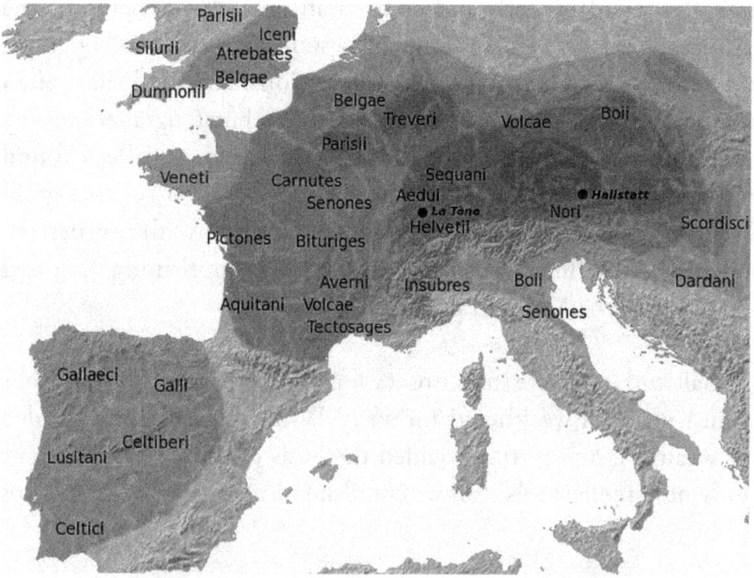

Overview map of the Hallstatt and La Tène Cultures.

Rise of Unified Dynasties

About this time, Hallstatt Celts had begun forming rich settlements run by unified dynasties over a broad range of central and Western Europe. They were settled chiefly in southern Germany and in part of Bohemia, which has preserved in its name that of the original inhabitants, the *Boii*. Everywhere they settled, Celtic society was evident by the establishment of citadels (or fortresses) in high places overlooking vast tracts of land. Archaeological discoveries have yielded much information showing the Celts of the Hallstatt period enjoyed a dynamic culture and a clan-based society ruled by powerful princes. In their early development, they lived alongside Germanic peoples in what is now southern Germany and Austria, but their social and political forms were distinct from that of their neighbors. By the late Hallstatt period, Celtic tribes occupied much of central Europe and were penetrating further south into the Spanish peninsula, and migrating to Britain and Ireland as well. The one essential element linking them was a common language. They all spoke dialects of a branch of Indo-European now known as Celtic.

According to archaeological information, the best example of an early Celtic nobleman's domain is that of Heuneberg near Hundersingen on the Upper Danube. In the sixth century BC, a fortified residence was built there on an area of about three hectares, on high ground. It was still in use in the fifth century BC. The building materials used were mainly stone, timber, and clay. Excavations revealed about ten phases of building, rebuilding, and reconstruction—evidence of unusual activity at the place in the sixth and late fifth centuries BC. There is evidence also that a foreign building technique, found for this period only in Sicily, was used during one of the building phases.

Finds of painted Greek pottery, wine amphorae, and other goods, mainly imported through Massilia (the Greek trading center founded in 600 BC in southern France) show evidence of increasing contacts with the south. Heuneberg and similar "castles" were typical of the fortified residences characteristic of the late Hallstatt period. Furthermore, for the first time in prehistoric Europe (north of the Alps), aristocratic residences of the authentic castle type, fortified with walls and gates, began to appear. (O'Driscoll, ed. 1982, 36)

The Hallstatt Celts were also known by the manner in which they buried their dead. Entombment had replaced cremation. Numerous archaeological finds of Late Bronze Age "barrow graves" from northeast France to Bohemia disclose aristocratic class members entombed in spacious chamber graves. These graves were surrounded by an array of personal belongings: a four-wheeled wagon, weapons, bronze horse harness trappings, pottery, and the essentials for an after-life feast. The largest barrow grave of this period (analysis dates the walls of the chamber to 550 BC) is the Magdalenenberg site in Germany's Black Forest district, measuring three hundred, twenty-five feet in diameter. For two centuries or more before the advent of La Tène, the Hallstatt Celtic elite along the northern edge of the Alps were building magnificent tombs, trading with the Mediterranean lands for luxury goods, and lording it over their poorer Celtic relatives further north.

By the middle of the fifth century, the political geography of Europe had changed dramatically. There was a war in 540 BC between the Greeks and the Carthaginians for western Mediterranean supremacy. In the final sea battle off the coast of Italy, the Carthaginians won and put in place a blockade that affected Greek trade with the Celts. At the same time, the Celtic dynamic of the Hallstatt culture took an unexpected twist upsetting the structure of its existing social order. Fortified residences lost their glory; there were fewer pretentious burials in richly furnished barrows. By the fourth century, barrow burial grounds, some of which were extensive, were replaced by simple graves in the ground in flat cemeteries. What stands out as particularly dramatic is that most of the original homeland of the west Hallstatt elite zone, so dominant in the late sixth and early fifth centuries, was now a cultural backwater. When trade relationships were reestablished half a century later there were major changes to the political geography of northern Europe. A more advanced Celtic culture had evolved, centered on the middle Rhone and Marne.

Historians have had difficulty coming up with an explanation as to why the Celtic tribes left their original homeland at this particular time. Some suggest that overpopulation was the cause. Celtic farming communities were forced to look elsewhere for new fertile lands to settle. Historians draw attention to the fact that Europeans were in a great state of flux throughout the first millennium BC and remained so into the first millennium AD. Over this period of time, there were great movements of peoples across Europe, settling for a while, establishing homelands, and then abruptly moving on. Perhaps a drought, several crop failures in consecutive years, forced farming communities to search for new lands and conditions; or perhaps the people would be forced to move on as more aggressive newcomers invaded their lands—this was the cause of the migrations of the Helvetti and Boii in the first century BC.

During much of the millennium preceding the Christian era, there were extensive movements of peoples throughout the Mediterranean world. When the Hittite empire collapsed at the end of the second millennium BC, it brought about a considerable uprooting of peoples along the eastern Mediterranean. Another movement came about when the Phoenicians established trading colonies at Gades (Cadiz) and at Utica and Carthage in North Africa. There was a further uprooting of people in the eighth century BC, when the Greeks began establishing colonies in southern Italy and in North Africa, Spain and at Massilla (Marseilles). In the fifth century, the Phoenician colony of Carthage had embarked on expanding its own empire with trading links across much of the Mediterranean. In the next century Macedonia expanded into a major empire in the east under Alexander the Great. Then came the rise of Rome; her victory over Carthage left the way clear for Roman expansion throughout the Mediterranean and beyond. (Ellis 2001, 21-22)

The expansion of the Celts was merely one of these movements. The difference being, once the Celts had moved into a new territory they did not set up trading colonies similar to those of the Phoenicians and Greeks, nor did they impose a military over lordship on the people they conquered, as did the Romans. They simply moved into the new lands, setting up pastoral and agricultural communities, and defending them with tribal armies raised from the people. So it is likely that the search for "living space" was the prime cause of the spread of the "Celtic empire" in the fifth and fourth centuries BC. (Ellis 2001, 22)

La Tène Cultural Phase

About the sixth century BC, a separate Celtic cultural phase began appearing. Archaeologists refer to it as La Tène with its more abstract and complex artistic style. The Celtic craftsmen of the La Tène era were masters in the arts, and their creativeness (particularly in jewelry) was dazzling. In literature the earliest Celtic epics:

> ". . . showed a feeling for heroic poetry, a sense of the marvelous, mingled with humour, and a dramatic conception of fatality which truly belong to the Celts alone . . . . All that was clearest and most valuable in the Celtic genius was incorporated in the mind of Europe. And that tradition has been kept up by the unending line of poets and prose-writers of Ireland, Scotland, Wales and Brittany who have adorned English and French literature by bringing to it the genius of their race." (Hubert 1988, 273-276)

La Tène retained many Hallstatt themes such as the transformation of one form into another—human into plant, and plant into abstract design. Henri Hubert writes that in craftsmanship the La Tène art was a direct extension of Hallstatt, it carried forward the legacy of Hallstatt. Its pottery preserves the Hallstatt form with regional uniqueness. The chief difference comes from the imitation of Greek objects and decoration. (Hubert 1988, 8-9)

From the abundance of archaeological evidence unearthed in recent times in the form of exquisite jewelry and metal work, it is widely acknowledged that during the La Tène era Celtic civilization evolved and flourished throughout Europe for several hundred years before the rise of the Roman Empire. Their mastery of technology was equal, and in some respects superior to that of their "civilized" Greek and Roman counterparts. La Tène style ornamentation reached the peak of maturity in the late fifth and early fourth centuries BC. Celtic art in Britain and Ireland can be traced from the middle of the third century BC onwards. It is believed that migrating groups brought it with them from the Continent. Today, the museums of Britain and Ireland can boast of remarkable Celtic works of art, which reveal the art of the islands as a distinctive style.

Societal Difference: Hallstatt Versus La Tène

La Tène society differed in many significant ways from that of the old Hallstatt chiefdoms; the geographical focus of the two barely overlapped. Instead of interning their dead elite on a four-wheeled wagon (as was the practice of the Hallstatt people), the La Tène folk buried their dead on a more elegant two-wheeled chariot, accompanied by weapons and the essentials for an after-life feast. Hallstatt tombs had featured weapons used mostly for hunting or as decorations; La Tène graves were filled with weapons made for war. In graves excavated in the south German region, in Burgundy, and in Switzerland, there were remarkably large finds of the goldsmith's craft, the gold having been washed from the sands of the Rhine and its tributaries.

A young girl buried in a timber barrow chamber at Sirnau (Wurttemberg) had gold bands on her arms and circles of gold in her hair. A barrow at Kappel in the Rhine valley yielded a neck torque of gold plate, a gold bracelet, and other jewelry. One of the most extraordinary Celtic tombs was discovered in the twentieth century near Mont Lassois in eastern France. It belonged to the so-called Princess Vix, a woman about thirty-five years of age who died about the middle of the sixth century BC. Princess Vix was most likely a powerful personage in her day, evident from the objects placed in her grave. Her remains were found lying on a small chariot, the wheels of which had been removed. Several ornaments and utensils were found alongside the chariot: an enormous bronze *krater* or mixing bowl for wine (one of the most famous treasures of archaic Greek art ever to survive), a silver cup with a gilded ornamented boss protected by a fiber covering, two Greek cups, and a bronze Etruscan wine flagon. Placed along the wall of the chamber were Etruscan bowls said to resemble ones depicted in frescoes at Tarquinia in central Italy. On the ground were blue and red pigments thought to be from clothes or decorative paintings.

The princess was adorned with a collar made of large gems and amber beads, bronze ankle rings, lignite (coal) bracelets, and fibulae with coral studs, and on her neck was a huge torque, a masterpiece in pure gold believed to have been crafted by a Celtic goldsmith familiar with Mediterranean techniques. (Laing 1979, 4) Excavations in the nineteenth century of La Tène-era cemeteries at Champagne in northwestern France revealed numerous graves in which men (obviously the more important ones) were buried on their chariots wearing bronze helmets, accompanied by their armaments and horse's gear.

According to eminent Celtic historian, Nora Chadwick, the concept of the two-wheeled vehicle and the inspiration for the new art style of the La Tène period came from the Etruscan world, almost certainly through the Alpine trade route which linked the Po valley to the Moselle-mid-Rhine region. She maintains there emerged (during the middle decades of the sixth century, in a great swath of territory from the Loire to the Vltava) a new cultural expression—archaeologically expressed as "Early La Tène"—a society where warrior prowess was celebrated and where local metalworkers of immense skill could produce works of great originality for their leaders. Chadwick further maintains that the relationship between the old Hallstatt chiefdoms and the emerging La Tène warrior aristocracies is not easy to distinguish from archaeological evidence. However, described in its simplest model, would be to suppose that the development of new centers of power was a cause of the collapse of the old system.

> Throughout the eighth and seventh centuries BC, extensive contacts were maintained between the innovating region of west central Europe and the more distant western lands as far as Ireland. These contacts continued into the La Tène era, but judging from the quantities of imported material found in Britain for the period, either the volume of exchange had decreased or there was a change to materials that have not survived in the archaeological record. This is particularly noticeable in Ireland, where there is almost no imported material dating from the La Tène era, which contrasts starkly with the comparatively large number of Hallstatt period items found there. Evidence would suggest that Ireland, together with much of northern and western Britain, developed in isolation outside the European-wide trading systems of the sixth and fifth centuries. (Chadwick 1997, 43-44)

Later La Tène Phase

The later decades of the fifth century were a time of rapid change in the La Tène phase. In the Marne, Moselle, and Bohemian regions, cemeteries grew in number and size—suggesting a considerable and constant increase in population—while the persistence of weapons in the graves stresses the warlike nature of society. At the end of the fifth century, a sudden decline in population occurred, as reflected in a marked decrease in the number of cemeteries in use. It is at this stage that classical sources take up the story, with accounts of mounting population pressures and conspicuous social tensions among the Celts north of the Alps. These pressures, it is explained, were relaxed only when selected chieftains led large hordes south through the Alpine passes to settle in the Po valley and east along the Danube to find new homes in Transdanubia and beyond. At this point, Chadwick writes, the migrations of the Celtic people had begun in earnest. (Chadwick 1997, 43)

The La Tène period marks the era when the Celts first extended their dominance across the last stages of western European pre-history and into the first pages of history. They initially extended their influence over the area formally occupied by their ancestors of the Hallstatt period. From the end of the second century BC the Continental Celts were subject to ever-increasing difficulties. Their domain was threatened by two powerful hostile forces which, in the end, completely encircled them: from the south there was increasing pressure from the Roman Empire, while from the north the Germanic tribes were closing in on them. The Romans first penetrated the south of present-day France, setting up the province of *Gallia Narbonensis* (later to become Provence). Before the middle of the last century BC, the Romans had spread into the other parts of Gaul. The greater part of Gaul then gradually became Romanized and subject to Roman administration. The pressure of Germanic tribes from the north is attested in classical literary sources for the year 113 BC, when the Boii held up the advance of the *Cimbri* (Germanic tribes) somewhere near Bohemia. The Celtic world was entering a new phase which, after a period of some resistance, ended with the fall of the Celts throughout Central and Western Europe.

Although the power and political importance of the Celts had declined throughout the Continent, by the beginning of the Christian era their legacy to civilization was of great significance for the progress of European culture, techniques, art, and literature. There is hardly a society in Europe which has not drawn directly or indirectly on the wealth of this Celtic heritage. (O'Driscoll 1981, 46-49)

Chapter V—

Celtic Military Expansion

Among the first inhabitants of the Apennine peninsula to lose their heads and much of their property to the Celts were the Etruscans. Around 400 B.C. this talented people had reached the peak of its five centuries of history . . . .

—Gerhard Herm, *The Celts*

The initial phase of Celtic military escalation began in the fifth century BC with movements of Celtic tribes across the Alps into the Po Valley. Polybuis, an Arcadian Greek, describes how the Celts without warning launched a large force against the northern Etruscans, drove them from their lands around the Po and settled the plains themselves. The first Celtic raids into Etruscan territory were so effective that the Celts not only occupied the region, they gave their collective name to it. It became known as *Gallia Cisalpina* (Gall this side of the Alps).

The Insubres, the first tribe to invade, established a center at *Mediolanum* (present-day Milan). They were followed by at least four other tribes who settled in Lombardy. Later, the Boii and Lingones settled in Emilia, and the Senones settled along the Adriatic coast near Umbria. Historians describe how their fierce armies of shaggy-haired, mustachioed half-naked warriors overran all in their path as they expanded their search for territorial advantage. Celtic bands moved south next, defeating a Roman army in 387 BC and threatening Rome itself.

The area settled by Celts, in what is now France, grew in size. They also crossed into Aquitania in southwest Gaul, moving their settlements south under pressure from their Belgae tribal relatives in the north. They penetrated into the Iberian peninsula as far as present-day Cadiz and, in a matter of two centuries, they occupied a large swath of western Europe. They re-colonized Britain and Ireland. In the course of the fourth century BC, the Celts were also spreading through Central Europe: into Bohemia, Moravia, Silesia, and Austria, and establishing a footing for a time in Transylvania.

In the east, Celtic tribes attacked Macedonia where, only a half century earlier, it had been the center of the greatest Empire the ancient world had previously known. In 279 BC, they attacked the Greek oracle at Delphi. By the third century BC, the Celtic world had reached the zenith of its European domain. (O'Driscoll, ed. 1993, 40-41)

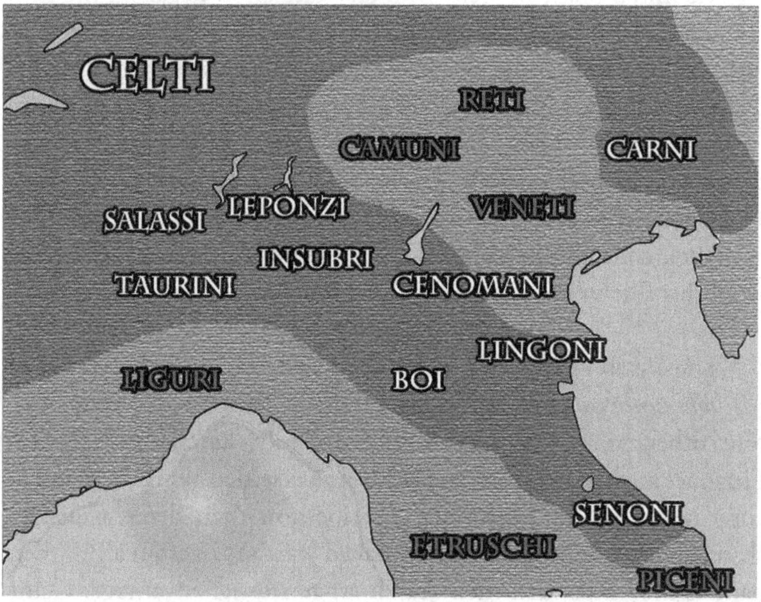

Map showing the peoples of Cisalpine Gaul (391-192 BC).

Hostile Neighbors

Celtic expansion led to the Celts sharing the Italian peninsula with several hostile neighbors. The Etruscans had been dominant, but their power was fading by the fifth century BC. In the region of the southern Apennines were the Samnites (descendents of the Sabines) whose power had been broken by Rome in the mid-fifth century BC. There was Rome itself whose year of foundation is given as 753 BC (even among classical authors there was considerable debate about the accuracy of that date). Rome, we are told, was founded after much tribal conflict between Latins, Sabines, and Etruscans. In 616 BC, Lucius Tarquinius (whose original Etruscan name was Lucumo) became the first Etruscan ruler of Rome. The Latins, defeated by the Etruscans under Tarquinius, were considerably less advanced than their conquerors. It was the Etruscans who introduced public sewerage and bridges to Rome. They also drained the marsh at the foot of the Palitine hill to create a public space, which eventually housed the Forum. (King 1998, 67) So when the Celts first invaded Italy, it was the Etruscans who were expelled from the Po Valley. In the south of the Italian peninsula, Greek colonies (collectively known as Magna Graecia) had been long established.

When Rome began to emerge as a power, Etruria (territory of the Etruscans) was its main rival. In 405 BC, Rome laid siege to the Etruscan stronghold of Veii, twelve miles north of Rome. After ten years of stalemate, the Romans finally conquered the city in 396 BC. The victory enhanced Rome's prestige and made her the undisputed master of Etruria. When the Senones, a Celtic tribe under a chieftain named Brennos, attacked and destroyed the Etruscan settlement of Clusium in 390 BC, the Romans retaliated. They dispatched an army of some forty thousand strong under the command of one of their consuls, A. Quintus Sulpicius, to take on the Celts. The Celts retaliated with a direct advance against Rome itself.

Celts Sack Rome

On hearing that the Romans were marching against them, the Celts, under their commander, Brennos, moved quickly to meet them. Brennos and his Celtic army met the Romans for the first time on July 18, 387 BC on the banks of the River Allia, a short distance north of Rome. It was a disastrous day for the Romans as the Celts smashed their way through Sulpicius' army. The Roman soldiers panicked. Thousands rushed into the river in an attempt to save themselves from the Celtic warriors, many meeting their deaths as they tried to reach the other side. Sulpicius and a few of his men managed to flee back to Rome. The city was in total panic. Three days after the battle, Brennos and his victorious Celtic army arrived outside the city of Rome. Only the Capitoline Hill, which was the most sacred part of Rome, was barricaded and defended. The rest of the city was wide open. (Ellis 2001, 27-28)

The besieged Romans had no choice but to enter negotiations and the Celts ransom settlement inflicted a lasting wound on Roman pride. Legend has it that when the Romans complained at the unjust way in which the ransom money was being weighed out on the scales, the leader of the victorious Celts threw his sword onto the scale, saying in Latin, "*Vae victis!*" (Woe to the conquered!) (King 1998, 70) The devastating blow to Rome's power and authority was in part responsible for the unrest that gripped central Italy throughout the next half-century or so. During this time, Celtic raids and Celtic mercenary forces made intermittent appearances and episodic contact with Roman forces. (Cunliffe 1997, 79)

Rome remained a prime target for Celtic attacks until the battle of Telamon in 225 BC, at which time the Romans won a decisive victory over a vast Celtic army. But it was not until 192 BC that Celtic domination of the northern Italian peninsula came to an end after the Romans defeated the Boii tribes on a battlefield near present-day Bologna.

Celts Pay Visit to Alexander the Great

Alexander the Great first encountered the Celts in 355 BC in what was one of the earliest face-to-face meetings between the Greeks and an almost legendary people from the unexplored forests and mountains of western Europe. According to Ptolemy, Alexander was sitting outside his tent when a group of warriors approached the camp and asked for an audience with the king. The delegation approached the surprised King and presented themselves as Celts who had traveled from the mountains of the west to seal a pact of goodwill with the victorious monarch. Alexander welcomed them warmly, assured them of his peaceful intentions toward their people, and invited them to share a drink of fine Greek wine. The Celts gladly accepted, though they refused an offer to dilute the wine with water, as was the Mediterranean custom.

Alexander, who had learned from Aristotle never to pass up an opportunity to discover something new about other people, queried his visitors about Celtic culture, history, and religion. As they were about to leave, Alexander asked his visitors: *What do you fear most?* Probably, he was expecting an answer that they feared the military might of the legendry general sitting across from them. Instead, their leader looked straight at Alexander and exclaimed, "Nothing! We honor the friendship of a man like you more than anything in the world, but we are afraid of nothing. Except," he promptly added, "that the sky might fall down on our heads!" The rest of the Celtic warriors laughingly bid farewell to the Macedonians. As they strolled out of the camp, Alexander turned to his aides and said, "What braggarts these Celts are!"

The Celtic warriors who showed up at Alexander's marquee in 355 BC were, most likely, La Tène Celts whose ancestors had migrated eastward out of central Europe and down the Danube River. About 400 BC, a huge influx of Celtic warriors, farmers, and families had moved into new areas along the Danube. This was immigration and settlement alongside indigenous cultures rather than a wholesale replacement of population. Jewelry and weapons from Celtic graves in present-day Slovakia, Hungary, and Romania from the mid-fourth century BC attest to this. (Freeman 2006, 50)

The few Greek records of the Celts before Alexander's time speak only of a wild and uncivilized collection of tribes known as the Keltoi, who dwelled in the distant lands of Italy, Spain, and beyond the Alps, all the way to the mysterious northern sea. But the Celts were rapidly becoming a force in the classical world. In the decades before Alexander, they had swept south over the alpine passes and breached the gates of Rome. Fifty years after Alexander, they attacked the sacred Greek site of Delphi, home to Apollo's oracle, and crossed the Hellespont into Asia Minor, ravaging the coast before settling permanently in their own kingdom of Galatia in the middle of the Greek world.

After Alexander died in 323 BC, the breakup of his empire made space for the aggressive Celts to begin moving south and east into Macedonia. They were successfully contained and repulsed until 281 BC when Celtic tribes seized and beheaded King Ptolemy Ceraunus I of Macedon. (King 1998, 73)

Mercenary Forces: Greece and Beyond

The presence of Celtic mercenary forces on the Italian peninsula provided a constant supply of warriors willing to fight for employment. They were accepted as a useful compliment to the fighting forces of aspiring tyrants. Henri Hubert writes there was no prince in the east who could fight without his corps of Gauls. Gauls appeared in the army of the Lagids that besieged Abydos in 186-185 BC in the repression of the revolt in Upper Egypt. Ptolemy II at the end of his reign (and Ptolemy III after him) enrolled mercenaries for their wars. There were likewise Gauls in the army of the Seleucids; some took part in the campaign against the Macabees. (Hubert 1988, 51-52) Dionysius of Syracuse managed to strike an alliance with a band of Celtic mercenaries, returning from service in southern

Italy, who helped with his naval expedition on the Etruscan port of Phrygia in 383-384 BC. For the next thirty years, Celtic bands continued to provide Dionysius and his son with mercenaries. For the most part they served in Italy, but one force was transported to Greece in 367 to take part in the conflict between Sparta and her allies against Thebes.

Celts Permanently Settle Phrygia (Galatia)

Celtic tribes moved eastwards through Macedonia, invading Greece via Thrace and Thessaly. Their attack on the temple of Delphi in 279 BC caused Greece to delay the opening celebration of the Pantheon. Earlier in the fourth century BC, the Greeks had come to recognize that the Celts occupied a large area of western Europe from Iberia to the Upper Danube. Ephorus (circa 405-330 BC) spoke of them as one of the four great barbarian peoples of the world, along with the Scythians, Persians, and Libyans. (Cunliffe 1997, 76)

The most curious adventure by Celtic tribes was that undertaken into Asia Minor. They were invited there, originally, by an aristocratic knight from Bythina on the Bosphorus who persuaded them to fight for him against Seleucid Aniochus, who claimed sovereignty over all Asia Minor and dominions beyond. By 270 BC, the Celts had permanently settled an area of northern Phrygia, thereafter named Galatia. Although they were cut off from their European roots, these Galatians (as they came to be known) managed to retain their Celtic customs and language into early Christian times. They are mentioned in the New Testament in Saint Paul's Epistle to the Galatians where he admonishes them not only against idolatry, sorcery, and jealousy, but just as strongly against hatred, murder, drunkenness, and the like.

Iberian Peninsula

The Iberian peninsula had been widely Celticized from early in the La Tène period, probably before 450 BC. Celtic tribes had crossed over the Pyrenees from Gaul where they intermarried with the indigenous population and became known as Celtiberians. Celtiberia as such was a relatively narrow area in the northwest of Spain. Iberians, as distinguished from Celtic and Celtiberian tribes, predominated in the eastern parts of the peninsula in its coastal regions and also in the south, though there were many areas of moving back and forth with the Celts and Celtiberians. Other tribes, such as the Lusitani and Vaccaei, are believed to have been of Celtic or part-Celtic culture and speech. There were also the Celtici, a southern Spanish tribe of Celtic disposition and connection. The Celtici lived near Gades and Tartessus.

Diodorus writing in the mid-fifth century BC recounts the many characteristics of the Celtiberians:

> "Celtiberes are a fusion of two peoples and the combination of Celts and Iberes only took place after long and bloody wars .... They are noted for their hospitality, and they regard strangers as being under the protection of the gods .... Celtiberes wear black clothes, hairy like goatskin: some have shields of the highly-constructed Celtic type; others a round shield of the kind more familiar in the Greek world. The iron in their two-edged swords, shorter than the Celtic great sword, is capable of cutting anything. The process of manufacture involves burying the iron from which they are to be made so that the softer layers of metal are peeled away by corrosion and only the harder part remains to be forged into a sword." (Rankin 1996, 166-167)

One of the founding fathers of prehistoric archaeology in Spain, Louis Siret was the first scholar to lead the way in claiming that the Celts arrived on the Iberian peninsula during the Bronze Age. This wave of settlers, according to Siret, was Goidelic-speaking. This correlates with the Irish tradition recounted in the *Leabhar Gabhala* (Book of Invasions), the earliest fragment of which survives in the *Leabhar na Nuachonghbala* (Book of Leinster), compiled about AD

1150 by Fionn mac Gorman claiming that it was from Spain that the Goidelic-speakers invaded and colonized Ireland. (Ellis 2001, 43)

By the time the Greek mariners began establishing their trading posts and settlements along the coasts of the Iberian peninsula during the seventh and sixth centuries BC, the Celtic population had switched languages. The Goidilic settlers in Iberia were replaced by a new wave of Gaulish (or Brythonic) speakers. Furthermore, Celtic peoples were well established throughout the land. Aristotle (384-322 BC) gives the name Celtica to the entire mountain mass of the Iberian peninsula. (Ellis 2001, 44)

Classical historians provide direct evidence for the existence of Celts in Iberia. The earliest of these, Herodotus the Greek historian (circa 490-425), writing in the mid-fifth century BC makes oblique and somewhat confusing references to the Celtic presence. In one passage, he mentions they were the most westerly people in Europe next to the Cynetes, who appear to have been the inhabitants of the extreme southwest of the peninsula. Elsewhere, he says that the Celts lived beyond the "Pillars of Hercules"—the area known as the Strait of Gibraltar. Professor Cunliffe suggests that "[B]oth comments provide a reasonable geographical precision and leave no doubt that Herodotus' informants believed there were Celts in western Iberia." Diodorus describes the Celtiberes as a fusion of two peoples: Celts and Iberes. (Cunliffe 1997, 136)

Celtiberians had a distinct ethnic character in the ancient world. There was a strong Celtic element in them. Other tribes, such as the Lusitani and Vaccaei, seem to have been of Celtic or part-Celtic culture and speech. Some of the Lusitani appear to have spoken, or understood, or at least used for inscriptional purposes, an Indo-European language which had some features in common with Celtic and which was of a very archaic and conservative linguistic type. (Rankin 1996, 166-167)

Gaul

The Celts occupied a large part of Gaul (present-day France and Belgium) from an early period. According to classical historians, they did not enter Gaul as a single nation. They appear to have arrived as military units, each occupying a more or less defined river valley; in the course of conquest and settlement, these separate elements formed political and military unions with the indigenous inhabitants of the area. As early as 400 BC, they had pushed south to the ancient territory of the *Ligurians* and formed the Celto-Ligurian League under a single chief who led them against the wealthy Greek trading colony at Massalia. To the north, Belgae tribes crossed the Rhine into Gaul in the fourth and third centuries BC, pushed forward by pressure from the German tribes. According to Caesar, the Belgae claimed to be of pure Teutonic origin, but spoke a Celtic language and their leaders bore Celtic names. It is possible they were of Celtic origin with a later Teutonic intermixture.

Hubert complains that positive information about the settlement of the peoples of Gaul is almost entirely lacking and goes on to say that the exploration of what was once Gaul is deplorably incomplete. He adds, ". . . their history is almost always impossible to follow. Moreover, the civilization of the Celtic countries in the Hallstatt and La Tène periods is in the main highly homogeneous, so that it is difficult to study local variations." (Hubert 1988, 121). By Caesar's time, however, the Celts dominated most of Gaul (present-day France, Belgium, and Switzerland).

Bronze Torc, 4th century BC (Saint-Remi Museum, Reims, France). A sign of nobility and high social status, torcs were large neck rings—often rigid, open-ended, and designed for near-permanent wear.

Celts or Germans

It is beyond doubt that the Celts had a great political and military influence on the Germans at an early period. This is shown by the words borrowed by Germanic from Celtic—words connected with politics, law, warfare, and civilization in general. On the whole, the Celts seem to have been—for hundreds of years, and in every matter—the educators of the Germanic peoples. (Hubert 1998, 93) But their influence was not due to their mere neighborhood; it can be assumed that it was enforced. In Germanic countries, there were Celtic kings, or kings after the Celtic mode, and where there was no king or kingdom we find Celtic officials or ambassadors. Celts and

Germans made treaties, exchanged oaths and hostages, did business, and made contracts of marriage or friendship.

In some instances, the two races formed what may be regarded as a single society; they combined in political associations and their tribes formed a confederation or confederations in which the Celts were the larger or predominant element. These relations did not always develop in peace; we must assume they engaged in wars, sometimes against each other and sometimes on the same side. Hubert goes to some length to provide proof of the closeness that existed between the Celts and the Germans by identifying names of Germanic peoples who he claims are Celtic in form, or are like Celtic names Germanized. The name of the Hessi, he points out, seems to be that of the Cassi. He believes the Burgondiones correspond to the *Brigantes.* The Nemetes, the Triboci, and the Marcomanni (who lived next door to the Gauls) had Gallic names, yet there is no doubt that these were Germanic peoples. (Hubert 1988, 93-94)

Hubert also writes that while there was a difference between German and Celtic languages, there was not much of a personal difference. Poseidonios, who was perhaps the first historian to speak expressly of the Germans, commented on their physical resemblance to the Celts. Strabo regarded the Germans as Gauls in their original pure state and suggests that this was what their name "germane" meant. He went on to say that while their speech was different, their institutions, manners, costume, and arms were the same. (Hubert 1988, 121)

Britain and Ireland

The question of when the first Celtic people migrated to Britain and Ireland has occupied archaeologists and linguists for a long time. There is general agreement that they came from the European continent. Disagreement surrounds what part of the mainland they came from, what language they spoke, and where they first settled.

In one theory, Ramon Jiménez describes that the first Celts bypassed Britain entirely and settled in Ireland as early as 2000 BC bringing with them Goidelic, an archaic Celtic language unknown in any other part of Europe. Jiménez adds that despite the most rigorous analysis of cemetery artifacts and language development, there is still insufficient evidence that there was a Celtic language or culture in Ireland or Britain before 700 BC. (Jiménez 1996, 131)

Historians are in agreement that Celtic influence in Britain first came about by trade and the occasional isolated settlement of Hallstatt immigrants who, for the most part, assimilated into the island's indigenous Bronze Age population. In Britain, as in Ireland, the La Tène culture became well established early on with the arrival of Gaulish and Belgae tribes from that part of Gaul which lies to the south of present-day Belgium. In the first century BC, there were further invasions by Belgae tribes, whose influence on Britain led to a greater flowering of Celtic culture, particularly in the south of the island. They are credited with establishing trade links with Rome, a move some historians believe set the stage for the Roman conquest of Britain. There were also tribal movements on the Atlantic seaboard, between Armorica (present-day Brittany) and southern Britain for centuries. (King 1998, 63)

The Pan-Celtic World

The third century BC marked the peak of Celtic expansion at which time Celtic people occupied a vast area stretching from Ireland in the west to the Black Sea in the east. They rubbed shoulders with the Hellenistic culture in the east, exposing their society to more affluence than that of their kinfolk in the west. But, as Gerhard Herm suggests, the Celts' greatest error was that they relied too much on "natural superiority" and never undertook the hard work of exploiting and organizing their resources. Creating the La Tène culture seemed easy to them, but they failed when it came to empire building. (Herm 1976, 127)

The Celts conquered Europe in the way the Romans were to do much later, the difference being the Celts did it with a loose alliance of tribal armies lacking unified leadership, whereas the Romans relied on centralized political and military power. In a nutshell, the Celts were great conquerors, but they failed in their attempt—if indeed they ever made an attempt—to establish an empire. In a still shorter time, the Celts lost their Continental dominions and most of Britain; being reduced to subjection in one place, driven out of another, and everywhere deprived of all political power except in Ireland. Henri Hubert writes that such was the destiny of the Celts; they were unable to create a lasting kingdom. Hubert also writes that, notwithstanding, they had failed politically; the Celts still made great contributions to western civilization.

Chapter VI—

The Fall of the Celtic Realms

Thus ended the war against the Celts, a war greater than any other known to history in the desperate bravery of the combatants, the number of battles, the list of the dead and the warriors who took part.

—Polybius, *History*

In the sixth century BC, the Romans were one of several tribes in the area of Latium on the west coast of the Italian peninsula under the rule of Etruscan kings. Living there in a collection of primitive abodes on the hills overlooking the Tiber River, they would evolve over the next six centuries to make Rome the most important city in the then known world. Toward the end of the century, Roman families of the aristocratic class joined together to overthrow the monarchy and establish an independent republic. They adopted a shared rule form of government comprising a Senate, an Assembly of citizens, and a hierarchy of elected magistrates headed by two *consules* (consuls). (Jiménez 1996, 7)

Exercising a combination of aggressive diplomacy and military might, the Romans steadily subdued and absorbed the various tribes around them over the course of the next several centuries. By 266 BC, they controlled the entire Italian peninsula below the Po River. Then, after three successful wars against the Phoenician empire of Carthage—the last against its legendary general, Hannibal—Rome took Sicily, Sardinia, and Corsica and most of Spain and made them into provinces. By 120 BC, the Romans had conquered and established provinces in Macedonia, modern Tunisia, western Turkey, Cilicia, and Further Gaul (the southern coast of modern France and the Rhône valley). Their domination of the Mediterranean world was such that they called its sea "*mare nostrum*" or "our sea."

Hostilities Between Celts and Romans

In 285 BC, the Celts renewed their hostilities against Rome but this time they suffered a major setback when the Romans assembled a powerful army against them. In a short time, all the tribal lands of the Senones were confiscated and Rome continued to make inroads northward into Celtic lands until Celtic tribes in most areas south of the River Po were brought under Roman influence. The Celtic world was starting to fall apart. Its domination in the eastern Mediterranean came to an end after meeting defeats at Macedonia, and at Pergamon in 244 BC. The Romans penetrated the south of present-day France, setting up the province of *Gallia Narbonensis* (later to become Provence); before the middle of the last century BC, they had spread into other parts of Gaul. The greater part of Gaul gradually became Romanized and subject to Roman administration.

Celtic armies went on to suffer further defeats. From the end of the second century BC, the Continental Celts were subject to ever-increasing challenges. Their domain was threatened by two powerful hostile forces, which in the end completely encircled them: from the south there was increasing pressure from the expanding Roman Empire; from the opposite direction, German tribes were pressing in on them.

At the Battle of Telamon in 225 BC, the Romans and the Celts of Cisalpine Gaul met in one of the fiercest battles of ancient times. The Celts were decisively routed. According to the account of the battle by Polybius, over forty thousand Celts were slain and ten thousand taken prisoner. These were men and women of the Insubres, the Boii, the Taurisci, and the Celtic mercenaries known only as *Gasaetae*, or sword-bearers. It had taken the Romans fifty years to recover and more than a century-and-a-half to extract vengeance from the humiliating experience of the Celtic attack on Rome in 386 BC.

After the Battle of Telamon, Rome embarked on the first significant stage of its territorial expansion. On all fronts (the Po valley, Asia Minor, Iberia, and southern Gaul), Rome confronted Celtic armies. By 192 BC, Celtic domination of the northern Italian peninsula had come to an end. After a century or more of fierce warfare on the Iberian Peninsula, the Romans succeeded in subduing the Celtic tribes in the Celtiberian Wars of 29-19 BC. The Romans went on to conquer the Celts in Britain in AD 47 and thereafter occupied the island for three hundred and fifty years.

The Battle of Telamon, however, did not end the hostilities between Celt and Roman. Many of the Gauls in northern Italy fiercely resisted the Romans for years. Seven years after Telamon, Hannibal invaded Italy in the Second Punic War, and the Carthaginian general found many willing allies among the Celts of Cisalpine Gaul. But, in the end, the Romans prevailed. By the start of the second century BC, Cisalpine Gaul was thoroughly subjugated. The Celts who survived were integrated into Roman society and even granted Roman citizenship. (Freeman 2006, 64-65)

The Iberian Struggle

From earliest recorded history, travelers from the eastern Mediterranean made the long journey to Iberia to cash in on its rich mineral wealth. The Phoenicians of Lebanon claimed they had sailed through the Strait of Gibraltar (then known as the Pillars of Hercules) long before anyone else, but their port in Cadiz, in the land of the Tartessus, wasn't established until the eight century BC. The Greeks were never far behind the Phoenicians when it came to seeking out new markets.

Herodotus tells the story of a Greek captain named Colaeus from Samos who was sailing to Egypt in 630 BC when a fierce wind from the east drove him and his crew across the entire Mediterranean to Tartessus. Turning calamity into opportunity, the Greeks loaded up with Spanish goods and made a killing when they returned to Samos. Soon, more Greek traders were sailing to Spain, followed by Greek trading centers that established colonies in the western Mediterranean. (Freeman 2006, 69)

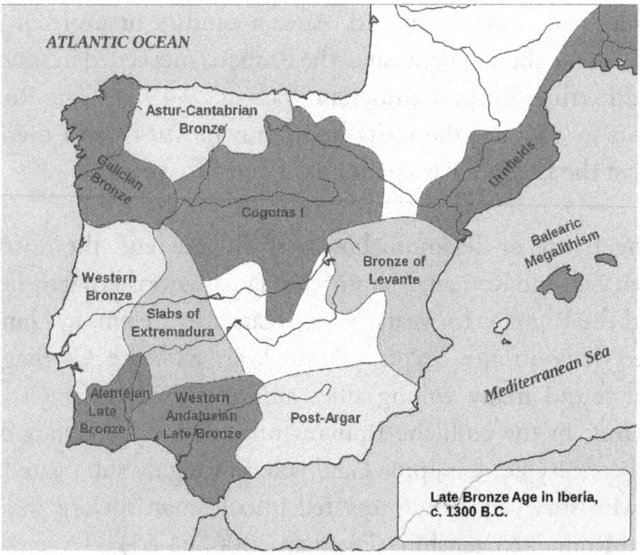

Map of Iberian Peninsula, Late Bronze Age (circa 1300 BC) showing the main cultural areas.

Conflict Between Carthage and Rome

The end of Celtic Iberian independence had its origins in the conflict between Carthage and Rome. Phoenician colonists established the city of Carthage at a strategic location on the Tunisian coast of North Africa about 814 BC. During the sixth century BC, Carthage grew to be a strong trading power and its interests began to conflict with Greek settlements throughout the Mediterranean. Forming an alliance with the Etruscans, the Carthaginians succeeded in driving the Greeks from Corsica and gaining control of Sardinia, Sicily, and several coastal towns on the Iberian peninsula. By 264 BC, Carthage was the center of a major empire. (Ellis 2001, 46)

Rome was now emerging as a dominant power. At the outset, Carthage was content to settle for commercial treaties with her. As Rome rose in power and influence, it was inevitable that a military conflict would sooner or later occur. The first conflict, known as the First Punic War, broke out in 264 BC and lasted until 241 BC. The Romans succeeded in defeating the Carthaginians; Carthage had to evacuate several of her colonies and was required to pay reparation to Rome. With its prestige severely undermined, the Carthaginian parliament (the Suffete) decided it must regain control of its lost territories as a first attempt to recover her status.

A Carthaginian general named Hamilcar Barca was sent with an army to reassert Carthaginian power in Iberia. He arrived at Gades in 237 BC. From there he proceeded to take control of the southeastern side of the peninsula and the Mediterranean coastline northwards towards the Greek colonies. In 229 BC, during the siege of the Greek colony of Helice, he accidentally drowned. His son-in-law, Hasdrubal, replaced him as commander of the Iberian campaign. Hasdrubal immediately launched a campaign to bring the Celtiberian and Iberian tribes under Carthaginian control. In 221 BC, a captured unnamed Celt from a defeated Celtic tribe managed to get close enough to Hasdrubal to assassinate him. With Hasdrubal's death, another family member, Hannibal (247-182 BC), became commander. For two years, he consolidated his position; then, in 219 BC, despite a Carthaginian non-aggression pact with Rome, he launched an attack against the rich city state of Saguntum. This attack precipitated war with Rome and thus began the Second Punic War.

In the spring of 218 BC, Hannibal dispatched an envoy to the chieftain of the Boii seeking his help against Rome. With a huge army of men and war-trained elephants, Hannibal embarked on a bold invasion of the Italian peninsula. Along the way, the Boii met up with the Carthaginians and led them through the passes of the Alpines. Hannibal, with his army of Celtiberians and Gaulish auxiliaries, passed through the Alps to their destiny on the Italian peninsula, and nearly seventeen years of continuous warfare there. Historians have never properly acknowledged the Boii role in that crossing. Without the Celts' knowledge of the mountain passes, Hannibal could not have journeyed successfully over the Alps in wintertime. (Ellis 2001, 46-58)

Aftermath of the Second Punic War

Not content with a policy of containing Hannibal in Italy, the Romans (with a master strategy of detaching Spain from the Carthaginian war effort) decided to move forces into Spain in 218 BC. In a series of actions, they successfully mounted a campaign against Carthaginian forces, both on land and at sea; by 211 BC, the Romans had taken control of a considerable portion of Spain and recovered Saguntum. At the same time, Hannibal's army was beginning to lose ground in Italy and the Carthaginians were not in a position to exploit their advantage in Spain. Gnaeus Cornelius Scipio was sent to Spain to liberate the Greek colonies from Carthaginian control. His brother, Publius Cornelius Scipio who had been defeated by Hannibal in the Po Valley, joined him a short time later. The Scipio brothers managed to retake the area as far south as Saguntum. Hannibal's brothers, Hasdrubal and Mago, launched a counter-offensive and, in a series of successes, both Scipio brothers were killed.

In 210 BC, Publius Cornelius Scipio's son (bearing the same name, though later taking the title "Africanus") landed with a new Roman army. A year later, he marched his army down the east coast to New Carthage where his legions stormed the city. The tide was turning against Carthage on the Iberian peninsula. In 206 BC, the Carthaginians were driven out of the Iberian peninsula altogether and control of the country was now in Roman hands. In 197 BC, with the Second Punic War ending in Rome's favor, the Iberian peninsula was divided into two colonial provinces: "Hither Spain" centered on the Ebro basin and "Further Spain," the area around Gibraltar across to the valley of the Guadalquivir. Rome sent officials and fixed annual taxes for these areas. This brought about the first of the general insurrections of the Celtiberians against their new imperial masters. (Ellis 2001, 49-50)

The Turdetani rebelled in 196 BC and were defeated at Turta. A year later, Consul Marcus Cato was sent to deal with other rebellious tribes. Cato's wars of pacification lasted several years, yet he did not make any significant headway against the Celtiberians. The Lusitani also rebelled, defeating the Roman general Aemilius Paullus in 190 BC. Paullus managed to regroup his legions and beat back the rebellious tribes later in the year. From Lusitania (substantially present-day Portugal), a leader called Viriathus emerged who was to succeed in carrying out a most effective guerrilla war against the Romans. Variathus was a survivor of the 153-151 BC siege on the Celtic hill-fort of Numantia where the Romans massacred the surrendering Lusitani. Between 147 BC until his assassination in 140 BC, Viriathus caused repeated destruction to the Romans. His death weakened Celtiberian resistance.

In 179 BC, Tiberius Sempronius Gracchus was sent to Hither Spain to pacify its rebellious Celtic tribes. Polybius confirms he destroyed three hundred Celtic towns. His subsequent pacification measures won him some fame for he revised the treaties with the Celtic tribes, placed the system of land tenure and taxation on a more equitable basis, and established several Roman towns in the interior of the country. He also encouraged Celtiberian enlistment into the Roman army, believing that this would keep the "wild spirits" among the Celtic population under control. The result was a twenty-year period of comparative peace. (Ellis 2001, 49-50)

Final Effort to Subdue Iberia

Toward the end of the second century BC, the Roman republican system of shared rule was upset by popular uprisings and by several foreign and civil conflicts that introduced a military factor into the political arena. The established methods of governing were repeatedly disregarded, and the practice of assigning important military commands to particular men by vote of the Assembly was instituted. This led to unmanageable rivalry among ambitious patricians, supported by their hired gangs, to use any means at their disposal to capture votes. (Jiménez 2001, 7) In 82 BC, a short and bloody civil war between two political factions resulted in the victor, Lucius Sulla, proclaiming himself as dictator. Two years later, he disbanded his legions, reestablished consular government, and abandoned his dictatorship. About this time, Quintus Sertorius, a distinguished Roman soldier, was put in charge of governing Spain. From his appointment until his death, he took firm control of the province and was successful in holding it against attacks from rival Roman armies, including one led by Pompey himself in 77 BC. Sertorius gradually lost his prestige and he ended up being assassinated in 73 BC.

It took Rome two hundred years to completely subdue the Celtic tribes of the Iberian peninsula. It was the campaign of Emperor Augustus in the Cantabrian Wars of 29-19 BC that finally brought about an end to the hostilities from the Cantabrians, Austurians, and Galicians. Historians tell us that a Celtic language was still spoken in many parts of Spain during the first century AD. Publius Tacitus (circa AD 56-117) records this fact. There is no mention of Celtic survivals afterward. Celtic scholar Peter Ellis writes that "we can only assume that by the following century Celtiberia had become merely a geographical label and that the Celtic language and civilization was lost in that area." (Ellis 2001, 56)

Yet, the presence of a Celtic people on the Iberian peninsula cannot be overlooked, particularly in the regions of Galicia and

Asturias. These were not survivors of the original Celtic inhabitants. They arrived there during the fifth century AD from southern Britain, pushed out by the Anglo and Saxon tribes who were making their way into Britain. Many Britons decided that migration was the only way to escape the pagan hordes flooding into their once prosperous homelands. The Armorican peninsula (present-day Brittany) was one source of escape. Other British tribes opted for northern Spain, mainly settling in Galicia and Asturias. Their settlements were recognized at the Council of Lugo in AD 567 as constituting the Christian see of Bretona. The see of Bretona existed until about AD 830 when the Moors ravaged it. In AD 900, it was merged with the see of Oviedo. (Ellis 2001, 57)

Offensive from Germanic Tribes

In the second century BC, Celts and Romans alike felt the scourge of Germanic tribes. Cimbri and Teutones from the shores of the North Sea besieged Celtic and Roman territories from 113 BC to their final destruction by the Romans in 101 BC. The Cimbri made their first appearance around 113 BC when a disastrous tidal wave forced them to leave their homeland in the Jutland peninsula and move southwards. Their attempts to resettle in Celtic territory met with fierce resistance from the Boii and other Celtic tribes.

Intelligence reports reaching Rome at the same time created fear once more at the prospect of a new barbarian horde approaching from the northwestern boarder of Italy. Rome, which still trembled at the mention of blond, blue-eyed giants from somewhere in the north, treated all these reports with deadly seriousness and right away sent an army against the unknown invaders. The Roman forces met the Cimbri and Teutones at Noreia, the Norician capital south of modern day Klagenfurt; it turned out to be a disaster. The Roman army under Papirius Carbo was annihilated. Like the warriors of the 386 BC disastrous Celtic attack on Rome, the warriors of this battle were equally "invincible in strength and courage . . . ." (Herm 1975, 63) While the Romans remained justifiably fearful of a second invasion of Rome, the intruders, instead of pressing on south, marched along the northern slopes of the Alps towards the west and vanished.

They did not appear until 109 BC when the Cimbri, Teutones, and Helvetii joined forces with a crack force of Ambrones and marched down the Rhone to Provence, which Rome had earlier annexed. There was a repetition of Noriea; two small senatorial forces were crushed and a third larger one suffered a defeat. Soon after at Arausio (modern day Orange), they met and defeated a Roman army led by Servilius Cepio and Mallius Maximus.

The Cimbri next pushed over the Pyrenees into Spain, while the Teutones continued southwards across Gaul destroying everything that stood in their way. Their only effective opposition came from the Belgae, but even they could not prevent the invaders from establishing a colony along the banks of the river Sambre near Namur. It was this colony of Teutones (the *Atuatuci* tribe) that was so challenging to Caesar during his Gaul campaign. The Helvetii journeyed back up the Rhone to settle beyond Lake Geneva only to be driven from the region later by the Surevi. (Lavin 1999, 20)

The Cimbri crossed back over the Pyrenees in 103 BC and joined the Teutons in a carefully planned advance on Italy. The Romans, all too mindful of the danger of a Cimbrian-Teuton coalition, recalled Consul Gaius Marius from Africa to confront them. Instead of following France's south coast, which they knew would be well defended by the Romans, the Cimbrian-Teuton coalition decided to cross over the Alps and surprise their foe from the rear. Marius, a skilled military leader, took on the Teutons first. His encounter with them came about in a battle near Pourrieres. It resulted in large-scale slaughter, not only amongst the two armies, but also among the Teuton women and children who followed their men everywhere. The battle of Pourrieres was long remembered by the Romans as a turning point in their conquest of Gaul. Meanwhile, the Cimbri continued to march through the northern Alps. Having routed

Consul Catulus at Adige, the road to Rome lay open before them. Instead of making straight for a defenseless Rome, they dispersed to look for plunder and to wait for their allied Teuton forces (unaware they had been decimated by Marius and his Roman legions).

Marius showed up to the surprise of the Cimbri, who then resorted to threatening the Romans with dreadful consequences when their allies arrived. "They are here," shouted Marius as he marched out the Teuton leaders in chains. When the Cimbri leader grasped what had happened, he asked Marius to select a site for a final encounter. The site selected was at Verceil and, on July 3, 101 BC, both sides met. The battle proved to be another massacre. The Cimbrians literally let themselves be slaughtered; the Romans were once again victorious. Marius was hailed as the third founder of Rome (after Romulus and Furius Camillus) because he had averted a grave danger to the capitol. (Herm 1977, 64-66)

The Greek philosopher, Posidonius, who journeyed deep into the heart of the Celtic lands of Gaul during the first century BC, maintains that the Cimbri as well as the Teutons were Celtic. Strabo, on the other hand, claimed they were Germanic tribes. The evidence suggests, however, the Cimbri were more Celtic than German: they spoke a Celtic language, associated themselves with Celtic tribes (the Helvetii, for example), all had Celtic names, and Cimbrian prophetesses were akin to the Celtic priestesses. All this collaborates the theory held by many historians that the Celtic world was no more than a mélange of different tribes and ethnic groups under a Celtic elite in which the indigenous peoples of the lands they conquered were first enslaved and then fused by a common Celtic language, culture, and religion.

Enter Julius Caesar

In the first century BC, an ambitious and brilliant young military leader by the name of Julius Caesar (who now ranks alongside Hannibal and Alexander as a remarkable military leader of ancient times) came to prominence in Rome. A sign of his growing importance was his election by the Assembly in 63 BC to the lifetime post of *pontifex maximus* (or chief priest), the highest religious office in the Roman state. In 78 BC, he had been appointed governor of Further Spain, giving him his first military command and his first opportunity to display his flair for tactics on the battlefield. He fought a campaign against the Celtiberians, capturing the hill-fort of Brigantium.

Events in Further Gaul, Rome's province on the French side of the Alps, soon gave Caesar an opportunity to distinguish himself. Caesar set his sights on conquering all of Gaul (the heartland of Celtic Europe), but had to invent some convincing pretense for his campaign to the Roman Senate. Rome already occupied northern Italy to maintain peace in the Po valley area between the warring Celtic tribes that had settled there. Rome had sent its legions into Iberia to protect its interests from Hannibal's conquering forces. Rome had also annexed a broad strip of land along the Mediterranean coast of France in 125 BC, turning it into the Roman province of Gallia Narbonensis—a link between Italy and Spain.

Up to this point in history, Gallic society had not been a threat to Rome's interests, and Caesar knew that any attempts at annexation would be met with fierce resistance from the Gauls. Gaul, however, was a hegemony of self-dependent tribal communities constantly engaged in armed conflict with each other, or with their Germanic neighbors to the north. Caesar was quite sure that, sooner or later, there would be opportunities to exploit the situation.

Roman Incursions into Gaul

As early as the sixth century BC, Rome had established an amicable trading relationship with the largest and oldest city in Gaul, the Greek colony of Massilia (Marseilles) at the mouth of the Rhone. Massilia had asked for and received aid from Rome against invading Ligurians, and again against Celtic tribes from the north. After the second rescue mission in 122 BC, the Romans stayed in the area and built a military base at Aquae Sextiae, modern-day Aix-en-Provence. (Jiménez 1996, 46)

In the Rhone Valley the next year, two Roman generals commanding more than thirty thousand men trapped a much larger Celtic army from the Arverni and Allobroges tribes, soundly defeating them. As a result of this battle, Rome took control of a large area of southern Gaul that would form the nucleus of its first province beyond the Alps. Over the next two decades, they occupied and then organized the entire southern coast of Gaul and the Rhone Valley as far north as Lake Geneva, as the new province of Gallia Narbonensis.

Caesar's first entanglement with Gaul came about in 58 BC when he led an army over the Alps to cut off the Helvetii and their allied tribes who were attempting to emigrate *en masse* from their Swiss homeland to southern Gaul (due to a mounting threat from invading German tribes). The Roman senate had not given him command or even permission to undertake this engagement. Caesar chose to interpret the migration of the Helvetii as a threat to Further Gaul.

It is believed that the Helvetii migrants, including their families, numbered three hundred and sixty thousand, twenty-five percent of whom were men bearing arms. Caesar's decision to prevent the migration would, in a few years, cost the Celts in Gaul their lands, their wealth, and their independence. It would put all but the fringes of Western Europe in Roman hands, and then put Rome in the hands of Caesar. His conquest of Gaul shielded Rome from invasions from over the Rhine for five hundred years. He imposed a Latinate culture and language on the area that remains to this day. Caesar had blocked the Helvetii migration by destroying a bridge over the Rhone near *Genava* (Geneva). When they tried to negotiate with him, he turned his legions upon them, massacring more than six thousand and forcing the remainder back to their homeland. Savoring victory, Caesar returned to northern Italy to attend to urgent administrative affairs and left his legions to watch over his newly acquired territory.

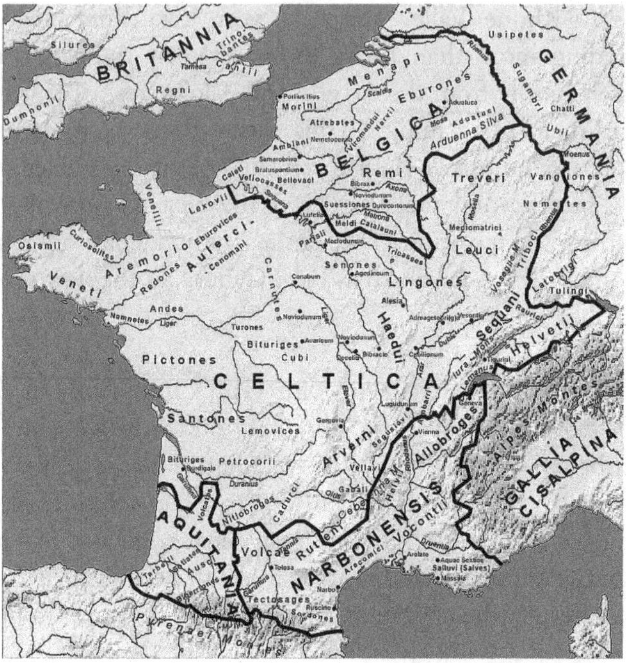

Map of Gaul, circa 54 BC. Prior to Gallic Wars, Gaul was divided into five regions: Gallia Cisalpina, Gallia Narbonensis, Gallia Aquitania, Gallia Celtica, and Gallia Belgica.

Caesar Defeats the Belgic Tribes

Soon after his success against the Helvetii, Caesar began receiving intelligence reports that the Belgic tribes had formed a confederation and were readying for war against the Roman invaders. The powerful Bellovaci tribe, from the Oise region, was leading the campaign. Among the others participating were the Suessiones, the Nervii, the *Atrebates*, the Ambiani, the Morini, the Calita, the Veliocasses, the

Viromandui, and the Teutonic Atuatuci. The Remi refused to join, preferring instead to aligning themselves with Caesar.

Alarmed by the reports, Caesar raised two new legions and intensified his intelligence-gathering network along the Belgae frontier. He moved quickly to thwart the Belgae siege of a fortress near Bibrax. Caesar's decisive battle against the Belgae out-maneuvered and pushed back the enemy. Determined to exploit this victory, Caesar entered the land of the Suessiones, besieged their capital, Noviodunum, and forced them to surrender. He next went against the Bellovaci and they also capitulated. Meanwhile, the Nervii, who had a reputation of tenacity, joined forces with the Atrebates and the Viromandui and took on the Romans at Sambre in a brutal encounter. The Roman side was stunned by a ferocious onslaught, which inflicted severe casualties. They were saved from massacre by the skillful maneuvering of their military leaders and by the arrival of reinforcements.

Caesar sent his legions into Armorica (present-day Brittany) in 56 BC against the Veneti, the greatest of the four Armorican peoples. The Veneti, relying on their powerful fleet and cross channel support, were nonetheless defeated by an armada of Roman ships under Caesar's lieutenant, Publius Crassus, at the battle of Morbihan Bay. They had staked and lost everything and were a conquered country.

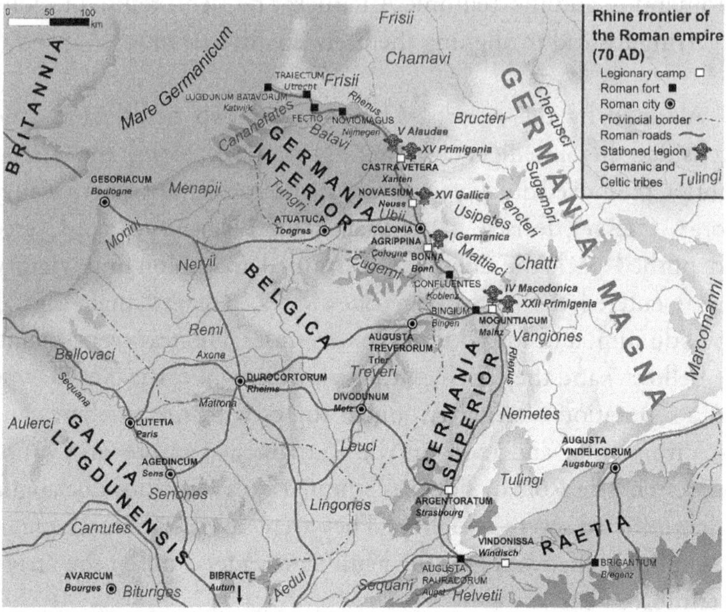

Map of Northeastern Gaul, circa 70 AD, showing tribes on the west bank of the Rhine.

Caesar Battles Vercingetorix

All of Caesar's carefully laid plans for a peaceful transition of Gaul to Roman rule began to unravel during Caesar's excursions into Britain in 54-55 BC. In the winter of 54 BC, the Carnute tribe attacked the Roman grain depot at Cenabum (modern Orleans), signaling the start of the greatest revolt yet seen in Gaul. One Belgic chieftain, named Ambiorix, managed to lure an entire legion out of its winter quarters near the Ardennes Forest and destroy it. The Nervii tribe of northern Gaul managed to besiege and almost destroy a second Roman army commanded by Caesar's brother, Quintus. It took a lightening march by Caesar from his camp north of Paris to relieve him. The most menacing force yet to face Caesar in Gaul soon overshadowed this brief success.

Celtic chieftain Vercingetorix (a nobleman of the Arverni tribe in south-central Gaul) tangled with Caesar in several places in central Gaul, including Avaricum, Gergovia, and finally the Burgundian stronghold of Alesia. Historians tell us that he was unlike anyone Caesar had encountered among the fiercely independent and uncooperative Gauls. Vercingetorix created a powerful army of Gauls that could stand up to and defeat the Romans. He forced Caesar to engage in a series of exhausting sieges of Gaulish towns while avoiding open battle. He adopted a policy to deprive the Roman legions of food by burning every Gaulish farm they might use to provide food.

This scorched-earth policy was effective against the Romans until Vercingetorix made the mistake of withdrawing his forces within the walls of the fortress town of Alesis. Whether he was seeking a brief rest for his army or hoped to tie down Caesar in a protracted siege, once he was within the walls of this formidable citadel, Caesar had him trapped. After several failed efforts to overcome Caesar's attacks, Vercingetorix surrendered. Caesar ordered that all the weapons and every warrior be brought forth to him. Thousands of warriors marched forth and threw down their weapons at Caesar's feet. Each was handed over to a Roman soldier as a war prize, to be quickly converted into cash by waiting slave dealers. Finally, Vercingetorix rode forth and presented himself to Caesar. Vercingetorix was bound and taken to Rome for public display and humiliation. Six years later, after Caesar had crossed the Rubicon and conquered all rivals in his bid to rule Rome, Vercingetorix was led on a parade of triumph through the Roman Forum and finally executed. (Jiménez 2001, 180)

Gaulish resistance continued for another year or so, especially among the Belgae in the north, but the days of independent Celtic rule on the European continent was over. The Galatians, Celtiberians, Italian Gauls, and now finally Celts of Gaul, had one-by-one fallen to Roman rule. (Freeman 2006, 187-188)

Caesar's triumph over Gaul brought about the collapse of a great alliance—but not of a great people. In exchange for individuality and pride, the Gauls acquired the amenities of a higher civilization and the confidence that Roman law would bring an end to centuries of restless warfare and inter-tribal feuding. Over the next few years, Caesar had just a few local revolts to contend with. Celtic Gaul was divided into four Roman provinces—Narbonenis, Aquitania, Lugdunensis, and Belgica. The tribal leaders had to submit to Rome's laws, administration, and agree to an annual tax of four million *sesterces* (equivalent to coins weighing forty-five tons in silver). Four thousand Gallic volunteers were inducted into the Roman military as an autonomous legion, and some Gallic leaders were even assigned to Caesar's personal staff.

Statue of Belgic chieftain Ambiorix who in 54 BC managed to lure an entire Roman legion out of its winter quarters near Ardennes Forest and destroy it.

Celtic Cultural Legacy to Western Society

Professor Jan Filip, University of Prague, in his address to the Symposium on the Celtic Consciousness at Toronto in 1978 said:

> "Although the power and the political importance of the Celts had declined throughout the Continent by the beginning of the Christian era, their contribution to civilization and art remained of great significance to the evolution of European culture, techniques, art and literature. There is hardly a nation in Europe, which has not drawn directly or indirectly on the wealth of this Celtic heritage. The mainspring of Celtic traditions and Celtic heritage, of course, remained in Britain and Ireland, where Celtic culture developed undisturbed when ancient Gaul was already markedly Romanized. Ireland and Scotland, in particular, where neither the Romans nor the Anglo-Saxons attained a permanent foothold, preserved their Celtic character. From there the ancient Celtic traditions reached back to influence England and the Continent, and came to a new flowering in the early centuries of Christianity and in the minor arts of the Middle Ages. Later the mysterious Celtic world of heroic deeds, legends and tales was a source of inspiration for the greatest minds at the birth of modern European culture. Man today does not always realize how great is the debt of our own age and of the whole of European civilization to that once courageous people." (O'Driscoll, ed. 1981, 49-50)

Chapter VII—
Celtic Britain

To judge from the descriptions of Classical writers, notably Caesar, the British Celts were every bit as good at putting on an act in the battlefield as were their Gaulish contemporaries. Caesar marveled at their expertise as charioteers, little guessing that the gymnastics they engaged in were rehearsed battle feats, intended to impress their opponents into submission . . . .

—Lloyd Laing, *Celtic Britain*

After the defeat of Gaul, Caesar turned his attention to the Celtic kingdoms in Britain. The peoples of the Mediterranean had known of Britain at least by the fifth century BC through the merchants of the ancient world. Britain was one of the few sources of tin, a necessary component of bronze in Europe. In the second half of the fourth century BC, Pytheas, the Greek explorer from Massilia, made a voyage north along the western coast of Europe and crossed to the islands, actually circumnavigating Britain and noting its neighbor, Ireland. The Greeks had named the islands the Cassiterides, meaning Tin Islands. Some historians have suggested that the name was Celtic and that the word meaning tin, first recorded by Homer (*kassiteros*), was borrowed from Celtic, as tin was a Celtic material. Polybius, Strabo, and Avienus referred to the Tin Islands as the Pretani Islands, thus implying that the inhabitants were Pretani. (Ellis 2001, 139)

During the Gallic war, Britons fought with the Gauls against the Romans and, after the war, continued the trading and cultural links that were long established between the two countries. Caesar, suspicious (or using it as an excuse) that the British Druidic religious leaders were aiding and abetting subversive activities across the Channel, made two armed explorations to southeastern Britain in 55 and 54 BC to consider the situation. On the morning of August 25, 55 BC, he led a Roman fleet ashore under the great white cliffs of South Foreland. Awaiting them along the cliff tops, as far as the eye could see, were massed thousands of British warriors alerted by the alarm of their coastal patrols. As the Roman legionnaires disembarked on the open beaches of nearby Walmer, in the land of the *Cantii*, there was a brief encounter after which the Celtic chieftains agreed to open peace negotiations with Caesar. (Ellis 1990, 149)

The peace talks went on for four days, during which time a great storm rolled into the area causing extensive damage to Caesar's warships sitting at anchor. The Celts saw this as a sign that the gods were on their side and they called off the negotiations. The situation looked bleak for the Romans. Roman legionnaires were on a hostile shore with no provisions and limited supplies for a protracted campaign. Caesar ordered his men into the countryside to forage for food and supplies. Along the way, a large force of Celtic warriors in war-chariots ambushed them. Caesar led a battalion into action to relieve his pinned-down party, and it was during this encounter that he observed firsthand how the Celts used their war-chariots in battle:

> "First of all they drive in all directions and hurl javelins, and so by the mere terror that the teams inspire and by the noise of the wheels they generally throw the ranks of soldiers into confusion. When they had worked their way in between the troops, they leap down from the chariots

> and fight on foot. Meanwhile their charioteers retire gradually from the battle, and place the chariots in such fashion that, if the warriors are hard pressed by the enemy, they may have a ready means of retreat to their own side." (Ellis 1990, 152)

Back in Rome, the news of Caesar's expedition onto the isle of Britain caused a stir. The Senate voted to celebrate twenty days of thanksgiving to the gods. From the Roman military viewpoint, the expedition was unsatisfactory. From Caesar's personal perspective, the British expedition capped a year of personal triumph. By the spring of 55 BC, he had to all appearances conquered Gaul and established Roman supremacy from the Alps to the Channel. During the previous summer, he had driven the Germans back across the Rhine. Finally, in the fall of 54 BC, he had invaded an island even beyond the border of his latest conquest, defeating the barbarian tribes he found there and had returned safely to Gaul.

In fact, Gaul was not conquered, only quieted. Caesar's climatic struggle with his most dangerous opponent, the Gaulish overlord Vercingetorix, was still three years away. The expedition to Britain was poorly conceived from the beginning and had achieved nothing substantial. Regardless of this, the reaction of the Senate and of the Roman public was all that Caesar could desire, and much of it was due to his own effort. For Caesar, the skillful manipulator of public opinion, his propaganda was as effective in Rome as his tactics were on the battlefield. (Jiménez 1996, 112-113)

Caesar later withdrew to the Continent where he began plans for a future campaign to establish a permanent garrison in Britain. He arrived a second time on September 25, 54 BC, but events in Gaul and a subsequent uprising against Rome dashed any hopes he had of bringing the island into submission. Caesar again departed without establishing a permanent settlement, and the turbulent political situation in the Roman world after his assassination in 44 BC delayed any further plans to occupy Britain for another century.

Caesar's brief campaign in Britain may not have achieved a great deal from a military point of view, but he did succeed in establishing relations with certain tribes on the southeast coast of the Thames, which secured for him clientage bonds that would be later used to Rome's political advantage. There are recorded instances in the early part of the first century BC of British chieftains who fled to Rome seeking help from the emperor in their inter-tribal disputes. The last recorded instance was that of Verica, king of the Atredates, whose appeal to Rome provided Emperor Claudius with the excuse he needed to mount a Roman invasion of Britain.

Kingdoms of Great Britain, circa 800 AD.

Britain Before the Celts Arrived

The question of when the first Celtic people migrated to the British Isles has occupied archaeologists and linguists for generations. The only generally accepted theory is they came from the Continent, but what part of the mainland they came from, what language they spoke, where they settled first, and, above all, when they came are still matters for scholarly discussion. There are intriguing stories that the first Celts bypassed Britain entirely and settled in Ireland, perhaps bringing with them Goidelic, an archaic Celtic language unknown in any other part of Europe. Some scholars believe that this may have taken place as early as 2000 BC, but despite the most thorough analysis of burial place artifacts and language development, there is still a lack of evidence of a Celtic language or culture in Ireland or Britain before about 700 BC. (Jiménez 1996, 131)

Whether the migrations were earlier or later, the islands to which the first Celts journeyed had taken their present shape thousands of years earlier. Before the warming climate caused the last glacier to begin receding from Northern Europe in about 10,000 BC, the British Isles were a single land mass still joined to the mainland from the Channel Islands to the coast of present-day Germany. As the northern ice cap melted, the rising Atlantic waters crept up the river valleys and across the lowlands, creating the Irish Sea and flooding the great Anglo-German plain to form the North Sea. Between eight and ten thousand years ago, water finally broke through the last chalk ridge connecting the receding peninsula with the mainland, and Britain from the continent.

Over a period of several thousand years, small nomadic tribes roamed the land, sustaining themselves by fishing, gathering wild berries, and hunting small animals. During the fourth millennium BC, this culture was gradually replaced by one based on simple farming and stock raising. In contrast to the circular huts of the nomads, these Neolithic farmers built rectangular wooden structures for themselves. They also used a new method of burying their dead, placing the remains in long barrows of earth and stone.

Toward the end of the fourth millennium BC, Stone Age tribes began building the first circular enclosures; more than ninety of these "henges," as they are called, have been identified from the Orkneys to Cornwall. Also toward the end of the fourth millennium BC, the first work was begun on the most famous henge, the mysterious monument at Stonehenge. About 2700 BC, inhabitants of the Salisbury Plain built the massive twelve-story mound of earth and chalk rubble, now called Silbury Hill—the largest prehistoric structure in Europe. (Jiménez 1996, 132-133)

The centuries following 2500 BC reveal the presence in Britain of the so-called Beaker People—named after the characteristic decorated handle-less drinking cups they used. The Beaker People are believed to have been the original inhabitants in Britain, although there may have been earlier inhabitants that originated in the Low Countries and the Rhineland. The Beaker People kept cattle, sheep, and pigs and planted barley, which they boiled and ate as porridge. These people had a knowledge of metalworking, notably of copper. Copper daggers from the third millennium BC are the earliest metal objects from Britain. The second millennium BC brought dramatic changes to Britain and Ireland. These changes were the consequence of extended trade routes linking the islands with France, Spain, and the Mediterranean. The process of converting bronze out of copper and tin, and the ability to make bronze objects, created new wealth. (Jiménez 1996, 133)

It is generally acknowledged that Celtic tribes began arriving into Britain and Ireland during the first millennium BC. They spread quickly into all areas, dominating the indigenous culture and instituting the Celtic language and society they had brought with them. Of all the European countries the Celts populated, it is in the British Isles where they left their most enduring legacy. Remains of their hill forts and outlines of their fields can be seen today in many areas. The contemporary names of many cities, rivers, and mountain ranges throughout western Europe have survived as Celtic words. (Jiménez 1996, 134-135)

Celtic influence in Britain first came about by trade and the occasional isolated settlement of Hallstatt immigrants which, for the most part, assimilated into the island's indigenous Bronze Age population. In Britain, as in Ireland, the La Tène culture became well established at an early period, with the arrival of Gaulish and Belgae tribes from that part of Gaul which lies to the south of present-day Belgium. In the first century BC, there were further invasions by Belgae tribes, whose influence on Britain led to a greater flowering of Celtic culture on the island, particularly in the south. They are credited with establishing trade links with Rome, a move some historians believe set the stage for the Roman conquest of Britain.

**Battersea Shield, 350-50 BC (British Museum, London).
This facing of a now-vanished wooden shield is made of sheet bronze and decorated in La Tène style.
Dredged from the Thames in 1857, it is believed to have been cast in the river as a votive offering to the gods.**

Romans Invade Britain a Second Time

Caesar had failed in his attempt to conquer Britain. Almost a century had passed before the Romans under Emperor Claudius attempted a new invasion in AD 43, which resulted in a solid Roman footing on the island. He appointed Aulus Plautius ("a senator of great renown") as commander of the expedition. The Romans went on to defeat the Britons in AD 47, finally establishing the Roman province. Unfortunately, unlike Caesar's expeditions, there is no first-hand account for this invasion. The only sources are *Gaius Suetonius Tranquillus* writing fifty years afterwards and *Cassius Dio* writing over one hundred years afterwards. Cassius Dio says the invasion fleet sailed in three divisions so they could outflank any attempt by the Britons to prevent the Roman legionnaires from landing on the beaches. Ptolemy mentions the landing was at a township called Routpoupiaci. (Ellis 2001, 196-197)

When Claudius and his legions arrived in Britain in AD 43, it was a country of separate tribal kingdoms without much political unity. The Belgic tribes occupied a large part of southeastern Britain and as far west as the Cotswolds. Tribes of the Cantii, *Trinovantes*, and Iceni, said to be already partly Romanized, were ready to enter into treaty relationships with the Romans as clients. Further, there were several stubbornly independent Celtic kingdoms, prominent among them the *Parisi* of east Yorkshire and the Brigantes who occupied much of remaining northern England. To the far west were several Welsh tribes, equally as independent: the *Cornovii* who occupied the Welsh Marches, the *Ordovices* of North Wales, and the *Silures* of South Wales. Northern Britain (present-day Scotland) did not emerge into recorded history until AD 80 when the Romans, under Julius Agricola, pushed northward to subdue the mostly "uncivilized" Picti tribes of Caledonia. Archaeological data would later reveal that the tribes of Caledonia were as advanced as their Celtic kinsmen elsewhere.

The first advance of the invading force captured Camulodunum, the capital of the *Catuvellauni* tribes. The Roman legions spread out across the core of the southeast to take jurisdiction of the territories either directly or indirectly under the control of the Catuvellauni, as well as those of the Atrebates whose king, Verica, had previously sought assistance from Rome. Next, the Romans successfully overpowered the *Durotriges*, *Dobunni*, and *Corieltolavi* (but not without considerable resistance from the Durotriges) and laid a military road through all three territories. The road was called the Fosse Way; it ran from one military base at Exeter on the Channel coast to another at Lincoln on the east coast. The southeastern area of the island was now under Roman administration, but for two client kingdoms which Claudius had created within it: the Iceni of Norfolk were left under the command of *Prasutagus*, while the Atrebates were put under the control of a leader named *Cogidubnus*.

Not All Plain Sailing for the Romans

As the Romans pushed ahead, they encountered strong opposition from a coalition of Celtic forces organized by *Togodubnus* and *Caratacus*, two sons of *Cunobelin*, king of the Catuvellauni who had died a year before. Togodubnus was killed in military action; Caratacus withdrew to his fortified capital of Camulodunum. At this point, Emperor Claudius sailed for Britain (with reinforcements and a detachment of elephants) where he took command of the Roman attack on Camulodunum. Descriptions of the battle that took place between the Romans and Caratacus' forces are sketchy. When the tide of battle turned against the Celtic chieftain, he and his followers managed to escape, fleeing westward into the Welsh mountains where he held out against the might of Rome's armies for another nine years before being captured.

The capture of Caratacus had not been an entirely military action. He was betrayed by another British ruler, *Cartimandua* (queen of the Brigantes), and handed over to the Roman commander,

Publius Ostorius Acapula. (Cunliffe 1997, 254) In return, Rome gave Queen Cartimandua backing to buttress her authority over anti-Roman dissidents in her kingdom. For the next ten years or so, she succeeded in retaining her position as queen—then lost it when Venutius, her estranged husband, gained control after organizing a revolt among anti-Roman tribes against her.

Desborough Mirror, 50 BC-50 AD (British Museum, London).
Discovered in Desborough, Northamptonshire, in 1908, the reverse side of this bronze mirror is decorated in Early Celtic La Tène style.

Caratacus Surrenders to Rome

Tacitus, the Roman historian, tells how the fame of Caratacus had spread near and far, beyond the British Isles, across the western provinces, and was well known in Rome itself. (Ellis 2001, 5) Now captured by Cartimandua's betrayal, Caratacus, his family, and retinue were paraded in chains from Britain to Rome and through the thoroughfares of the imperial capitol. Romans were eager to see the man who had so long defied the Empire. Tacitus tells how Caratacus, standing on the spot where four hundred years earlier the Celts had stormed and sacked the city, addressed the Emperor and his senate:

> "If to the nobility of my birth, and the splendor of exalted station, I had united the virtues of moderation, Rome had beheld me, not in captivity, but a royal visitor and a friend. The alliance of a prince, descended from an illustrious line of ancestors; a prince, whose sway extended over many nations, would not have been unworthy of your choice. A reverse of fortune is now the lot of Catatacos (Caratacus). The event to you is glorious, and to me humiliating.
>
> "I had arms, men and horses; I had wealth in abundance; can you wonder that I was unwilling to loose them? The ambition of Rome aspires to universal domination; and must the rest of mankind, by consequence, stretch their necks to the yoke?
>
> "I held you at bay for years; had I acted otherwise, where, on your part, had been the glory of conquest, and where, on mine, the honor of a brave resistance? I am now in your power. If you are bent on vengeance, execute your purpose. The bloody scene will soon be over and the name Catatacos will sink into oblivion. But if you preserve my life, then I shall be, to late posterity, a monument of Roman clemency." (Ellis 2001, 6-7)

Caratacus' speech to his conquerors was audacious and moving; he evidently impressed Claudius and the senate with his address. He, his family, and retinue were granted their lives. There would be no orgy of bloodshed to appease the Roman crowds that day. Caratacus, his family, and retinue were ordered held in permanent exile within the confines of the city of Rome. (King 1998, 149)

While these events were taking place, Roman legions took control of the English midlands, the southwestern peninsula, and much of Wales; the only significant remaining resistance coming from two major Welsh tribes, the Silures in the south and the Ordovices in the north. The fighting was fierce, but the superior skills and discipline of the Roman legionnaires ultimately prevailed. Rome next negotiated a pact with the Brigantes, a coalition of clans occupying most of northern Britain.

Southern Britain was now firmly in Roman hands. Yet, in other areas, the Romans achieved only limited success as resistance to their occupation mounted. The Romans, suspecting that druidism was behind much of the resistance, attacked the island of Mona (Anglesey) in northern Wales, destroying the shrine of druidism, and slaughtering most of the druids operating there. Reports show that the Romans encountered no difficulty in occupying the unprotected island, because it had never occurred to the Britons of the area that anyone would dare attack this sacred sanctuary. But the sacrilege committed at Mona turned more Britons against the Romans.

In AD 61, a rebellion by the Iceni, led by their Queen Boudica (wife of the Roman client King Prasutagus), spread rapidly and ferociously as other disaffected Britons joined in. The Roman colony of Camulodunum, the town of Verulamium, and the port of London were destroyed and many of their inhabitants killed. The Romans eventually put down the revolt in a battle where supposedly eighty thousand Britons were killed. Boudica ended her life with poison. She has been described as the most formidable single opponent encountered by the Romans in Britain, with the possible exception of the Caledonian chief Calgacus who commanded the northern tribes against Agricola at Mons Graupius.

The Wandsworth Shield, 2nd century BC (British Museum, London).
Dredged from the River Thames at Wandsworth, London, sometime before 1849, this bronze shield boss is considered a masterpiece of British Celtic Art. A round, convex, or conical piece at the center of a shield, the boss was designed to deflect blows and provide a place to mount the grip.

Agricola Appointed Governor

Meanwhile the situation in the north of Britain had deteriorated. Rome appointed Julius Agricola governor of the province in AD 78. He served eight years, during which time he steadfastly pushed the area of Roman domination northward to the line later chosen for Hadrian's Wall. Agricola penetrated further north into the Perthshire Highlands to Inchtuthill on the Tay where he built a vast legionary fortress. This was as far north as the Romans got a foothold. Thereafter, they made their way eastwards, via Strathmore and Kincardineshire, and up the east coast as far north as Kintore on the River Don.

Agricola led seven campaigns to complete the subjugation of the Caledonian tribes, fighting the last successful battle against the army of Calgacus at Mons Graupius in AD 84. This was the last occasion when a Celtic army used chariots against a Roman force. (Cunliffe 1997, 255) Mons Graupius marks the culmination of Rome's military victories against the Britons. The submission of the Orkney Islands tribes brought Agricola's victorious campaign to an end. However, the Roman hold on northern and western Caledonia was fragile at best, and the Romans ended up withdrawing to the Tuyne-Solway line. By this time, however, the greater part of Britain was under Roman administration. Only Caledonia and the Welsh area of Powys, then occupied by Ordovices and *Scotti* (Irish) tribes, remained independent.

About AD 100, Roman control in Scotland was at least partly abandoned for a time. A rebellion in northern Britain about AD 117 subsequently brought the Emperor Hadrian to Britain, and it was decided to abandon northern Britain entirely. Hadrian's Wall—from Wallsend on the Tyne to Bowness on the Solway—was built to secure the line of defense against the Picti and Caledonian tribes. Twenty years later, the building of the Antonine Wall (under Antoninus Pius) extended the boundary further north to the Clyde. Later rebellions and risings in the Scottish lowlands and the north of England destroyed the Roman defenses. Hadrian's Wall was repaired, but advance forts beyond the Wall were abandoned. Further forts were built southwards and westwards to prevent hostile Scotti landings on the coast. (Chadwick 1997, 71)

The Picts of Caledonia remained a continuing threat. In AD 306, they penetrated Roman defenses but were contained by Constantius Chlorus who died in York the same year. Another Pictish force reached London in AD 364 but was driven back by Theodosius the Great. From the fourth century onward, the situation grew more critical for the Romans as Pictish and Scotti tribes increasingly stepped up their attacks on Roman fortifications—so much so that before the end of the fourth century, the Romans had to abandon Hadrian's Wall. Niall of the Nine Hostages, High King of Ireland, raided Chester and Caerleon in AD 395, and a series of pirate wars continued until Niall was killed in a sea battle in AD 405. Saxons (Germanic tribes) made frequent raids on the east coast.

Emperor Constantine died in AD 337. He converted to Christianity on his deathbed; it was a significant conversion. According to the preponderance of historical sources, he was the architect of the "Edict of Milan" which reversed the policy of hostility of the Roman Empire to the Christian faith and accorded it full legal recognition. (Johnson 1995, 67) In AD 436, Roman troops left Britain for good. Almost immediately, waves of Angles, Saxons, and Jutes attacked, invading from the east and bringing with them new dialects and new gods. Anglish replaced Celtic in many places. Woden, Thor, and Freya supplanted Lugh, Bel, and Brigid. (King 1988, 100)

Welsh survived intact as a language; Wales survived as a political and cultural entity. The Romans had failed to conquer the Picts in Scotland. The Picts remained dominant until at least the fifth century AD when *Dál Riata* (Dalriada or Dalriata) tribes from northeastern Ulster, who had earlier formed the Scotti colony of Argyle, began expanding. As the Dál Riata people became dominant, the Gaelic language and influences came to prevail throughout the western islands and the Highlands. By the ninth century, the Picts ceased to exist as an autonomous nation, though some aspects of their culture lingered on into the Anglo-Norman ascendancy.

The Waterloo Helmet, 150-50 BC (British Museum, London). Dredged from the River Thames near the Waterloo Bridge in the 1860s, this Celtic bronze ceremonial helmet—decorated in La Tenè style—is the only Iron Age helmet with horns ever to have been found in Europe.

Administering Britain

Under Roman domination, few of the average Britons became Romanized; only their leaders adopted Roman customs and chose to live in Roman-style villas. The old socio-economic divisions at the time of the conquest remained unchanged throughout the Roman interlude. Outside the Roman-occupied areas, Roman institutions had little effect on the native population. In Cornwall, Wales, and the north, traditional patterns of Celtic living remained unchanged. The natives outside the areas of intense Romanization scarcely ever spoke Latin, the language of the rulers. Southern Britain, on the other hand, became integrated into the Roman Empire. Like Gaul a century before, Britain already consisted of political units which corresponded quite closely to the patterns which Rome was accustomed to dealing with: substantial and productive policies already sustaining, and controlled by defined aristocracies. The Romans did not seek to destroy annexed tribes; on the contrary, they sought to maintain much of the status quo, coalescing their resources with minimal disruption. With the exception of localized areas under the control of the military, there was no mass colonization of the island. (James 1999, 100-102)

Chapter VIII—
Post-Roman Britain

Over the two or more centuries after the exit of the Romans, increasing numbers of Germanic tribesmen (Jutes, Angles, and Saxons) from the continent, akin in language, religion and customs, overran much of Britain, undoing the political and social institutions Rome had instituted. According to Welsh tradition it was British treason that enabled the Saxons to settle in Britain.

—Jean Markale, *The Celts*

Soon after the death of Emperor Constantine, the Roman Empire began to unravel. Franks and Goths crossed the Rhine in AD 406, attacking Rome's western territories, while fierce Huns pounded away at her eastern frontiers. Rome began calling its military forces home from the peripheral regions of her Empire, leaving many of the outlying provinces (including Britain) to defend themselves. Rome began vacating Britain in AD 407. In AD 410, Honorius wrote to the Britons informing them that henceforth they would have to be responsible for their own defenses. (Rankin 1996, 227) The Roman withdrawal created an organizational upheaval of British institutions which, for the Britons (like the Gauls), meant taking on the responsibility of fighting off the hordes of invading barbarians. Teutonic peoples from the east, Picts and Scotti from the north, and Irish from the west rushed in to take over.

In spite of centuries of Roman influence and in spite of the blending of Italic and other foreign military elements into the population, most Britons stubbornly hung on to their native Celtic customs and way of life. (Rankin 1996, 213) During the Roman occupation, there was little cultural assimilation of the Celtic population. Under Roman domination, only the Briton leaders adopted Roman customs and chose to live in Roman-style villas. In Cornwall, Wales, and the northwest, traditional patterns of Celtic living remained unchanged. The language of the rulers was Latin. It was scarcely adopted by the native Britons outside the areas where significant Romanization had taken place. Of these areas, the Lowlands of Scotland, northern England, Wales, and the Cornish peninsula spoke Briton. North of the British periphery, the Picts were at least part Celtic; the Irish to the west were totally Celtic. In the end, it was within this impregnable region the struggle for the survival of Celtic civilization would take place.

Teutonic Incursions

While it is difficult to discern historical fact from mythological clouding during this period, it is quite probable that the Britons had resumed the old and dangerous game of appealing to one enemy to help rid them of another: The *Aedui* had called in the Romans; the Roman military had used Saxons and others as *foederati* (mercenaries) from before the end of the second century to fight off the troublesome Picts and Irish. It was now the Britons' turn to call in the Saxons in their defense against the Picts and the Scotti, who continued their incursions on the western and northern boundaries. (Markale 1993, 164)

The employment of mercenaries also contributed to an upsurge of foreigners seeking permanent homes, which is substantiated from archaeological sources showing the earlier Saxon arrivals were non-aggressive groups, opting instead for new settlements. Archaeologists confirm that, east of a line between York and Bedford, there is scarcely a Roman walled town. Instead, pottery and similar items uncovered have revealed Roman technique combined with

Saxon decoration, which suggests a close association of Roman and Saxon in the areas of the Saxon Shore and East Riding near York. Professor Myles Dillon states there is good reason to believe that, by the end of the third century, the Saxon Shore area was already partially settled, or the forts themselves had been partially manned by Saxons. These forts were the focal points of more-or-less organized trading relations with the Teutonic tribes across the North Sea. In Britain, as was the case with Gaul, what apparently began as relative small-scale enterprises led into settlements and, as Roman power weakened, into a military occupation. The creation of alien communities had displaced Roman and Celtic dominion alike. (Dillon 2003, 48) Furthermore, it was only a matter of time before the new migrants were calling themselves Anglo-Saxon and their newly adopted land England.

Historian and author T. W. Rolleston writes that the role of the Celtic peoples of Britain, to a large extent, has been acutely suppressed in popular thought from an early period even though they played a decisive role in the cultural and economic development of the island. He believes that the use of the term "Anglo-Saxon" to identify the British people as a description of ethnicity is largely responsible and especially misleading. The Anglo-Saxons, or the Romans before them, did not get rid of the Celtic or Celticized populations whom they found in control of Britain when they occupied the island.

Rolleston further claims there is little to support this singling out of "two Low-German tribes" (other than their conquest of Celtic Britain) to proclaim the ethnic character of the British people. He maintains that it is mistaken to label the inhabitants of Britain—and for that matter their descendents in North America and Australia—Anglo-Saxon. Rather, they should be identified as Anglo-Celtic, for it is about these people that the early history with its underlying account of the religion, and the heroic, mythical, and romantic literature of the Celtic peoples is told. (Rolleston 1911, Preface)

Historical Versus Mythical Allusions

Not a great deal is known about the period between the departure of the Romans in AD 407 and the Anglo-Saxon conquest some two centuries later. Documentary evidence is limited to a small number of inscriptions and a random selection of writings, of which those of Gildas, Nennius, and the Anglo-Saxon Bede are the most important. From what is available, it is difficult to separate factual accounts from those that are mythical—many of which have been passed down in the Arthurian legends. What is known is that during this intervening period (generally referred to by historians as the "Dark Ages"), a remarkably civilized society which the Romans had shaped came apart. In its place, the embryo of Anglo-Saxon Britain was planted.

Some historians argue that the collapse stemmed from the decline of strong central institutions after the Romans withdrew. Others believe its root cause was in the return to the tribal system of independent petty kingdoms, which was accelerated by the arrival of large numbers of Germanic tribesmen. Historians have a tendency to paint the "Dark Ages" as a period of anarchy and violence; archaeologists, on the other hand, take a less callous view of the period. Dr. Lloyd Laing, for example, describes it as a historical "Dawn," a time when documentary corroboration was easily attainable. (Laing 1991, 14)

In the areas formally subject to Roman jurisdiction, progress in the post-Roman period was markedly dissimilar from those areas outside the Imperial boundaries. The areas within Roman jurisdiction had been more exposed to Continental influence, and the inhabitants were generally familiar with their Germanic neighbors—those, in particular, recruited into the Roman army. It was also to these areas the Angles, Saxons, Jutes, Franks, and others arrived when they crossed the Channel from their homelands in the fifth and early sixth century. These people are credited with changing the name of the island from Briton to England, and they emerged as the dominant tribes. (Laing 1991, 123)

Vortigern: Celtic Hero or Traitor?

According to tradition, a Celtic prince named Vortigern came to prominence around AD 425. He assumed command in eastern Britain after the Romans had exited, and he assembled an armed force to push back the Picts and the Scotti. He appealed to the Saxon chiefs Hengist and Horsa for military aid and, in exchange, ceded them territory. He fell in love with Hengist's daughter and, to obtain her hand in marriage, surrendered Cantium (present-day Kent) to Hengist and the land bordering Hadrian's Wall to Hengist's son.

The Saxons, however, continued to be increasingly troublesome to deal with, so Vortigern is said to have fled to Wales where he built a stronghold at Mount Eryi (Snowdon). Vortigern's eldest son Guortepir (Gwrthevyr)—sometimes identified as Vortiporius, king of the *Demetae*—was much less appeasing to the Saxons than his father had been, and he waged several successful attacks against Hengist and his followers. It is believed that he killed the Saxon chief Horsa. After Guortepir's death, Vortigern assumed the leadership of the west Britons. When the Saxons renewed the offensive and were seizing increasingly more of his territories, he offered to negotiate peaceful terms. Thereupon, Hengist craftily invited him and several hundred Britons to a banquet where he had ordered his servants to take Vortigern prisoner and slay the remainder of the guests. This episode is substantiated in the *Gesta Regum Anglorum*:

> "Hengist deceitfully invited his son-in-law and three hundred British chiefs to a feast. His guests were deliberately inflamed by drink and angered by provocative speeches until they quarreled, first verbally, then physically. Every one of the Britons had his throat cut and gave up the ghost in the midst of the drinking. Their king was taken prisoner and paid for his freedom with three provinces." (Markale 1993, 166)

After the massacre and the loss of his three provinces, Vortigern retires to Wales. It is at this stage that Geoffrey of Monmouth relates the episode of the fatherless child and the two dragons. The child declares himself to be *Merlinus Ambrosius* (the Welsh texts call him *Myrddin Emrys*). Jean Markale writes that this is the first written allusion to Merlin whom Geoffrey was ultimately to make one of the best-known literary characters in Europe. (Markale 1993, 167) While the legend of the dragons is used by Geoffrey to symbolize the struggle between the Britons and the Saxons, the ritual significance of the dragon is from the Welsh tale, *Ludd and Llevelys*, dealing with three plagues that had fallen upon Britain. After Vortigern's death, the core resistance to the Saxons appears to have been confined to Wales. Traditionally, it was Uther Pendragon, the successor of Vortigern, who is believed to have avenged the honor of the Britons.

At the time of Vortigern's death (circa AD 461), much of the southeastern region of the island was in Anglo-Saxon hands, and the core of the resistance movement had moved to Wales under Uther Pendragon. It is through him that the story enters the Arthurian cycle where the struggle against the Saxons is told through the magical world of heroic deeds and legends in which the tribal chief Arthur is transformed into the authentic King Arthur. Like the Continental Celts, the Britons were constantly trying to consolidate their forces which invariably escaped them. Their Celtic world was crumbling: first it was the Roman invaders, then the Saxons. Although embittered and disillusioned, the Britons still hoped for military success, and it is through the adventures of the legendary King Arthur that the final chapter of the great struggle between the Britons and their Saxon foe is told.

The Legendary King Arthur

The earliest mention of the legendry Arthur occurs in the extant manuscript, *Gododin*, by the bard Aneurin, which dates from the thirteenth century but is believed to contain passages from a much earlier text. The second allusion to Arthur comes in the *Historia Brittonu*, which contains a blend of data from different writers, including the ninth century chronicler Nennius. Here, Arthur is described as *dux bellorum* (a war leader). The medieval, courtly tone now associated with Arthurian romance came from Geoffrey of Monmouth. Arthur is the son of Uther and Ygene Ingerna (wife of Gorlois, Duke of Cornwall) who are brought together by the help of Merlin's magic. Arthur defeats the Saxons, the Irish, and the Romans and conquers a good part of Europe. In doing so, he achieves great glory. His court is a meeting place for the bravest knights of the Celtic world who, on closer examination, become the gods and heroes of Irish and Welsh mythology. It is Arthur who sends his knights in quest of the Holy Grail. The discovery of the Grail, which represents the fulfillment of the quest, is a signal that the Celtic world is approaching its end. (Markale 1993, 171-173)

Arthur is accredited with twelve battles, most of which took place in the forest of Celyddon (Scotland). This suggests that the Britons of the time were concentrating their war effort on the northern frontiers. According to the *Annals of Cambri*, Arthur fought and won a fierce campaign against the Saxons at Mount Badon (identified as Baydon Hill) on the western border of Wessex in AD 516. The victory of Mount Badon is also mentioned in Gildas' *De Excidio Britanniae* where the victorious leader is named Aurelius Ambrosius, leading many historians to believe that Aurelius and Arthur were one and the same person.

Arthur and his contemporaries managed to halt the Anglo-Saxon expansion into the west until the middle of the sixth century; but soon after AD 550, the Saxons defeated the Britons at Salisbury and pushed westward again. Twenty-seven years later, a stunning defeat was handed to the Britons at Dyrham (AD 577), which delivered the strategic towns of Bath and Gloucester to the Saxons. The enemy had now reached the Severn valley, thereby cutting off Cornwall from Wales. It was at this point that several of the British tribes began to migrate. The Cornovii, who had first settled on the Welsh borders, were now in the Cornish peninsula and some crossed the Channel to find refuge in Brittany. The *Dunmonii*, whose home was in Devon, also went to Brittany to the area of Malo and Dinan where they founded the kingdom of *Donmonia*. Meanwhile, some Welsh and northern Britain tribes found refuge in Finistere. According to historian Jean Markale, Wales was then becoming overpopulated from the influx of refugees fleeing there from other parts of the island.

There was a brief period (AD 515-540) when the Britons held the Anglo-Saxons in check, but it is quite certain that the Britons were defeated about the end of the sixth century. Around this time, various chiefs tried to organize anti-Saxon resistance but were repeatedly fighting among themselves over questions of dominance. Now more fragmented than ever, Britain fell prey to all kinds of adventurers. One such notable was Geraint, son of Erbin, the hero of the Welsh tale of *Geraint and Enid*. Geraint was, in fact, King of the Britons who fought the King of Wessex in AD 710. (Markale 1993, 176)

Arthurian literature is animated by what seems an excess of Celtic energy, later to be cultivated by the Plantagenet dynasty. With its blend of Saxons, Normans, and Britons, it assumed control of England. The Plantagenets, and especially Henry II, came to realize how much could be gained from exploiting British pan-Celticism in the fight against continental Capetian (Charlemagne) influence. "The insular Celtic emperor Arthur rose to challenge the continental Charlemagne whose throne had passed to the Capetians." (Markale 1993, 171) Arthur came to represent the Celtic spirit; he was the emblem of Celtic resistance to the Anglicization of Britain.

Irish Settlements of Wales and Cornwall

During the fifth century and earlier, the weakening power of the Roman Empire gave great momentum to the movements and expansion of the Insular Celtic peoples, who were always seeking to extend their territory. The Irish, in particular, took advantage of the military weakness of the Roman defenses of western Britain to penetrate the western peninsulas of Wales. From the fourth century, Irish raids were no less fearsome than those of the Picts and Saxons from the north and east. The Irish Sea had always been, and continued to be, a purely Celtic area—both politically and culturally. The Romans did not rule here, and there was no unified Celtic power to preclude the free movement of the individual Celtic communities to and fro across this Celtic waterway. Among the most significant of the Irish expansions was the occupation of southwestern Wales, an area somewhat larger than Pembrokeshire (later known as the kingdom of Dyfed). This area was occupied by a dynasty from Leinster, who led a migration and settled in sufficient numbers to render the population bilingual in the fifth century. (Dillon 2003, 38)

During the same period, Irish penetration of the Caernarvonshire peninsula left abundant traces of place-names and archaeological evidence of Roman defenses. The northern peninsula was known, and is still known today, by the name of *Lleyn* (from Irish *Laigin* meaning "the Leinstermen"). According to late Welsh tradition—preserved in what is believed to be the oldest part of the *Historia Brittonun* and dating perhaps from the seventh century (though finally compiled by Nennius in the early ninth century)—a certain Cubnedda came to North Wales with his eight sons and grandsons from Manau Gododdin (the ancient territory of the *Votadini*) to the south of the Firth of Forth. They drove out the Irish from these regions; it is believed there was immense slaughter. The Irish never returned again to inhabit this area. Historians tell us that there is no corroboration to support this story. (Dillon 2003, 41)

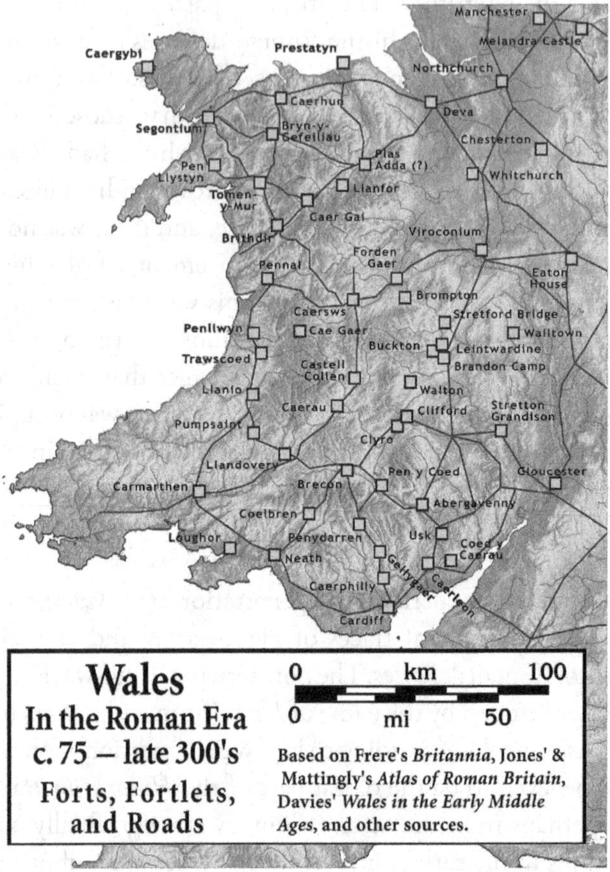

Wales in the Roman Era, circa 75-late 300's AD.

The Final Chapter in Celtic Britain

In the waning centuries of the Anglo-Saxon conflict, several Briton chieftains tried to pick up the pieces and organize anti-Saxon resistance, but their efforts were futile due to continuous infighting among themselves. The Anglo-Saxons continued to expand their dominance over the native Britons: first in the kingdoms of Kent and Anglia and next in Devon. By the mid-seventh century, Northumbria emerged out of the alliance of two kingdoms, Bernica and Deira, and this alliance was later extended to include all of the territory from Yorkshire to the Lothians. Still, later in the eighth century, Northumbria was incorporated into the central Anglo-Saxon kingdom of Mercia, which became important under the distinguished leader Offa. The various kingdoms continued to coalesce; around AD 927, under the leadership of Athelstan, there emerged a unified Anglo-Saxon England.

But the Britons were determined to make one more attempt at overthrowing the Saxons. In AD 937, Howel Dda, king of south Wales and Powys, reunited the Britons by forming a coalition composed of Welshmen, Cornishmen, the men of Strathclyde, and even including Picts, Danes, and Irishmen in an attempt to drive out the Saxons. The Saxon leader Athelstan eventually defeated Dda's forces. England was now firmly in Anglo-Saxon hands. However, to what extent the Celtic population of Britain was displaced by the Teutonic invaders is not known. From historical accounts, some of the Celtic-speaking peasantry were enslaved (a usual practice of the conqueror), others fled to hilly regions in the west and the north, while yet others took refuge across the Channel in Brittany.

The Celtic world (which at an earlier date had encompassed most of western Europe and the British Isles) was now confined to Ireland, Wales, the Scottish Highlands, Brittany, and to a lesser degree Cornwall, where the inhabitants held tightly to their Celtic language, customs, and ways. Like the Celts elsewhere, the Britons were constantly seeking unity—though only, perhaps, in theory for they never realized it in practice. The Saxon invasions were, in a sense, the last straw for a Celtic society already subjugated by the Romans. In the words of Jean Markale:

> "The bitter taste of defeat gave the Britons a natural longing for revenge; but since there could be no question of retaliation on the material level, and since the ancient Celtic world was crumbling away, vengeance became a matter of ideas. And it was through these ideas that the

> Britons ultimately achieved their finest victory. In any case, myth-making was an essential characteristic of the Celtic mind, and by some process of reversal, the Britons succeeded in turning every defeat into a magical adventure where the erosion of Celtic society could be attributed only to supernatural events. In this way the tribal chief Arthur is transformed into a real king." (Markale 1993, 70)

During the eighth century, new barbarian invasions took place from Scandinavia, sweeping east over Russia and west over the British Isles and the peripheral countries of western Europe. But it was the conquest of England by William of Normandy in the eleventh century which had a profound influence on the development and future of the Celts, despite the fact that in the initial stage it mattered only to the Anglo-Saxon population. A number of Breton Celts came with William to avenge the Saxon conquest of their ancestral homeland; they were rewarded for their help with gifts of land taken from the Saxons, and in the end they became more English than Briton.

The last of the Welsh kings was Llywelyn ab Gruffyd (1246-1282). Llywelyn spent his life trying to safeguard Welsh independence. For a short time, Wales managed to retain a certain degree of autonomy. In AD 1277, Llywelyn was forced to surrender all claims to homage from other Welsh chiefs. He died in AD 1282 in a battle against the Anglo-Normans near Buelt. Welsh self-determination had reached its final stages. Edward I of England accorded the title Prince of Wales to his son, the future Edward II. (Markale 1993, 190)

Aberlemno Cross (Angus, Scotland). Located in the Aberlemno kirkyard, this eighth century sandstone sculpture bears a Celtic high cross on the front and Pictish symbols on the back.

Scotland

Scotland did not emerge into recorded history until Julius Agricola attempted to conquer it in AD 80-84. Scotland's early history, at the time when contemporary written records were emerging in the early seventh century, is particularly difficult to trace. This is due to the fact that Scotland was divided among four peoples: Picts, Dál Riata (Irish), Britons, and Angles. They differed widely from one another in origin, and all spoke different languages.

Of these, the Picts north of the Firth of Forth and Clyde—whom the Romans regarded as wild and barbaric—were the most ancient both in language and tradition. Some historians believed them to be a pre-Celtic people. The Venerable Bede (circa AD 673-735) regarded their language as different from Celtic. Later, historians discounted this view and considered the Picts to be unquestionably Celtic, speaking a language (long lost) which was part Celtic and part belonging to some more ancient tongue, probably that of an indigenous people who were occupying the region when the Picts arrived. Little of the early Pictish tradition has survived, but according to some sources their kinsmen the Cruitins ruled small kingdoms in Ireland. (Dillon 2003, 78)

The Picts were the dominant tribes until at least the fifth century when Dál Riata tribes from northeastern Ulster, who had earlier formed the Scotti colony of Argyle, began expanding. As early as the third century, the Dál Riata began moving off their lands in western Munster (west Cork and county Kerry). Heading for the northeastern area of Ulster, they formed a new community among the Cruitin tribes. Shortly after, a band crossed over to Caledonia where they established a colony in the peninsulas and islands that make up the present Argyle area of western Scotland. A century or so later, the Argyle Dál Riata tribes were joined by another party of their Kerry kinsmen under a leader named Fergus.

Over the next century, the Dál Riata steadfastly battled the Picts as they sought to expand beyond their original settlements to accommodate their ever-growing population. It was not until the late fifth century, however, and with the aid of the Irish king Niall of the Nine Hostages, that the Picts along the western seaboard were brought under submission. From the sixth century onwards, the struggle for supremacy between the northern and southern Picts on the one hand, and the Irish kingdom of Dál Riata on the other, formed the most important episode in the history of Scotland until the union of the two peoples in the middle of the ninth century. The nation of Scotland as we know it emerged from this union.

The Dál Riata in Scotland remained closely linked, and possibly tributary, to their kinsfolk in Ireland until AD 576, at which time they were granted independence. A decree issued by the Assembly of Druim Ceata under the guidance of Saint Columba made the king of the Scotti in Scotland independent of the authority of the High King of Ireland. A treaty was also adopted: In case of war, the Irish kingdom of the Dál Riata was obliged to serve the Irish high king with its land forces and the king of the Scotti with his sea forces.

For the next two-and-a-half centuries, relations between the Dál Riata and the Pictish communities were relatively calm. However, near the end of the eighth century in the reign of Don Coirce, the Dál Riata were attacked by the Norsemen. They were pushed eastward from their west coast settlements, and they in turn pushed the Picts further east and northeast. The windfalls of war changed several times before destiny ordained that the Dál Riata and the Picts be fused into one kingdom (Scotland). The driving force behind the unification was the Dál Riata king, Cinead (Kenneth) MacAlpin. He became the first king of the Scotti; his death is recorded for AD 858. (Dillon 2003, 110-111)

Now that the Dál Riata were the dominant people in Caledonia (except in the southeastern area ruled by the Angles), the name Scotia Minor was applied to the area. Scotia had then been the name applied to Ireland. Later, the title Scotia was dropped completely from Ireland and it became the exclusive name for former Caledonia. The Gaelic language and influences came to prevail throughout the west and the Highlands; by the ninth century, the Picts had ceased to exist as an autonomous nation, though some aspects of their culture lingered on into the Anglo-Norman ascendancy.

Lastly, Briton tribes occupied the whole of the southern territory between the two Roman Walls, at least from Roman times and probably much earlier. By the middle of the sixth century, a new Teutonic dynasty had superimposed itself in the eastern territory of northern Britain, founding the Anglian kingdom of

Bernicia. This new political element rapidly extended its authority along southeastern Scotland, annexing the British area of Manau Guotodin and the whole of the old area belonging to the Votadini. (Dillon 2003, 78-79)

The Hunterston Brooch, circa 700 AD (Royal Museum of Scotland, Edinburgh).
Discovered in Hunterston, Ayshire, in the 1830s, this ornate silver brooch—with detailed silver and gold filigree and amber studs—is considered to be one of the earliest and finest of Celtic brooches to survive.

Chapter IX—

Celtic Ireland Beyond the Mists

When the Celts arrived in Ireland, the island had been inhabited for over 7,000 years. These pre-Celts have left no written records: they were literary pre-historic. But they have left extensive archaeological evidence, of which Newgrange is the most celebrated example.

—Laurence Flanagan, *Ancient Ireland: Life Before the Celts*

At a site near Ballycastle in northwestern County Mayo, archeologists discovered an extensive Neolithic field system preserved beneath a blanket of peat bog. Now known as the Céide Fields, the site has an impressive system of fields covering an area of four square miles, separated from one another by long parallel stone walls running down towards the sea, with offset subsidiary walls dividing the long enclosures into individual fields. Arguably the oldest of its kind in the world, the site provides an incredible snapshot of the Irish countryside from five millennia ago. According to archaeological evidence, Céide Fields was farmed for several centuries between 3500 BC and 3000 BC. Radiocarbon dating for a hearth beside the remains of a house confirms that humans lived here a few centuries before 3000 BC. Shreds of broken pottery found at the site are similar to those found in Stone Age tombs in western Europe. The cutting part of a primitive plow unearthed provides a clue to what was once a settled agricultural community. (Flanagan 1998, 42)

The Stone Age dwellings at Céide Fields suggest a developed social order for the many families who resided there and thousands more scattered throughout North Mayo. Archaeologists are of the opinion that the folks of Céide Fields belonged to a common west European farming tradition, which began before 6000 BC in the Middle East. Regrettably, they had no written language to pass on more about themselves. However, their elaborate structures tell us they must have been accomplished in many skills for Céide Fields provides an incredible picture into Ireland's distant past. The site near Ballycastle by no means represents Ireland's earliest human inhabitants. Radiocarbon datings, ranging from circa 7010 BC to circa 6490 BC, have been found at half a dozen earlier Mesolithic sites scattered throughout the country.

After the Ice Age

For the story of Ireland's Celtic past, we must first journey back in time into the island's remote past. During the last Ice Age, which lasted from 100,000 until about 15,000 years ago, Ireland was part of the European land mass. At various stages in its duration, much of the land was covered by an icecap similar to what one finds in Arctic areas today. The ice cover was not continuous, for alternating warm and cold stages caused the glaciers to retreat and expand accordingly. The question arises as to whether humans may have been present in Ireland during one or another of those warm phases when the glaciers were in retreat. To date, there is no scientific evidence of that possibility; no Old Stone Age tools from the Paleolithic period have been unearthed, and no extraordinary animal paintings (such as those on cave walls in France and Spain) have been discovered. Conditions were too cold over much of Europe for vegetation to grow.

Ice covered the highlands of the north and the mountains of central Europe. On the lowlands there were rich and fertile grassy plains with great herds of deer and horses. In southern France, and in parts of Spain in particular, a large population survived by hunting big game. They lived in caves. At Lascaux and other places, they painted wonderful pictures of the animals they hunted on cave walls. Then, over the next several thousand years, enormous masses of ice began slowly withdrawing northwards as, century after century, the climate improved. These hunters followed the game into England, for the English Channel did not then exist. They left no pictures in England, but their first implements have been found, and their living conditions are believed to have been much the same as in France. Despite the efforts of many historians to establish their presence in Ireland, or to find any of their tools, these early hunters do not seem to have reached there. (Moody, ed. 1967, 31)

The first people to set foot in Ireland arrived about 7,000 BC. Later, Mesolithic people were believed to have migrated across the North Channel from Scotland. Settlement sites of Mesolithic people have been found in several sites scattered throughout the country. They arrived after the ice retreated and are known mainly from the remains of their more durable implements, those of flint or stone from sites at Mount Sandel (County Derry) and Lough Boora (County Offaly). It is a meager record, from which little can be reconstructed except some information on their basic economy.

While little is known about the Mesolithic people of Ireland, it is relevant to start out with them. According to archaeologists, they lived on a varied diet of seafood, birds, wild boar, and hazelnuts; they lived in seasonal shelters, which they constructed by stretching animal skins over simple wooden frames, and they had outdoor hearths for cooking their food. There is no evidence of deer in the Irish Mesolithic Age, and it is unlikely that the first red deer were introduced until the early stages of the Neolithic Age. The human population hunted with spears, arrows, and harpoons tipped with small flint blades called microliths. During the Mesolithic Age, the population of Ireland was probably never more than a few thousand. (Flanagan 1998, 20)

Neolithic Peoples

Archaeologists describe the Neolithic or new Stone Age as a revolutionary era and perhaps the most significant step forward in the history of man. From that time on, instead of being at the mercy of nature, man could control his environment. He learned to polish rough stone tools and to make a more effective hoe or axe. He invented the felling axe to clear the forests and make more land available for cultivation and, hence, more food for his family.

It was the expanding population in the Middle East that forced Neolithic people to spread out in a never-ending search for new land. They pushed west along the Mediterranean to Spain and France, moved up through France to the Channel coast and on to Ireland, Britain, and the Low Countries. This expansion took a long time, but by various dating methods archaeologists can say that the Neolithic colonizers reached northwest Europe and Ireland about 3500 BC. (Moody 1967, 35)

Neolithic folk were the first farmers, and they introduced agriculture and animal husbandry to the island, as well as the skills of pottery making and weaving. They also started a custom of burying their dead collectively (usually cremated) in large stone-built chambered burial places known as megalithic tombs. Ruins of many such structures still dot the Irish countryside. Data extracted from Neolithic sites—such as the court tomb at Annaghmare (County Armagh) and the passage tomb at Knowth (County Meath)—attest to the presence of a variety of domesticated animals: cows, goats, and pigs. As mentioned above, the extensive Neolithic field system at Céide Fields in northwestern County Mayo is the site of an impressive system of fields covering an area of four square miles where Neolithic man tilled and herded around 3500 BC. These pre-Celtic folk left no written records. We know little of their beliefs, their institutions, or their traditions. A clue to their religious beliefs may be in the spirals, lozenges, and zigzag patterns which decorate the stones in tombs such as the one at Newgrange in County

Meath. They did, nonetheless, leave behind extensive archaeological evidence in the form of sites and megalithic monuments. (Moody, ed. 1967, 39)

We do know more about the immigrants that followed them. We know them as the Celts, and they made Ireland their home for more than twenty-six hundred years; even today, some vestiges of their ways survive in the Irish-speaking households of western Ireland.

Celtic Tribes in Ireland

Ireland entered a new phase of her history with the arrival of the Celts. They came in successive waves of migration from Britain and mainland Europe in the millennium before the Christian era. They brought with them their culture and social structure which they superimposed on that of the island's indigenous population. It was a social structure that divided the island into many tribal kingdoms based on family ties. Families were loosely joined together in aggregations of three or four into local kingdoms, which in turn were grouped with several other kingdoms to form a provincial-kingdom.

The historical period in Ireland did not begin until the fifth century AD, when writing was first introduced with the coming of Christianity. Therefore, many of the stories passed down relating to Celtic invasions and the colonization of ancient Ireland have mythical overtones. The oldest-surviving native historical record (believed to be the most reliable) is the *Annals of Tighernach*, a history of Ireland prepared in the late eleventh century at Clonmacnoise. During the twelfth century, a new book appeared in Ireland titled *Leabhar Gabhala* (*Book of Invasions*). This book was a compilation of the traditions of Ireland's ancient past—presumably both oral and written—detailing an account of the origins of the Celtic Irish, the various invasions, and the formation of the monarchy. While it is classified as a work of mythology, there is undoubtedly much in it that is historically true. There are dim echoes of the Bronze and Iron Ages, and echoes of a society similar in many ways to the one the Romans found in Gaul in the first century BC.

Celtic culture in Ireland, however, is generally believed to have found its roots in the last millennium BC, during the Iron Age. The first Celtic-speaking tribes are believed to have arrived on the island about 600 BC in what is referred to as the Hallstatt era. Other colonists followed them, the main thrust arriving in the later La Tène era sometime between the third and first centuries. They came from neighboring Britain, Gaul, and Iberia—tribes from two main stems of the Continental Celts. They were fleeing the Roman legions as they advanced across Europe at that time. By the time Julius Caesar had completed his conquest of Celtic Europe in the first century, the beginning of the end of Celtic society on the European mainland had arrived. The imperial armies of Rome next invaded Britain and again the Celts capitulated. Only in Ireland, untouched by the Romans, would Celtic culture survive and flourish, similar in many ways to what it had been in the centuries before the first Roman legions marched across the Alps to transform the face of Europe.

Medieval Accounts of Celtic Incursions

Native historical renditions from medieval accounts describe four separate Celtic incursions into Ireland in pre-historic times. They were, firstly, the *Priteni* who settled in both Ireland and Britain; next, the *Euerni* who invaded Ireland from Britain; following them were the *Laginian* tribes who came from Armorica (present-day Brittany) and who may have invaded Ireland and Britain more or less simultaneously; and, lastly, the *Goidels* who reached Ireland from northern Iberia and southern Gaul.

The earlier invaders are believed to have spoken a Brythonic dialect of Celtic recognized linguistically as P-Celtic. It was the language of Gaul and Britain, and it survives today as Welsh, Cornish, and Breton. The Goidel invaders spoke the Gaelic dialect, recognized linguistically as Q-Celtic, which they brought with them from Spain. Gaelic replaced Brythonic over time as the dominant idiom of the Irish Celts and it survives today in the Irish, Scottish, and Manx languages.

The First Wave—Priteni

The Priteni tribes (Ireland and Britain were known to the early Greeks as the Pritenic Islands) are believed to have arrived sometime after 700 BC. Their origin as Celts is questionable and, according to some sources, they were more likely to have been the indigenous descendants of the earlier Neolithic inhabitants of the island. Probably, they were a mixture of both. Their descendants in Ireland were the Cruitini tribes, later living alongside the powerful Dál Riata that dominated northeastern Ulster up to the ninth century AD. The Romans, who never fully succeeded in conquering them in northern Britain, referred to them as the Picti, meaning painted people.

The Second Wave—Euerni

The second wave, known as the Euerni (and also referred to as *Erainn*, *Menapii*, *Bolgi*, Belgae, and the mythological *Firbolgs*) by annalists and historians, arrived after 500 BC. They called their new home *Eueriio*, which would later evolve through the old Irish *Eriu* to Eire, and from Eire to Ireland. The second century Greek geographer Ptolemy drew a map of ancient Ireland showing branches of the Euerni widely dispersed throughout the island, but with their strongest connection in the areas around Cork and Kerry where they first settled. According to historian J. Rhys (1890), the Euerni were a seafaring people who wore breeches, wielded improved weapons, and traced their origins to the goddess *Bolg*.

Norman Mongan, in his well-researched book *Menapia Quest* (1995), traces their origin to the Menappi, a confederation of Belgae Celts from north Gaul and the area now known as Belgium.

Mongan suggests that many Euerni survived into early historic times as "tributary" tribes. He also suggests that many of today's name places in Ireland and elsewhere containing syllables such as *mong*, *muin*, *maion*, *maine*, *managh*, *monach*, *manach*, and *mannog* attest to the presence of the Euerni in the area at some stage. Branches of the Euerni identified with early historical times in Ireland have been identified as Corcu Loige (West Cork); Corcu Duibne (Kerry); Muscraige (allies of the Goidels in a number of detached districts between the River Lee and the extreme north of Tipperary); Corcu Baiscinn in west Clare; Calraige (Westmeath, Longford, Roscommon, Mayo, and Sligo); Dal Fiatach in east Down; Dál Riata north Antrim; and Osraige, *Ui Bairrche*, Ui Liathain, and Desi of east Munster. (Mongan 1995, 74, 126-128) Father Hanlon's edited version of the *Life of St. Greallan, Patron of the Ui Maine* refers to the Euerni people as the earliest noted aboriginal inhabitants of the province of Connacht.

After the beginning of the La Tène era, the Euerni were followed by other Belgae colonists. They contributed greatly to their adopted country with their art forms: swords, torcs, and vessels very similar to those produced on the Continent. However, there is little evidence that their technological capabilities had any effect on the archaic life-style of the natives. They seem to have set up very few oppidum-like hill settlements, common in Britain and the Continent at the time. Instead, they made do with the natives' style of dwellings: rudimentary circular beehive-shaped stone houses built without mortar.

The Third Wave—Laginian

The third colonization of Ireland is believed to have taken place sometime about 300 BC. These folk, named the Laginians and mythologically referred to as the *Tuatha De Danann*, are believed to have come from the northwestern region of Gaul, later Normandy. Their name association with *Laighi*, the ancient name for Leinster, suggests that this was where they first settled. Another branch of the same people, called the *Galioin* (or *Gailenga*), settled in an area north of Dublin. Eventually, the Galioin extended their dominance to Connacht, and in the process forced the Euerni tribes into the remote parts of the province. The remains of many great stone forts built by the Euerni in their defense against the *Laigain* tribes can still be seen in remote areas of western Ireland. Within a few generations, the Laigain and Galioin tribes were well established in northern Connacht, where in County Sligo their descendants include O'Hara, O'Gara, and other families. Their strength, nonetheless, was uppermost in southeastern Leinster where they remained the dominant power into historic times. In Munster and in Ulster they made little impact, suggesting that their conquest was limited to parts of present-day Leinster and Connacht. Like the Euerni, the Laginian tribes were linguistically P-Celts and had kinsmen in Britain.

There is mention in the *Táin Bo Cualnge* tale of three thousand Gailioin warriors serving under Queen Meave of Connacht and her consort Ailill in their expedition into Ulster against King Conchobar. The *Táin*, one of the great Irish heroic sagas, depicts warfare between the men of Connacht and the men of Ulster in which Cuchullian and his "ardent and adored foster brother" Ferdia face each other in a deadly single combat. The story, we are told, has many similarities to the Gaulish world of pre-Roman times—druids, feasting, heroic warriors, fearless women, and greedy kings—but all are seen through the eyes and imaginations of the medieval Irish audience. Just as Homer fused the world of Bronze Age Greece with elements of his own era centuries later, the *Táin* combines the lost age of pre-Christian Ireland with the culture of the Irish Middle Ages. (Freeman 2006, 193)

The Fourth Wave—Goidel

The last major Celtic settlement in Ireland is believed to have taken place sometime between 150-50 BC. These invaders have been identified as the Goidel or *Milesians* (sons of Mil) who, according to tradition, fled Roman incursions into northern Iberia and southern Gaul. They were Iron Age Celts and their ensuing dominance over the island was to last well over a thousand years. The ancient manuscript, *Leabar-Gabala*, has them landing at two locations—Kerry in the south and the Boyne estuary in the east. Those who landed through the Boyne estuary pushed the earlier Laighin settlers from their land in north Leinster and established their kingship at Tara. The southern Gaels had no fixed location in the beginning; instead, they pushed inland moving from one district linking to another until eventually they made Cashel their headquarters.

The early annalists describe how the Euerni people survived as distinct tribes well into early historical times. In Connacht, they were the *Ui Maine*, *Conmhaicne*, and other tribes farming alongside the *Ui Fiachrach* and *Ui Briuin* families of the ascendancy Goidel. In Leinster, they were the *Ui Failige*, Ui Bairrche, and *Ui Enechglaiss*. In Ulster and in Munster, many tribes can be identified whose pedigrees can be traced to the Euerni. Likewise, tribes of the Laigain people flourished alongside their Iberian Goidel masters. In the Midlands, Laigain warriors entered the service of the Goidel who assigned them "sword-land" in return for their services and tribute. Laginian tribes (*Gailing*) also aided the Goidel in their conquest of Connacht and were rewarded with a grant of territory in Mayo where the barony of Gallen preserves their name.

Goidel subjugation of the Euerni and Laighin occupiers of the island was, according to O'Rahilly, still incomplete as late as the beginning of the fifth century AD. The Ulaid tribe still ruled Emain and was challenging the midland Goidel for supremacy, and it was only in AD 516 that the conquest of the midlands was finally achieved when "the Plain of Mide" was wrested from the Laighin. (O'Rahilly 1946, 92-97)

Should the medieval account (with mythical overtones) of successive waves of invaders be accepted as the manner in which the Celts colonized Ireland? Much of what is recounted about Ireland's Celtic invasions would undoubtedly fail serious critical analysis. Archaeologists and historians alike are not convinced, believing that it is not supported by archaeological evidence. Professor John King suggests that the overall pattern seems to have been more complex than a single series of tribal incursions, that archaeological data shows that continental influence was trickling onto the island for hundreds of years before the main body of Celtic people began to arrive, and that the indigenous inhabitants who previously occupied the island were not eliminated, nor even conquered. However, the stories provide a key to unlocking a genuine long-lost history and help somewhat in unraveling the real story of ancient Ireland and from whence the various colonists originated.

Without the classical sources of information on Ireland (such as that which is available from Roman and Greek sources about the Continental Celts), historians are limited to what archaeology and the vernacular literature can reveal. As always, archaeological evidence raises questions of interpretation, and the vernacular evidence is limited and imprecise because it was written down largely by Christian scribes many centuries after the events described actually took place.

Chapter X—
Pre-Christian Ireland

Unfortunately, we know practically nothing about the religious beliefs of the pre-Christian population . . . . The entire pre-fifth-century Irish experience has been filtered through the prism of later Christian writers, and those aspects, which would have been of most interest to the modern student have been irredeemably diluted.

—Dáibhí Ó Crónin, *Early Western Ireland 400-1200*

Historians have been challenged in their efforts to reconstruct the early history of Ireland. The Irish thought of their history in mythical terms; written corroboration comes from mythological tales, poems, and the *Leabhar Gabala* (or *Book of Invasions*, a scholarly compilation of various oral traditions, annals, and genealogies). These accounts were, of course, not recorded in writing until after the arrival of Christianity in the fifth century AD. Professor Thomas O'Rahilly writes in his *Early History and Mythology* that much of what they tell us of the history of pre-Christian Ireland should not be looked upon as dependable. But he goes on to qualify this remark by writing, after criticism has done its legitimate upmost, there remains a modest residuum from which important historical deductions can be drawn.

There are, of course, other sources: the contemporary evidence provided by Greek and Latin writers, although their supply of information concerning Ireland is somewhat sparse. There is also the valuable account of Ireland preserved in Ptolmey's *Geography*. The island Ptolmey describes is regarded as the oldest account of Ireland that exists. It is an Ireland dominated by the Euerni tribes where neither the Laginian invaders nor the Goidels have as yet arrived. According to Ptolmey, Ireland is Celtic-speaking of the Brittonic type. O'Rahilly goes on to provide a list of Irish tribal and place-names, which he believes must have been derived, directly or indirectly, from some geographer who lived several centuries before Ptolmey's time.

Still, other sources of information can be derived from the close contacts that existed between Ireland and Britain, and no discussion of the history of pre-Christian Ireland could ignore the history of the neighboring island. In pre-Christian times, Belgae and Domnonii tribes occupied considerable parts of both countries. Earlier still, the Priteni tribes (known to the Romans as Picti) were chief in Britain and Ireland. There were Irish raids against Roman Britain, and Irish settlements in Wales and Cornwall. And, finally, we must not overlook the information supported by archaeological discoveries. All of these areas provide much information which help in formulating an image of early Ireland. (O'Rahilly 1999, v)

Historical Map of Ireland by artist Wenzel Hollar (1607-1677).

Society of Tribal Overlords

Celtic society in pre-Christian Ireland was remote and beyond the influence of the civilized world in the centuries following the Goidel (Milesians) ascendancy. Because of this, life continued to function as it had in Britain and Gaul prior to the Roman conquest. The lifestyle was rural, strongly tribal, and loosely organized into largely autonomous communities bound together by family ties. This was in marked contrast to the centralized and urban characteristics of Celtic societies that had come under the sway of Roman influence.

It was a heroic age that kept alive traditions that the settlers had brought with them from their ancestral homes. Kings fought kings; warriors stole wives and massacred each other. Conflict flared mainly on issues of livestock, where the rustling of cattle was a usual pretext for a call to arms. It was very much a society of tribal overlords and Iron Age warriors with a culture akin to that of Homeric Greece and pre-Roman Gaul. The steady arrival of settlers over the centuries and their inevitable assimilation has made it difficult for historians to distinguish, with any certainty, which tribe belonged to which people. Most pre-Goidel tribes—particularly those belonging to the Euerni and Laginian peoples—remained in place, forming the basis for the future society that would be dominated by the less numerous but more powerful Goidel people. Many were reduced to subsidiary status; others, powerful enough to maintain a substantial degree of sovereignty within their well-established territories, coexisted with the new rulers.

Verse passed down from the *filidh* (ancient poets) describes how tribes from the Goidel, Euerni, and Laginian peoples coexisted and intermarried. In his introduction to *Leabhar-I-Eadhra* (*Book of O'Hara*, 1980), Lambert McKenna, S.J. writes that the filidh (who were also family historians) tell of the existence of two distinct kinds of ruling families in early Ireland. To the first kind belonged the families of the conquering Goidel people who had established themselves as ascendancy masters. To the second were the leading families of the pre-Goidel tribes, such as the Euerni and Laginian peoples who, although reduced in importance to the level of tributary folk, were in many instances permitted to carry on a certain measure of influence and freedom within their communities. Their chieftains, many of whom were men of wealth and influence, were often granted noble ancestry linking them to the ruling Goidel families.

But coexistence didn't necessarily mean social equality. *The Book of Genealogies* (a genealogical treatise), compiled in 1650 by Sligo native Duald MacFirbis from older authorities, describes the attitudes of the Goidel toward the Euerni and Laginian folk. They were spoken of in unflattering terms while the Goidel themselves were heaped with praise. Of the Goidel it was said that, "Everyone who is white of skin, brown of hair, bold, honorable, daring, prosperous, bestowal of property, wealth, and rings, and who is not afraid of battle or combat, they are the descendants of Milesius of Erinn." The Laginian, on the other hand, were judged as, "Everyone who is fair-haired, vengeful, large, and every plunderer; every musical person, the professors of musical and entertaining performances, who are adept in all Druidical and magical arts, they are the descendants of the De Danann." The Euerni received the least complimentary accolades and were said to be, "Everyone who is black-haired, who is a tattler, guileful, tale-telling, noisy, contemptible; every wretched, mean, strolling, unsteady, harsh, and inhospitable person; every slave, every mean thief, the disturbers of every council, and every assembly, and the promoters of discord among the people, these are the descendants of the Firbolgs." (Joyce, vol. 1, 1977)

Social Structure of Pre-Christian Ireland

The social structure of pre-Christian Ireland was similar in many ways to that of Celtic Gaul in pre-Roman times in that the island was divided into many tribal kingdoms based on family ties. A group of families occupied a division of land called a *tuath* within which the members equally owned the land. The members of the tuath, collectively known as the *deirbhfine*, consisted of all relations in the male line of descent for five generations. Included were a man's sons, his father's brothers, his grandfather's brothers, and so on, all sharing alike in the family's belongings and privileges, achievements, and misfortunes. Each tuath was presided over by a chieftain elected by its freemen (who alone had that privilege) from among the many eligible members of the ruling family. The king had certain delegated powers which included leading the army in time of war and representing the tuath in time of peace, but did not include making or enforcing the laws which belonged to an assembly of freemen. Several tuaths, when allied together, made up a local kingdom which was ruled by an over-king. Local kingdoms in turn formed confederated alliances ruled by a provincial king.

Ancient Ireland had a well-developed and complex tribal culture consisting of a highly codified legal system that regulated relationships within and between classes, families, larger kin-groups, and inhabitants of tuaths. The early Irish law tracts tell us that society within the tuath was precisely defined. Below the *ri tuaithe* (petty king) was an aristocracy composed of noble ranks whose status was measured partly by the number of their *celi* (clients). In early Irish law, clientship was known by the Gaelic term *ceilsine*. Beneath the aristocracy were the *boaire* (freemen), persons who belonged to the franchise-holding classes whose property had a value of at least twenty-one *cumals*. Also included were the learned, certain skilled craftsmen and (alone among the musician class) the harpists. Beneath the boaire were the non-free who constituted the majority of the tuath members. "Non-free" did not mean slaves only, though there were slaves. The non-free were those who did not have the legal rights of the freemen. They had no property or possessions; they were tenants, laborers, herdsmen, inferior craftsmen, squatters, and interlopers from other territories.

Agreements were transacted collectively as all deirbhfine property was communal. Members were given only limited rights. Leadership of the tuath belonged to members of the great families. Noblemen of lesser rank would attain, at most, the position of retinue leader. Mastery of an art or craft enabled a man to climb the social ladder. There were no towns or centralized authorities.

The ri tuaithe was elected to office by a gathering of the privileged classes, who in fact represented a minority assembly as it excluded the non-privileged members. All male descendants of a former king, extending to and including great-grandsons, were eligible to compete for the kingship spot. Primogeniture was not an advantage; superior military aptitude and leadership talent were the essential requirements. Much was expected of the person who would occupy the highest office in the tuath. By present day standards, one could reason that it was a democratic system in a way. There were flaws, nonetheless, in the *modus operandi.* The rule precluding primogeniture succession often meant many rival contenders for the kingship, thus producing many disgruntled competitors believing they had better qualifications and a more rightful claim.

The situation was further aggravated by a custom which prescribed that a family whose contention for the kingship had failed over four generations thereupon lost its noble status, privileges, power, prestige, and its eligibility to seek election another time. Families faced with this plight stopped at nothing—murder, war, or both—to avert the stigma this brought upon them. Fathers ended up fighting sons, sons fighting brothers, uncles, and cousins, and so on. Family feuds were sparked off and lasted for generations. Feuds with neighboring families added to the hostilities; young warriors, determined to demonstrate their fighting qualities and suitability for kingship, led random raids into adjoining territories.

On the whole, there was little impetus toward the creation of centralized political and administrative institutions because society had little use for them. Celtic society's strength and stability lay in a generally diffused body of social customs and laws enforced entirely within the context of closely integrated neighborhood units.

Political power, somewhat detached from this, was grounded not in social institutions but in tribal loyalties, in charismatic qualities of leadership, and in military skill. (Joyce 1997, Vol. 1, 155-166)

Recurring Power Struggles

Throughout the centuries before the arrival of Christianity, there were recurring power struggles between rival tribal leaders. Accounts abound telling of conflicts and battles between the north Leinster Goidels and their Laginian neighbors. An ancient poem describes Laginian tribes doing battle with the Goidel rulers of the Midlands. King Cormac Conloig was killed when his fortress at *Da Cloga* in Meath was destroyed in the first century AD. The *Attacotti* (rent-paying tribes) led by Carbri Cinn Cait temporarily overthrew Goidel dynastic rule. The story of the Attacotti revolt is told in one of the ancient tracts called *Histories*, a copy of which is in the *Book of Leinster*. Tradition has it that Goidel rule was restored only when the legendary Tuathal Feachtmar arrived in Ireland at the head of a foreign army. It is not certain from where he arrived; some sources suggest he returned from exile in Britain to put an end to the Attacotti rebellion. Other sources describe him as a great Goidel warrior who led the ancestors of the Midland Milesians to Ireland, and overcame the Attacotti who had previously ruled the country.

Conchobhar mac Nessa of Ulster

Among the names of the early pre-Christian Goidel kings of Ireland (many obviously mythical) was Conchobhar mac Nessa of Ulster who reigned at the time of Christ. According to tradition, he was the great-grandson of Rory Mor, a powerful Ulster ruler and the founder of the Rudrician line of Ulster kings. The memory of Conor mac Nessa is preserved in the tale of *The Sons of Usnach* and in the greater tale of *The Táin Bó Cúailnge*. It was during Conchobhar's reign that the warrior's of the Red Branch Knights reached their heroic prominence. Their deeds have been recorded by succeeding generations of poets and annalists. Conchobhar's first wife was *Medb* (Maeve), a daughter of the high king *Eocaid.* Later, as queen of Connacht, Medb is remembered as the instigator of the great Connacht-Ulster war described in the *Táin Bó Cúailnge.* (MacManus 1971, 24)

Conchobhar married several times. After Medb, he had the misfortune of marrying Deirdre, usually referred to as Deirdre of the Sorrows. When Deirdre was born, the druid Cathbad prophesized that she would be the most beautiful woman in Ireland, she would marry a king, and she would cause death and destruction throughout the land. She fulfilled the prophecy by marrying Conchobhar when he was an old man and then leaving him for the younger Naoise, precipitating terrible wars between Conchobhar and Naoise's king, Fergus mac Roth. According to the scribes, Conchobhar died from a "brain ball" that had lodged in his skull. It is said that he fell into a rage causing the ball to explode killing him. (King 1998, 177)

Political Development and Characteristics

At the time of Conchobar, Ireland was divided between the kingdoms of Connacht, Ulster, Leinster, Munster, and Meath. This period was known as *Aimser na Cćicedach* (the Time of the Five Fifths). During this time, the political development of Ireland evolved from a primitive pastoral society into an embodiment of rivalry and hostility. Its zenith, in the time shortly before the advent of Christianity, was the vibrant period known as the Heroic Age. This epoch is preserved in extravagant detail in a series of tales known as the Ulster cycle. The tales describe the feats, journeys, loves, and battles of a circle called the Red Branch Knights, warriors of the court of the arrogant King Conchobar of Ulster. Ulster was a province perpetually at odds with the rest of Ireland. Its hereditary foe was led by the equally arrogant King Ailill of Connacht, who ruled with his combative queen, Maeve, from Rath Cruachan in County Roscommon. The Connacht court had its own circle of knights, and "contention between the two sets of hero-warriors was a tradition indulged in with passion." The classic contest between the two proud realms is enshrined in the magnificent epic *Táin Bó Cuailnge* (The Cattle Raid of Cooley).

A century and a half later, the people of Connacht were occupying Uisnech, a territory east of the River Shannon. From there they acquired Meath and its capital at Tara. Later, they gained access to all of Ulster, except counties Down and Antrim. The kingdom of Conchobar was, by this time, no longer recognizable; moreover, it was almost entirely occupied by Cruitin tribes. Political development continued to advance with the occupation of Tara by Cormac mac Airt. The kingdom of Ulster was further divided into the kingdoms of Airgialla and Ulster. During the reign of Niall of the Nine Hostages as high king in the early fifth century, Ulster was further reduced in area, and his sons took all that was left of it in the northwest. Instead of five, there were now seven provinces: Meath, Connacht, Aileach, Airgialla (or Oriel), Ulster, Leinster, and Munster. (Hubert 1988, 169-170)

The early Irish literary tradition includes a group of writings called *dinnseanchas* which, collectively, ascribe a series of characteristics to each of the five fifths or provincial kingdoms. Connacht in the west is described as the kingdom of learning, the seat of the greatest and wisest druids and magicians. The men of Connacht are depicted as renowned for their eloquence, their charm, and their ability to pronounce true judgment. Ulster in the north is described as the seat of battle heroism, of arrogance, strife, and boasting. The men of Ulster are said to be the fiercest warriors of all Ireland, and the queens and goddesses of Ulster are associated with battle and death. Leinster in the east is characterized as the seat of prosperity, hospitality, and the importing of rich foreign wares. The men of Leinster are said to be noble in speech, and their women exceptionally beautiful. Munster in the south is exemplified as the kingdom of music and the arts, of harpers, of skilled *ficheall* players, and of expert horsemen. The last kingdom, Meath, is represented as the kingdom of kingship and stewardship. In Meath lies Tara, the traditional seat of the high king of Ireland.

Túathal Techtmar

Túathal Techtmar is another of the prehistoric Irish kings who stands out as a great leader. He became king of Tara and carved out a kingdom for himself in the Midlands and is credited with imposing a permanent tribute called *bórama* on the pre-Goidel tribes of the region. Túathal is believed to have ruled thirty years and was succeeded by Cathair Mor, who in turn was succeeded by Túathal's grandson, Conn-of-the-Hundred-Battles. Conn, a half-legendary, half-historical figure, is said to have been king of Connacht before he crossed the River Shannon to settle in central Ireland where he founded the kingdom of Meath. Conn wrestled the high kingship from *Mogh Nuadhat* of Leinster in 180 AD and moved to Tara. Mogh fled to Spain where he married Beare, a Spanish princess. A few years later, he returned to Ireland, assembled a great army, and marched on Tara. Conn then took off for Rathcroghan in present-day county Roscommon. He later made a treaty with Mogh, dividing Ireland between them along the ridge of sandhills, called *Esker Riada*, running from Dublin to Galway. Mogh got the southern half, naming it *Leath Mhogha.* Conn got the northern half and it became known as *Leath Chuinn.* But peace was short-lived between the two antagonists, and constant warfare ensued until Conn was assassinated in 212 AD. His son-in-law, Conary II, is said to have succeeded him, although some historians have him succeeded by his son, Airt.

The Illustrious Cormac mac Airt

It was Airt's son, Cormac, who became high-king in 227 AD. Cormac was, unquestionably, the most celebrated of all the ancient kings who ruled at Tara. He is described in the *Book of Ballymote* "as a great ruler and a noble, illustrious king." *The Book of Leinster* tells how Gauls, Romans, Franks, Saxons, Caledonians, and other foreigners would call upon him to seek his wisdom and counsel.

Three great literary works are attributed to Cormac. The first, *Teagasc an Riogh* (*Instructions of a King*), is set in the form of a dialogue between him and his son, Cairbre, whom he was preparing to assume the kingship. The second, *The Book of Acaill*, is a code for criminal law forming part of the Irish Brehon Laws. The third, *The Psaltair of Tara*, is known only by the frequent references to it by ancient writers. Cormac's literary work would appear to confirm the tradition that there was a considerable amount of scholarly enlightenment in pre-Christian Ireland of the third century. Cormac died in 267 AD, more than a century and a half before Saint Patrick arrived. However, there is a belief that he had become a Christian before his death and, inspired by his new faith, had made a dying wish to be buried at *Ros-na-Riogh* facing the east and not with the other pagan kings at *Brugh-na-Boinne*.

Finn mac Cool and the Fianna

During his kinship, Cormac had to contend with the autocratic Finn mac Cool and his warrior militia group, the Fianna. Finn mac Cool belonged to one of the great Irish cycles of storytelling, that of the Fianna. According to the annalists, Finn is the leader of a band of hunters and warriors who acquired great prestige and extended their sphere of influence over much of Ireland during the reign of Cormac. In contrast to the Red Branch Knights who were of Ulster, the Fianna was of Munster and Leinster origin. In Connacht, the Fianna was distinguished as *Clan na Morna*. It was in the reign of Conn, at the end of the second or beginning of the third century, that the Fianna was founded by Fionn's grandfather, Treun-mor. Although the Fianna was supposed to uphold the supremacy of the high king, their oath of fealty was not to him but to their own leader. In the course of time, in the reign of Cormac's son Cairbre Lifeachar, they rebelled against the levying of the *Boru* tribute. Both sides met at the battle of Gabra in AD 284. According to the annalists, the Fianna was wiped out. The *Annals of Tighernach* report Finn's death for that year and it is most likely he was killed in battle. Professor O'Rahilly writes that while much of what has been ascribed to Fianna exploits is probably mythical, Finn himself was undoubtedly a historical personage who existed about the time at which his appearance is recorded in the annals. (O'Rahilly 1999, 272)

Emergence of the Midland Connachta Dynasty

From Conn's descendants emerged the Connachta dynasty in the Midlands. They were an ambitious people who did not rest content with ruling only the kingdom of Meath. At an early period, some pushed westward across the River Shannon to their ancestral territory, making themselves master of much of the present-day province of Connacht. They subordinated the pre-Gael tribes long established in the territory called *coiced-Ol-nEcmacht*. By the seventh century, coiced-Ol-nEcmacht came to be known as *coiced-Connachta*, and the term Connachta (first applied to Conn's descendants in Meath) became more narrowly applied to emulate the Goidel rulers west of the Shannon.

Niall of the Nine Hostages

Another of Conn's descendents was Niall of the Nine Hostages (circa AD 380-405). Tradition tells us that when Cormac mac Airt became king of Ireland, he gave the kingdom of Connacht to his son, Eochaid Muigmedon, who in turn (when he became high king of Ireland) transferred the Connacht kingship to his son, Niall of the Nine Hostages. When Niall succeeded to the throne at Tara, he gave Connacht to his four half-brothers—Brian, Fiachra, Ailill, and Fergus. (O'Rahilly 1999, 396)

Niall was the protagonist in a tale about his stepmother which has been preserved in the *Yellow Book of Lecan*. As the story is told, Eochaid had five sons, including Niall. Whereas the mother of his brothers was Mongfionn, Niall's mother was Cairenn, daughter of a British king. She gives birth to him out on the plain of Tara while being pursued by Mongfionn, described as a bitter, jealous, and ambitious woman who was set on having her son, Brian, succeed his father as high king. "She [Cairenn] did not dare take the child with her; she left it there exposed to the birds. And none of the men of Ireland dared take it for fear of Mongfionn, so great was her magic power and so great the dreads she inspired. Then Torna, the bard, came to the meadow, and saw the lonely infant being attacked by the birds. Torna took the child, carrying it against his breast, and it was revealed to him what was to follow. And he said, 'Welcome to you, little guest, you will be Niall-of-the-Nine Hostages. There will come a time when you will colour a whole crowd red. Seven and twenty years you will rule over Ireland and you will be heir to Ireland forever.'" (Markale 1993, 117)

When Mugmedon became high king in AD 358, the Connacht kingship went to Mongionn's brother, Criomhthan. Resentful that it wasn't her son, Brian, Mongfionn poisoned her brother so that Brian could be crowned. Niall, his father's favorite, was made king instead. Only after Niall assumed the high kingship did Brian accede to the kingship of Connacht. Brian was killed (allegedly by his nephew, Daithi) in a battle near Tuam. Then Daithi became king and ruled Connacht until he acceded to the high kingship in AD 404. Amalgaid succeeded Daithi; in turn, Oilill Molt succeeded Amalgaid.

Niall was the most remarkable of the fourth century rulers in Ireland. He was founder of the longest, most important, and most powerful Irish dynasty in the history of the island. Almost without interruption, his descendants claimed high kingship of Ireland for six hundred years. From Connacht, Niall expanded his realm, first into the midlands and later into Ulster. In the course of time, his descendents emerged as two powerful dynasties: the northern Ui Neill, with its seat at Aileach in Inishowen; and the southern Ui Neill, with its seat at Tara.

For several generations, the *Ui Neill* sought to assert power over all of Ireland but the *Eoghanacht* of Munster never accepted their claim. Following the battle of Ocha in AD 438, Ui Neill succeeded in acquiring what had previously been Connacht's claim. The Ui Neill finally declined in power in the twelfth century when the O'Conors, heirs to the Ui Briuin dynasty in Connacht, succeeded in acquiring the high kingship.

Niall of the Nine Hostages was a formidable invader of foreign shores. His first foreign expedition was to *Alba* (Scotland) to subdue the Picts. The small Scotti colony in Argyle across from County Antrim had gradually been growing in numbers and strength, until they aroused the enmity of the native Picts who rose up against them. Niall assembled a fleet and crossed the narrow strait dividing Alba from Ulster in support of his Scotti countrymen. Niall succeeded in securing Argyle and Cantire for the Scotti. Historians write of Niall's many subsequent incursions into Britain and Gaul and the hostages and booty he brought back to Ireland. It was on one of these expeditions that he supposedly captured the young boy, Succat, in a sweep of captives and sold him into slavery upon his return. Succat would eventually be known as Saint Patrick who would, several years later, bring Christianity to the people of Ireland. (MacManus 1971, 80)

On another occasion while on an expedition to Wales, Niall was forced to withdraw after an encounter with the Roman general Stilichon. While on an expedition to the continent, he is supposed to have died on the banks of the Loire after being wounded by an arrow shot by the king of Leinster who had an old score to settle with him. After Niall's death, his nephew, Dathi, became high king. He followed in Niall's footsteps, leading his armies abroad on foreign expeditions. As Niall had followed upon the heels of Maximus and his Roman legions in their departure from Britain, Dathi is said to have hastened the retreat of Constantine from the kingdom. Dathi is said to have followed the Roman legions into Gaul where he was killed by lightening at the foot of the Alps. (MacManus 1971, 82)

About this time, Christianity was spreading its web across Ireland under the influence first of Palladius and then the celebrated Saint

Patrick who died in AD 461. Although Patrick endeavored to impose a form of Christianity, which was entirely Roman in organization, the institutions he established barely survived him and the Irish adopted a form of the religion more suited to themselves and their ideas. The age of heroes in Ireland gave way to the age of saints. The monasteries so characteristic of Irish Christianity became not only religious centers but cultural and learning centers as well. Their leadership grew powerful, replacing that of the increasingly less authoritative kings. Ireland prospered during the next few centuries, and during this time its cultural achievements surpassed those of the rest of Europe. (Markale 1993, 118-119) As Europe languished in the barbarism of the Dark Ages, Irish monks and scholars succeeded in saving western civilization.

Chapter XI—

Celtic Mythological Tradition

One thing is evident, confirmed by Caesar and the insular Celtic literatures that the Celts did not look upon their gods as their creators but as their ancestors—more as supernatural heroes and heroines, in which form they also appear in Hindu myth and saga.

—Peter Berresford Ellis, *The Druids*

It is Ireland, more than any other of the Celtic nations, which best managed to take care of its ancestral traditions and retain its mythical anthology. The myths and popular epics of pre-Christian Ireland have given us the most detailed picture that exists of the Celts. The myths and epics of ancient Ireland enthrall us with heroes, enchanted maidens, and heroic deeds, handing down a lively and exciting portrayal of the culture, and opening a window into a world astonishingly similar to that which the Greek philosopher Posidonius encountered when he journeyed deep into the heart of the Celtic lands of Gaul in the first century BC. These mythic stories emphasize that Celtic Ireland of the Heroic Age was a society of aristocrats and warriors with a culture in many ways similar to that of Homer's Greece. Hence, it was the Irish, among the great kindred of Celtic peoples, who have the unmatched distinction of having carried into modern historical research many of the characteristics of a native Celtic civilization.

The mythology of Celtic Gaul, on the other hand, did not survive owing to the fact that no Gaulish literature has survived.

The oral traditions of Gaul, including its mythology, were never written down and, because of the Roman conquest and occupation, Gaul rapidly adopted Roman culture, including the art of writing. If Gaul had no developed system of mythology, it did, on the other hand, provide information on its Celtic religion, which according to Alexander MacBain was at best "sufficiently meager." (MacBain 1996, 61) This differed from Ireland where there was a wealth of mythological tradition in a highly developed literary form, but practically no evidence directly bearing on its pagan beliefs.

Celtic Britain formed a bridge between the two Celtic realms of Gaul and Ireland. In material matter, Britain had much in common with and was directly influenced by Gaul. She has retained fragments of mythological traditions, which can be shown as identical in origin with those of Ireland. Owing to the Roman conquest, both her material matter and mythological traditions are relatively sparse. (Dillon 2003, 134) The most recent form embraced by British Celtic myths is the Round Table cycle which grew up around the mysterious King Arthur. Arthurian romances were first written at the direction of the Plantagenet dynasty who sought to glorify the English (and, therefore, the British) monarchy in order to counterbalance the popularity given the Continental Capetian (and, therefore, Carolingian) dynasty by the *chansons de geste*. A personage had to be found who could match the stature of Charlemagne. When Arthur became that figure, the outlook of a conquered race found their way back to the surface and through him dominated western Europe throughout the Middle Ages. (Markale 1993, 255)

Mythology: Man's Search Through the Ages for Truth

The term "mythology" embraces a complex set of ideas and perceptions. It is described as a sacred tradition, which tells us who we are and why we are. It embraces a whole range of tales, sacred beings, and theologies that make up the religious backdrop of belief systems. Myths have many functions and concerns, the most important of which is to answer difficult and imponderable questions where explanations cannot be rationalized in terms of human experience. Such questions may relate to the creation of the world, life, death, the afterlife, the seasons, and the behavior of natural phenomena (like the sun, lightening, and thunder). Thus, such matters can be explained by means of the construction of a myth. The other related purpose of mythology is to account for traditions existing within a given society and for natural, habitual, or extraordinary ritual practices (such as repeated festivals) or sacrifice. (Green 1997, 21) American mythologist, writer, and lecturer Joseph Campbell (1904-1987) describes myths as stories of man's search through the ages for truth, for meaning, and for significance. (Campbell 1988, 148)

The Sumerians became the first humans to record for succeeding generations the fact that the essential events of their lives—the growth of crops, the rising and falling of rivers, the mating and birth of animals, and all the other marvels of the world—seemed to be in thrall to the movements of the sun, the moon, and the stars. They learned that celestial events corresponding with earthly events could be used as markers, reminding people when to go about the various tasks involved in carrying on a livelihood. When a certain star that had not been seen for many months rose just after twilight, it was time to sow. Another star called in the harvest. And they began to recognize and record whole groups of stars, tracing the outlines of deities or extraordinary animals between the distant points of light—the constellations. (Judge 2005, 16-17)

The mythologies with which most of us are best acquainted, those of the Greeks and Romans, have come down to us as a collection of written stories. The myths of Greece form a remarkable example of the value of what early legendary and poetic records are to nations. In the Greek creation myth, Uranus (the sky) wed Gaia.

Their lovemaking produced the oceans and the lands, trees, flowers, and animals. The marriage of heaven and earth finally produced men and women who saw, in the connection between the cycles of the sky and the cycles of the earth, proof that they and their world were together children of the gods. (Judge 2004, 21)

Four Waves of Irish Mythic Beliefs

British author and historian Michael Dames writes that ever since the first human communities settled in Ireland, the island has experienced at least four major traditions of myth. First, he describes, were the myths of the Mesolithic hunter-gatherers and the later New Stone Age (Neolithic) farmers who occupied Ireland from circa 7000 BC to 2000 BC. The myths of this era (termed "Old European" by pre-historian Marija Gimbutas) revolved around the figure of a female goddess of birth, death, and regeneration, matched by a matrilineal human order. Second were the myths of Indo-European warriors which stress a male sky god, reflected in a patriarchal human society. This mythic wave, Dames writes, is most clearly identified with the Celtic-speaking colonists of the Iron Age onwards from circa 800 BC (but possibly from as early as circa 2000 BC). Dames classifies the third wave (originating from AD 500) as Christian mythology with its concepts of "Original Sin and a dualistic division between body and soul, world and spirit," concepts previously unknown in pagan Ireland. Out of this was formed the partition of the Christian myth between Catholic and Calvinist following the seventeenth-century settlement of Ulster by an Anglo-Scottish population. Dames includes a further mythical wave which he describes as the consequence of Scientific Rationalism introduced into Ireland by English and Anglo-Irish urban populations in the 1700s. However, he has his doubts about the rationale for this wave, "as it rejects all supernatural accounts of reality, preferring to describe the cosmos through an ostensibly objective language of numerical abstraction (mathematics) . . . ." (Dames 1992, 10)

Irish Mythological Traditions

Ireland has preserved the richest store of mythological traditions of any country north of the Alps. This legacy sometimes caused bafflement to those trained in the Christian tradition. For example, a medieval Irish monk wrote, in a colophon to his copy of the *Táin Bó Cuailnge* myth: "I do not accept as matter of belief certain things in this history, or rather fiction, for some things are diabolical superstitions, some are poetical inventions, some have the semblance of truth, some have not; and some are meant to be the entertainment of fools. Every generation tends to assume that it is 'fact,' and others are 'fiction;' for some things are diabolical superstitions." (Dames 1992, 9) Despite the size of the original Celtic realm, Celtic mythology has survived only in Ireland and to a lesser extent in Britain and it comes from an assortment of oral sources. The Irish material did not achieve written form until about the seventh century AD; the British (Welsh) probably not until about three centuries later. In both cases, this was after the arrival of Christianity and the transcribers are likely to have been monks who, viewing this blatantly pagan matter through Christian eyes, censored where they thought necessary. (Rutherford 1993, 26)

The romantic stories of Ireland of the Heroic Era are presented in vivid and copious detail in a series of sagas handed down orally over the generations by poets and storytellers. Most of the Irish legends fall under four cycles: Mythical, Ulster, Fianna, and the Historical cycle. In the Mythological cycle, the chief characters belong to the Tuatha De Danann (The Peoples of the Goddess Danann) who are said to have occupied Ireland before the coming of the Sons of Mil, the ancestors of the present inhabitants. The stories of the Ulster cycle are mainly about the warriors of King Conchobar of Ulster, and especially about the exploits of the foremost among them, Cú Chulainn. The Fianna cycle stories are about Finn mac Cumaill and his roving war bands. The Historical cycle is a more miscellaneous group of stories centered on various high kings of

Ireland and on a number of provincial and lesser kings. Each of the four cycles contains material which appears to belong to a common Indo-European heritage, and which presumably was part of a tradition of the Celtic peoples before they ever set foot in Ireland. The personages about whom the tales are told are arranged in a chronological sequence extending from the time of the Deluge to the time of the Viking raids in Ireland. (Rees 1995, 26-27)

Mythological Cycle

The Mythological cycle describes a series of invasions that led to the establishment of Celtic Ireland. The story, which is told in the medieval manuscript *Leabhar Gabhala* (*The Book of the Taking of Ireland*), is the embodiment of the people of Ireland's impressions of the history of its peoples. Celtic tradition has preserved no native story of the creation of the world and of man. Even in the oldest documents that have survived, the Biblical Adam and Eve have already been accepted as the first parents of mankind. Nevertheless, *Leabhar Gabhala* is undoubtedly a challenging attempt to combine parts of the native teaching with Hebrew mythology, overstated with medieval legend. The account proceeds from the Creation to the story of Noah and the Flood, the Dispersal of the Nations, and the descent of the Gael of Ireland from Japheth son of Noah. For the early Christian Celts, the acceptance of the new Faith (with a cosmogony of its own) inevitably involved severing the stem of native tradition at some point or other and grafting it on to Christian roots. *Leabhar Gabhala* performed this grafting as far as the Irish were concerned.

This Biblical history, as set out in *Leabhar Gabhala*, culminates in the story of the "Sons of Mil." After journeying through Egypt, Crete, and Sicily, these ancestors of the Irish eventually reached Spain. One of their company, Bregon, built a tower there; from the top of this tower, Ith (the son of Bregon) saw Ireland across the waters and set sail to investigate the land he had seen.

In *Leabhar Gabhala*, the story of the Sons of Mil is not a continuous narrative. After tracing the fictitious history of the Gael until they are ultimately at Bregon's Tower in Spain on the eve of their voyage to Ireland, the narrative changes course and the story goes on to tell of five successive groups of invaders who occupied Ireland before the ancestors of the Gael eventually settled there.

The first three groups are known by the names of their respective leaders—Cessair, Partholón, and Nemed. The last two, by group names—namely Fir Bolg, and Tuatha Dé Danann. The narratives describing the voyages of these groups are several and differing. The *Annals of the Four Masters* talks about Cessair who came to Ireland "forty days before the Deluge, with fifty girls and three men." MacFirbis, in the *Book of Genealogies*, tells us that Partholon first took possession of Ireland shortly after the Deluge; he also mentions the coming of Cessair. The account given in the *Leabhar Gabhala* tells of the race of Nemed coming out of the Caspian Sea into the Northern Ocean and fighting the Fomorians, said to be African sea rovers, for possession of Ireland. (Rolleston 1911, 96-100)

The story continues with the famed battle at Moytura on the Mayo-Galway border in which the De Dananns, described as a "beautiful people descended from the goddess Dana," met and overthrew the uncultured Firbolgs. It was at this battle that King Eochaid of the Firbolgs was slain and King Nuada of the De Dananns had his hand severed, thus depriving him of the kingship of his people, since under De Danann law no king could rule who suffered a personal blemish. The De Dananns therefore chose King Bres, who was the son of a De Danann woman named Eri (whose father was unknown) to reign over them instead. Next, the De Dananns took on the Fomorians in a great battle at Northern Moytura in County Sligo. It was there that the most infamous Formorian chief of them all, Balor of the Evil Eye who ruled Tory Island off the northwest coast, was slain by a stone from the sling of his own grandson. After the defeat, many of the Firbolgs followed their Formorian allies to the Western Isles of Scotland, only to be oppressed by the Picts. They returned eventually to Ireland and, upon crossing the Shannon into Connacht, were received with open arms by their Firbolg kin and were given lands by the celebrated Queen Maeve. From then on, the De Dananns were the undisputed rulers of ancient Ireland until they had to make room for the Sons of Mil who, upon displacing the De Dananns, became the ruling people of Ireland.

Journey of the Sons of Mil

Next to take Ireland were the Sons of Mil. They were called the Goidel (Gael) people, supposedly after a remote ancestor named Goidhal Glas who lived during the time of Moses. An ancient tale described in the *Yellow Book of Lecan* gives an intricate account of their origin and arrival in Ireland:

> "We are born of the children of Mile, of Spain. After the building of the tower of Nimrod and the confounding of languages, we went to Egypt on the invitation of the Pharaoh, king of Egypt. Ne, son of Fenius, and Goedel Glas were our chiefs when we were in the South. That is why we were called Fene, from Fenius and Gaels from Goedel Glas.
>
> "When we were in Egypt, Scota, daughter of Pharaoh the king, was given as wife to Ne, son of Fenius. That is why she is our ancestor and why we are called Scots from her. The night when the children of Israel escaped from Egypt and crossed the Red Sea dry-footed with Moses, son of Amran, the leader of God's people, and when Pharaoh and his army were drowned in the sea after keeping the Hebrews in captivity, our ancestors did not go with the Egyptians in pursuit of God's people and therefore feared Pharaoh's anger. They feared least the Egyptians reduce them to slavery as they had previously done the children of

> Israel. So they fled one night on Pharaoh's vessels across the shallow Red Sea to the boundless ocean around the North West of the world. They passed the Caucasian Mountains, Sythia, and India, crossed the Caspian Sea, which lies there, crossed the Palus Maeotis and arrived in Europe; from the South East Mediterranean to the North West, right of Africa, they passed the columns of Hercules on their way to Spain and thence to this island . . . . It was Ith son of Breogan who saw the mountains of Irrus from the top of Breogan's tower in Spain and it was he who came to this island leaving a path for us to follow . . . ." (Markale 1993, 107)

There is not much to be learned from this rambling story, except that the Gaels like the other Celtic tribes originated in Central Asia. According to one rendition of the story, Milesius died before ever setting foot in Ireland. After his death, Scota with his uncle Ith together with his (Mil's) eight sons and Ith's nine brothers sailed for Ireland. As they neared the southwestern coast, a dreadful storm overtook them dispersing their fleet. Many in the flotilla were lost at sea. Those who survived made it ashore only to meet stubborn resistance from the Dé Dananns. In due course Mil's side prevailed, conquering the Dé Dananns in a great battle at Taillte in County Meath. The two races then agreed that the Sons of Mil should keep the earth and that the Dé Dananns should have the underground and island regions. The Dé Dananns may have been banished, but their memory has endured until the present time in the guise of what the Irish country folk respectfully call "the good people," or the fairies.

The island was then divided among Milesius's kin as follows: Eber was given the southern half of the land; Eremon the northern half; Ith's son, Lughaid, was given the southwestern corner of Munster; and to the children of Ir went the northeastern corner of Ulster. In time, a dispute arose between the followers of Eber and Eremon. Eremon was victorious and, hence, through him was established the lineage and succession to the over lordship of the Gaels in Ireland. Another version has the land divided between Eogan Mor (alias Mug Nuadat) and Conn and tells of the struggle for supremacy between the two, ending in the battle of Mag Lena.

Ulster Cycle

The second, the Ulster cycle, consists of tales and sagas of the powerful Ulster king, Conor mac Nessa, and his Red Branch Knights. The stories of this cycle form the finest part of Ireland's ancient romantic literature. The most celebrated tale, the *Táin Bó Cuailnge*, telling of the long drawn-out struggle between the warriors of Ulster and the warriors of Connacht, is a stunning epic about a classic encounter between two self-important monarchs: Conor of Ulster and his ex-wife, Meave of Connacht.

In the prelude to the epic, there is the story of the beautiful young Deirdre whom the old king, Conchobar, insists on marrying. Instead, she falls in love with Naisi and elopes with him to Alba. Conchobar, although infuriated at their elopement, pretends to forgive them and sends his trusted servant Fergus mac Roth to Alba to entice them to return to Ireland. Conchobar, however, goes back on his word and has Deirdre's husband Naisi and his two brothers (who eloped with them) put to death. Fergus and his followers, enraged with Conchobar for breaking his word, defect to Queen Meave, Conchobar's chief enemy. Meanwhile, Deirdre flings herself from a fast-moving chariot to her death.

The story continues recounting the rivalry between Meave and her consort, Ailill, as to their respective possessions. It happened that Meave possessed a famous bull named Finnbenach. One day when she and Ailill were counting up their respective herds and matching them against each other, Ailill taunted her about Finnbenach attaching himself to his herd. Impatient, Meave asked her steward where in Erin he could find a bull the quality of Finnbenach. "I know of one," responded mac Roth. "The Brown Bull of Culigne.

It belongs to Dara mac Fachtna and is the mightiest beast in all the land." It is so huge "that a hundred warriors could find shade from its shadow," and it is remarkably virile in that "every day it would bestride fifty cows, which calved the very next day." But this bull was in Ulster and Meave knew that the Ulstermen would not let her have the animal without a fight. Meave was determined, so she mobilized a great army of Fir Domnainn knights (Connacht's equivalent of Ulster's Red Branch Knights) under their leader Ferdiad. They were joined by forces from other parts of Ireland, mostly defectors from Ulster under Fergus (eager to strike at Conchobar for having killed their brave comrades). They marched on Ulster to do battle with Conchobar and his Red Branch fighting men led by the gallant Cuchullian.

The contest for the brown bull, which is the central theme of this the greatest and most exciting of the Irish heroic epics, goes on to describe how the Ulster hero Cuchulian single-handedly held back the forces of Connacht as well as his soul-friend, the yellow-haired Ferdiad whom Meave pitted against him. Throughout the story, Cuchullian is shown to embody the archetype of the Celtic warrior-aristocrat, possessing courage, honor, unmatched haughtiness, and a disregard for death; he is henceforth the hero and the great central figure of the *Táin*. There is also Cuchullian the demigod who, in preparation for battle, transforms into a figure with the hideous malformation of one of the Celtic gods:

> "His body made a furious twist inside his skin, so that his feet and shins switched to the rear and his heels and calves switched to the front . . . . On his head the temple sinews stretched to the nape of his neck, each mighty, immense, measureless knob as big as the head of a month-old child . . . . He sucked one eye so deep into his head that a wild crane couldn't probe it onto his cheek out of the depths of his skull; the other eye fell out along his cheek . . . . His cheek peeled back from his jaws until the gullet appeared, his lungs and liver flapped in his mouth and throat . . . .

> The hair of his head twisted like the tangle of a red thorn bush . . . . If a royal apple tree with all its kingly fruit were shaken above him, scarce an apple would reach the ground but each would be spiked on a bristle of his hair as it stood up on his scalp with rage . . . . Then, tall and thick, steady and strong, high as the mast of a noble ship, rose up from the dead center of his skull a straight spout of black blood darkly smoking." (*Tain* references: Scherman 1981, 30)

A detailed account of the battle follows, describing how Cuchullian single-handedly fights Meave's army: "One by one the great warriors of Connacht were sent against him and one by one he fells them." Meave, infuriated at the number of her men he is slaying, sends one hundred warriors against him all at once. He slew them "two and three at a time day and night and for three months he knew no rest except for short naps whenever he could." Cuchullian overcomes Connachtman after Connachtman until finally he has to do battle with his foster-brother, Ferdiad. Meave offered her daughter, Finnabair, in marriage to Ferdiad if he would fight his old friend. From O'Curry's translation of the *Tain*, we have the following description of the hand-to-hand fighting between Cuchullian and Ferdiad:

> "Each of them began to cast spears at one another, from the full middle of the day till the close of the evening; and though the warding off was of the best, still the throwing was so superior, that each of them bled, reddened and wounded the other, in that time. 'Let us desist from this now O Cuchullian,' said Ferdiad. 'Let us desist,' said Cuchullian. They ceased. They threw away their arms from them into the hands of their charioteers. Each of them approached the other forthwith, and each put his hands around the other's neck, and gave him three kisses. Their horses were in the same padlock that night, and their charioteers at the same fire; and their charioteers spread beds of green rushes for them, fitted with wounded men's

> pillows. The professors of healing and curing came to heal and cure them, and they applied herbs and plants of healing and curing to their stabs and their cuts and their gashes and to all the wounds. Of every herb and of every healing and curing plant that was put to the stabs and cuts and gashes and to all the wounds of Cuchullian, he would send an equal portion from him westward over the ford to Ferdiad, so that the men of Eirinn might not be able to say, should Ferdiad fall by him, that it was by better means of cure that he was enabled (to kill him). For several days the two warriors fight more fiercely, more terribly than ever until Ferdiad finally manages to thrust his sword into Culchullian's shoulder. It is then that Cuchillian calls on Laegh for his most famous weapon, the Gae Bulga, or belly spear, and with it he finally brings down Ferdiad. 'The end has come at last, O Cuchullian,' Ferdiad whispers, and he drops to the ground." (Source: MacManus 1972, 31)

Here, we are reminded of the striking parallelism between the fight of Cuchullian and Ferdiad and that in the Greek epic between Achilles and Hector. As in the fight between Achilles and Hector, there is something inequitable about this contest: like Achilles, Cuchullian is shown to be semi-divine, and as Achilles has divine protective covering, so does Cuchullian who possesses a secret weapon which he ultimately uses to kill Ferdiad.

The young Ulster warrior fights valiantly, just as he had in many other sagas describing his feats. Again and again, we encounter him in the traditional affrays defending his hero's role. On one occasion while walking with his sweetheart, Emer, he is confronted by an unusually brash youth challenging him to a fight. Although Emer has warned him that the youth is in fact his son, Cuchullian takes up the challenge, for he "would not let even a youngster call into question the honour of the men of Ulster." After striking the fatal blow, he picks up the limp body in his arms and carries it back to the camp where the men of Ulster are gathered. "This is my son," he tells them, and from that time on he is seen by his friends to have become despondent.

But noble as Cuchullian was, he was destined to die young. Of the several myths surrounding his death there is the one where Meave is reputed to have used her magical powers to enfeeble him in battle against Erc—the battle that resulted in his death. Knowing that he was dying, Cuchullian ties himself to a column so that he may die erect and honorably, having the war-goddess *Badh* in the form of a raven perched on his shoulder.

As a portrayal of Irish civilization in pagan times, the stories of the Ulster cycle are of the highest significance. Preserved in manuscripts dating from the twelfth to the fifteenth century, these sagas in most cases go back to a much earlier period, some having been transcribed from originals written as early as the eighth century. The culture portrayed is in general that which prevailed in Ireland before the beginning of the Christian era.

The population, not yet united under a central direction headed by a "high-king," is divided into groups, each inhabiting their own district, or province known as a *coiced* (fifth). The *Ulaid* (or Ulstermen) occupy the north with their capital, Emain Macha; the *Connachta* (or Connachtmen), the west with their capital at Rath Cruchan in county Roscommon. In the southeast, the province of Leinster comprising the *Laiginian* (or Leinstermen); and in the southwest is the province of Munster. The historical district of Meath, carved out of the center of Ireland after the establishment of the high-kingship in the second century AD, is unknown in the earliest sagas, as is Tara which did not become the seat of the high king until much later. Each coiced was comprised of numerous *tuatha* (tribes) which again were subdivided into still smaller groups bound together by an elaborate system of blood kinship and ruled over by kinglets and chieftains of varying degrees of importance, all subject (at least in theory) to the king of the province. (Cross and Harris, eds. 1996, 128)

In the ancient sagas, Ulster occupies the position of a proud and haughty antagonist to the rest of Ireland, though her special hereditary enemy is Connacht, ruled by Queen Meave and her husband Ailill who, like Conchobar, are represented as surrounded by a court composed of distinguished warriors. Rath Cruchan, the ancient capital of Connacht, is often referred to in the sagas of the Ulster cycle.

The way of life of the heroes in the *Táin* replicates that of the heroes in Gaul, as described by the Greek philosopher Poseidonios in the first century BC. It is also a way of life similar to that of the Homeric warriors in the *Iliad.* Still further east, the Sanskrit epic poem, the *Mahábhárata*, depicts a similar society of chariot-driving warriors in northern India some centuries earlier. (Moody 1967, 43)

Finn Cycle

The third of the great cycles of Irish mythological literature is known as the Finn cycle. It is sometimes described as the Ossianic cycle because most of the poems which belong to it are attributed to Finn's son, Ossian. The stories comprise tales of Finn, the chief of a warrior band, whose heroes include his son Ossian and his grandson Oscar. The exploits of Finn and his companions have formed a part of the popular culture of Gaelic-speaking Ireland and Scotland for several centuries. The tales of Finn are founded on events that happened at the end of the third century AD, but the earliest references to him in literature do not appear until several hundred years later. The vast majority of the tales about him are found in manuscripts dating from the twelfth and later centuries.

The Finn cycle differs markedly from that of the Ulster cycle. The tales are more numerous and were in general written down at a much later date than those of Ulster. Moreover, sources tell us that few of them furnish linguistic evidence of having been composed before the twelfth century. Nor do they as a rule, according to the same sources, contain references to ancient manners and customs such as those that give the Ulster epics their value as pictures of pre-Christian culture. It appears from early references in the annals and other sources that Finn's army of warriors was only one of many such bands of warriors, which existed in ancient Ireland and were a recognized feature of the social structure. Since the oldest traditions represent Finn as having his chief stronghold on the hill of Almu, it has been inferred that his Fianna belonged primarily to Leinster.

The Fianna epic begins before the birth of its hero, Finn, with the struggle of two rival clans, each claiming to be the real and only Fianna of Ireland. They were Clan Morna (whose leader was Goll mac Morna) and Clan Baoisgne (led by Finn's father, Cumhal). In a battle fought at Cnucha, the Clan Morna was routed and Clan Baoisgne' leader Cumhal was killed. Cumhal's wife gave birth to a posthumous son, who was secretly raised in the Slieve Bloom Mountains for fear of his father's enemies. The boy, who was at first named Deimne, grew up to be a skilled sportsman. Later, he took the name Finn. Legends describe that he made himself known to his father's old followers, mystified his enemies with his magic, and turned them into faithful servants. Gradually, he welded the two opposing clans into one Fianna, over which he ruled, taking tribute from the kings of Ireland. He warred against the Fomorian "Lochlannach," destroying every kind of giant, serpent, or monster that infested the land and finally carried his mythical conquests over all Europe.

The legends of Fianna exploits are numerous. All are heroic, romantic, wild, and fantastic. Hunting is a prominent feature of the Fianna tales, for the Fianna were essentially a band of mighty hunters. But the creatures of their chase were not always earthly. Enchanters who wished the Fianna ill could always lure them into danger by taking the shape of a boar or a deer, and many a story begins with an innocent chase and ends in a fatal encounter. But out of such struggles, the Fianna always emerged successfully.

Ever fortunate in war, Finn found tragedy in love. *The Pursuit of Diarmuid and Grainne* is the most striking and tragic tale of the Fianna cycle. Grainne, Finn's betrothed wife, falls in love with Diarmuid, Finn's favorite warrior, and both elope from Tara. Briefly, the tale begins with Finn seeking a wife in his old age. Grainne, daughter of Cormac (the high king of Ireland) was his choice. Finn received the consent of both King Cormac and his daughter, and he headed for Tara with Diarmuid and other members of the Fianna to claim his bride.

At a reception in their honor in the great banquet-hall at Tara, matters became complicated when Grainne placed her eyes on Diarmuid. He was so fair and noble to look on that no woman could refuse him love, and it was said that he never knew weariness. She fell instantly in love with him and with the help of her father's druid placed him under a *geasa* (bonds which no hero could refuse to redeem) and begged him to elope with her. After the feast, Diarmuid went to his comrades, one by one, and told them of Grainne's love for him, and of the geasa she had placed upon him to take her from Tara. He asked each of them what he ought do. All answered that no hero could break a *geis* put upon him by a woman. He even asked Finn, concealing Grainne's name, and Finn gave him the same counsel as the others. That night, Grainne and Diarmuid fled from Tara cross the River Shannon to a place called the "Wood of the Two Tents," where Diarmuid built a hut for Grainne to shelter in.

Meanwhile, Finn learned of their elopement and sent Clan Neamhuain to track them down. They located the hut in the woods with Diarmuid and Grainne inside. When Finn himself arrived, he called out to Diarmuid, asking if he and Grainne were within. Diarmuid replied that they were, but that none should enter unless permission was given. Then Finn instructed the Fianna to surround Diarmuid and capture him. Thereupon, Diarmuid rose up and gave Grainne three kisses in the presence of Finn "so that a burning of jealousy and rage overcame Finn upon seeing that, and he said that Diarmuid should give his head for those kisses." Diarmuid now found himself matched single-handed against Finn.

The tale continues narrating (in a somewhat perfunctory manner) several episodes in which Deirmuid is attacked and besieged by Finn's warriors, and his and Grainne's eventual freeing by way of miracles and the exercise of magical procedures of his foster-father, Angus of the Brugh. They are chased all over Ireland, and after sixteen years, peace arrives at last to Deirmuid by intercession of Angus and King Cormac with Finn. Deirmuid received his proper patrimony, the Cantrad of O'Dyna, and other lands far away in the west, and Cormac gave another of his daughters to Finn. (Cross 1996, 355) Whether there is any real personage behind the enduring figure of Finn is difficult to say. But for the reasoning here, it is not necessary to focus on this question. He was, no doubt, the creation of the Celtic mind and like most Irish heroes had a mythical ancestry. His mother, Murna of the White Neck, was granddaughter of Nuada of the Silver Hand, who had wedded Ethlinn, daughter of Balor the Fomorian.

The end of the Fianna is told in several versions, generally without any of the supernatural and mystical atmosphere in which nearly all of the Finn legends are steeped. After the death of Cormac mac Airt, his son Cairbry replaced him as high king. By this time, the Fianna had grown into an autocratic influence, extracting heavy tributes and burdensome privileges from kings and chieftains across Ireland. Cairbry had a daughter named *Sgeimh Solais* (Light of Beauty) who was being wooed by the son of a neighboring king. When the marriage was arranged, the Fianna stepped in to claim a tribute which, by all accounts, was the custom on these occasions. Cairbry, determined to break their power, took this opportunity to refuse their demand and he called for all the kings and chieftains of Ireland to help him against the Fianna who were now in rebellion for what they deemed was a denial of their rights. The decisive battle of the war that ensued took place at Gowra (present day Garristown, county Dublin). As for Finn himself, he seems to have melted away, but not without myth. There is a popular tradition which says that he and his companions never died, but rest spell-bound in an enchanted cave where they await the appointed time to reappear in glory and redeem their land from tyranny and destruction. (Rolleston 1911, 307-308)

Historical Cycle

The so-called Historical cycle is a more miscellaneous group of stories centered on various high-kings of Ireland and on a number of provincial or lesser kings. Each of these cycles contains material that appears to belong to a common Indo-European heritage, and which presumably was part of the tradition of the Celtic peoples before they ever arrived in Ireland. But in the works of early Irish historians, the personages about whom the tales are told are arranged in a chronological sequence extending from the time of the Deluge to the time of the Viking raids in Ireland.

A certain amount of supplementary information concerning the characters and events of these four groups of stories is supplied by various learned works compiled in the early Middle Ages. *Lebor Gabala Erin* (*The Book of the Taking of Ireland*) is, in particular, a history of the Irish and of the peoples who occupied Ireland before them, with an accompanying "Lists of Kings." Another is the Glossary attributed to Cormac mac Cuilennain, the King Bishop of Cashel who was killed in the year AD 908. Others include the *Dindśenchas* which contains lore associated with hills and other features of the Irish landscape; and *Cóir Anmann* (*The Fitness of Names*) which gives brief stories explaining the origin of the names of traditional personages. And finally there are poems, *triads*, and genealogies which record celebrated names. (Rees 1995, 27)

King Arthur and the Knights of the Round Table

The last cycle of Celtic mythical tales is that of King Arthur and the Knights of the Round Table. This cycle recounts events of that period in Britain commonly referred to as the Dark Age, which followed the withdrawal of the Romans and the later invasions of the Saxons. For the Britons, whose Celtic society was already severely weakened by Roman subjugation, the Saxon invasions were the last straw. Their Celtic world was crumbling around them as the Saxons drove them into the western areas of the island. Too weak to recover their lost lands, they turned to mythmaking. So the myth of King Arthur as the supreme king or leader came into existence and with it came the Arthur who reigned over Wales where his legend was first born, over the rest of Britain (excluding Scotland), over Brittany and Gaul, and even over Rome itself.

Nennius, a ninth century monk, wrote in his *Historia Britonnum* (*History of the Britons*) that Arthur fought with other British kings against the Saxons and was their commander-in-chief. Nennius also describes how the Britons fought in twelve battles with the Saxon invaders, the last of them on Mount Badon where "there fell in one day nine hundred and forty men." Arthur killed them at the first attempt. No one other than Arthur was capable of defeating these enemies. He was the victor in all the action.

Whether the real Arthur ever existed may not be that significant, for it is the legendary Arthur who has illuminated the history of Britain's "dark centuries" after the withdrawal of the Romans. Following the departure of Roman rule in the fifth century, Saxon tribes pushed the native Britons further west out of their communities. Many took refuge in Wales where they re-established themselves among their western kinfolk; others fled to Cornwall or to Gaul. As the annalists describe it, they took with them the memories of their hopeless struggle and tragic downfall, not only in their songs and ballads, but also in the myths that safeguarded for them the essence of the Celtic soul from worldly influences. It suited the Celts' style, for they were a people who never came to terms with reality; if conditions became intolerable, they invariably found sanctuary in their imagination—the most successful of which for the Britons was the creation of the kingdom ruled by King Arthur.

Arthur becomes king and Britain enters the heroic epic. He selects Camelot (a place no one has yet identified) as his residence and marries Guinevere, daughter of the dwarf-king Leodegrance. He selects one hundred and fifty knights (the number that can be seated at his huge round table) with swords vastly superior to those in the hands of all mortal foes. Arthur defeats the Picts, Saxons, and Scots (Irish) and, when summoned by the Roman legions to pay tribute, he heads to the Continent where he forces the Roman legions back to the Tiber. Returning from this campaign, he does battle with rebellious British chiefs and from time to time embarks on unusual adventures. His fairy-tale biography fills in a century of British history in such a way that historians have yet to discern where it overlaps with factual history. Charles Squire writes that Arthur's rise to prominence is one of the many problems of Celtic mythology. He points out that it is not mentioned in any of the Four Branches of the *Mabinogi*, which deal with the races of the British gods equivalent to Gaelic Tuatha de Danann. (Squire 2000, 406)

Mythological Tales Versus Factual History

The mythological tales of Ireland are so intertwined with factual history that it is difficult to know where mythology ends and fact begins. This blurring of the two, it has been described, is part and parcel of the culture formed to some extent by an oral tradition that kept alive the great sagas of a heroic age (later put into writing by the Christian monks). However, a comparison of Celtic mythology with that of others of the same ethnic origin reveals countless parallels. Rutherford points to an incident in the Táin Bo Cuailnge where Fergus, king of Ulster, is persuaded by his wife Nessa to abdicate in favor of his son. In the Hindu epic, *The Ramayana*, Kaikeyi persuades her husband, Dasfaratha, to make a similar sacrifice. Cú Chulainn's inadvertent killing of his son also occurs in the German *Hildebrandslied*. Other examples, cited by Rutherford, are the linking of the horse and agriculture gods, and the Cattle Raid Myth, central to the Ulster cycle. The Irish Second Battle of Moytura may well have derived from the myth of the final battle, which occurs *inter alia* in the Norse *Ragnorok* and the Hindu epic *The Mahabharata.* There are also numerous relics in British material for which parallels are found in Indian, Iranian, Greek, Roman, German, and Hittite contexts. (Rutherford 1993, 28) Such examples are capable of infinite multiplication and go on to prove that the Celts brought with them, as they spread, a mythology and beliefs whose roots went back to a past before Indo-European migrations, and hence long before they themselves had emerged as a separate and identifiable people.

It is often said that the Age of Myth is over and that the gods of humanity's childhood have been supplanted, first by the *real* Christian God, and then by the reality of scientific reason. Ireland, more than any other country in Europe, has retained its Celtic mythological heritage, which lives today in the oral tradition of folk tales, in literature, in place-names, and language. In legend-haunted Ireland, the hills and dales still retain memories of the ancient gods of times past. Mountains and lakes are the homes of gods and goddesses, of saints and monsters, and pattern, beauty, and cyclical logic are revealed in their stories. (Dames 1992, 9)

Chapter XII—

Celtic Deities and Traditions

. . . of all the races of antiquity, outside Egypt, the Celts seem to have cherished the most ardent belief in the world beyond the grave, and to have been preoccupied with its joys.

—J.A. MacCulloch, *The Religion of the Ancient Celts*

Ancient Celts had a strong sense of the supernatural, survival of the soul beyond death, and the presence of the gods throughout the universe. Many divinities were worshipped, often in groups of three or triads, and there was a recognized hierarchy of gods and goddesses, possibly making it easier for the pagan Irish to understand the doctrine of the Trinity when it was presented to them by Saint Patrick. (Jiménez 1996, 34) Feminine divinities were notably present in Celtic thinking, and the Celts had a great sense of the sacredness of places, particularly woods, groves, rivers, and springs. In contrast to the beliefs of the Greeks and Romans, Celts believed strongly in reincarnation of the soul; to them the soul did not die, but passed into another body, in effect, another life after death. (Chadwick 1997, 154) In Celtic belief, man was not so much created by gods as descended from them.

According to Caesar, the Gauls declared they were descended from Dispater, and the druids, they say, passed this on to them. Dispater was a Celtic underworld god of fertility. We do not have a complete surviving Celtic myth on the creation of the world; however, from a marginal note to the *Senchus Mór*, we learn that the druids, like the Brahmans, boasted they had made the sun, moon, earth, and sea—a boast in keeping with their supposed powers over the elements. (MacCulloch 2003, 228-229) When Saint Patrick arrived in Ireland in the fifth century AD, he found a flourishing spiritual tradition already in existence among the Irish people. There is an abundance of Irish legendary literature, much of it originating from pre-Christian sources, which describes a strong belief in the mystical and a devotion to a variety of ceremonial observances. Yet, there is practically nothing bearing on a religious, or even an ethical, social formation to administer the whole array of beliefs that existed.

Celtic Pantheon

The Celtic pantheon consisted of a multiplicity of gods and goddesses, of whom more than two hundred have been recorded. If we accept that individual deities could have been known by several titles or epithets, then at least the plethora of divine personages might be reducible to a more manageable arrangement. Julius Caesar attempted to do so in a passage in Book 6 of his *Commentaries on the Gallic War*. (Cunliffe 1997, 184-185) Our knowledge of Celtic deities and beliefs has been largely derived from Caesar and the classical historians. Caesar's sketch of the Gaulish pantheon and religious beliefs is the best we have although, overall, what he wrote is relatively meager; at best, three chapters on the subject. Additionally, we have a few lines each from Diodorus, Mela, and Strabo, some scattered allusions in Pliny and Lucan, and a statement from the Greek Timagenes reproduced in *Ammianus Marcellinus*. (MacBain 1996, 61) These sources have enabled us to know the names of many Celtic gods, especially those surviving on inscriptions in Latin (and occasionally in Greek).

The nature of Celtic beliefs has been the subject of extensive speculation by both ancient and modern writers. The archaeological record sheds little light on the matter; the main evidence is literary, and is found in passages from classical writers beginning as early as the second century BC. They describe the beliefs of the Celts as being based on the worship and appeasement of a great variety of gods and goddesses who influenced all aspects of their lives: matters of war, agriculture, weather, and the household. Jiménez writes that more than four hundred deities have been identified, although only twenty-five percent of them occur more than once, suggesting that the majority were local or tribal. (Jiménez 35, 2001)

Transmigration of the Soul

Many ancient writers claim the Celtic idea of immortality embodied the Oriental conception of transmigration of souls; to account for this, they claim the Celts were following the doctrine of Pythagoras from classical antiquity. Caesar writes, "The principal point of their (Druids) teaching is that the soul does not perish, and that after death it passes from one body into another." Diodorus writes: "Among them the doctrine of Pythagoras prevails, according to which the souls of men are immortal, and after a fixed term recommence to live, taking upon themselves a new body." Traces of this doctrine certainly do appear in Irish legend. T.W. Rolleston writes that Mongan, a historical personage whose death is recorded about AD 625, is said to have made a wager as to the place of death of a king named Fothad, slain in a battle with the mythical hero Finn mac Cumhal in the third century. He proves his point by calling upon Keelta, the actual slayer of Fothad, from the Otherworld. Keelta correctly describes where the tomb is to be found and described its contents. He begins his tale by saying to Mongon, "We were with thee," and then, turning to the gathering, he continues: "We were with Finn, coming from Alba . . . . Hush," says Mongan, "it is wrong of thee to reveal a secret." The secret is, of course, that Mongan was a reincarnation of Finn. (Rolleston 1911, 80-81)

But the evidence on the whole, according to Rolleston, shows that the Celts did not hold this doctrine in the same way as Pythagoras and the Orientals did. Transmigration was not, for the Celts, part of the order of things. It *might* occur, but universally it did not. The new body, which the dead took on, was a body not of this world. The question of moral reckoning connected with the adopted form in the future life was not a matter of consideration. It was not so much a statement of belief as an idea that haunted the imagination; as Mongan's caution indicates, not to be brought into transparency.

Then again, the belief that immortality had a basis in Celtic Druidism is not evident. Caesar affirms this distinctly and declares the druids fostered the doctrine principally for the promotion of bravery rather than for purely religious reasons. An intense Otherworld faith, such as that held by the Celts, is certainly one of the most effective modus operandi in the hands of a priesthood who hold the keys of that world. (Rolleston 1911, 81-82)

Sacrificial Rituals

Celtic religions were sacrificial religions. Little is known of the ritual; there were blood sacrifices and others (offerings of first fruits, for example). The ancient writers speak of human sacrifices among the Gauls and massacres of prisoners which had a sacrificial character. In Ireland there are very few allusions to human sacrifice, except the sacrifice of newborn infants to the idol Cromm Cruaich. In the ancient Christian tract "Dinnsenchus," preserved in the *Book of Leinster*, it is stated that on *Moyslaught* (the Plain of Adoration) there stood a great gold idol, Crom Cruach. The Gaels used to sacrifice children to it when praying for fair weather and fertility. However, no trace of a being like Crom Cruach has yet been uncovered in the pagan literature of Ireland, nor in the writings of Saint Patrick. (Rolleston 1911, 85)

There is reason for believing the blood-sacrifices (for which the Celts have been accused) were not so gruesome: the victim most often was a divine victim who died transcendentally. Hubert writes that when one reads of the long series of deaths of heroes commemorated at the festivals, one cannot help thinking that these legends were derived from myths of divine sacrifices renewed in the form of human, animal, and vegetable victims. (Hubert 1988, 244)

The poet Lucan names three Celtic deities—*Teutates, Taeanis,* and *Esus*—whom he said were appeased by human sacrifice. The victims of Teutates were drowned, those of Taranis burned, and those sacrificed to Esus hanged. Teutates, likely from the same root as the Gaelic tuath, has been identified with various deities; he was probably a war-god, defender of the people, at whose altars captives poured forth their blood. His name does not appear in British literature. Taranis was the Northern Jupiter, worshipped by the Britons sometimes under epithets derived from the words for thunder and rain. He answers to the Norse god Thor, the head of the "meteorological" gods who regulated the weather and the seasons. The Irish *Dinnsenchus* mentions this "thunder" god as Etirun, an idol of the Britons. Esus was probably synonymous with Lugh, a widely revered deity of the Celtic world. Lugh's name is preserved in a number of places such as Lugudunum (Lyons) and Luguvallum (Carlisle), and also in Ireland where he is celebrated at the harvest feast of Lugnasad held on the first of August. (MacBain 1996, 65)

We should bear in mind that the practice of human sacrifice is not exclusively druidic or Celtic. It has been practiced by all pre-historic cultures at a certain stage of their development and, according to historical sources, may have been a survival from the time of the Megalithic People.

The Celtic Otherworld

The "heaven-world" of the ancient Celts, unlike that of the Christians, was not located in some far-off, mysterious region of terrestrial space, but here on this planet. Sometimes it was a subterranean world entered through caverns, or hills, or mountains, and inhabited by many races and orders of invisible beings—such as demons, fairies, or even gods. We are told that the Tuatha de Danann or *Sidhe*-folk, after their defeat by the Sons of Mil at the Battle of Tailte, retired to this underground world and took possession of its mansions beneath the green hills and vales of Ireland; and how they, as gods of the harvest, continued to exercise authority over their conquerors.

More frequently, in the old Irish manuscripts, the Celtic Otherworld was located somewhere in the center of the western sea. Manannan mac Lir was one of the divine rulers of its fairy inhabitants, and because he was one of the Tuatha de Danann, his mansion was there rather than in Erin. When he traveled between the two locations, it was in a magic chariot drawn by horses that moved over the sea-waves as on land. According to the pagan Irish, it was a place where there was neither death nor pain nor humiliation; only everlasting youth, and endless joy and feasting. In Irish manuscripts, the Otherworld is known as *Tír-na-nÓg* (Land of Youth). To enter this realm before the appointed hour of death, consent was necessary. This was usually in the form of a silver branch of the sacred apple-tree bearing blossoms, or fruit, given by the queen of the Land of the Ever-Living and Ever-Young to those mortals whom she wished to have as companions.

In Greek mythology, one is reminded of the parallel between the expedition of Proserpine as shown in the journey of Aeneas and the Otherworld of the Celts. In Virgil's classic poem, the priestess Sibyl commanded the plucking of the sacred bough to be carried by Aeneas when he entered the underworld; without such a bough, plucked near the entrance to Avernus from the wondrous tree sacred to Infernal Juno (Proserpine), none could enter Pluto's realm. From this, we may perhaps acknowledge that the Otherworld of the Celts is like the invisible realm of the Ancients called Hades and is also like its mythological counterpart in the Elysian Fields to the west, reserved by the Greeks and Romans for their gods and heroes, and in the Happy Otherworld of Scandinavian, Iranian, and Indian mythologies. (Wentz 1981, 336)

Gaul: Pagan Deities and Beliefs

The only Celtic religion of which we have any description is that of the Gauls; but the information is meager. According to Caesar, Diodorus, Siculus, and other classical writers, the ancient Gauls taught (as one of their tenets) that the soul was immortal. After death, it passed from one human body to another. In Irish literature, however, it is doubtful the pagan Irish believed the souls of all men were immortal, or that the spirits of those who died were rewarded or punished in the "Otherworld" for their conduct in this, or whether in fact their spirits existed at all after death. Nevertheless, there were a few individuals who became immortal in "Fairyland," and others who lived on after death as other men, or in the shapes of animals. Connla, son of Conn, king of Ireland in the second century, was carried off in a crystal boat by a fairy maiden before the eyes of his father and friends, and was never seen on earth again. (Joyce 1997, 297)

At the time of the Roman invasion, the myths of the Gauls were the only myths prevalent in Western Europe. We know that many survived well into the Christian era because resolutions passed at Church councils (Tours in 567, and Nantes in 568) provide evidence of such. Also, Charlmagne's edict of 789 decreed against the worshippers of stones and those who practiced their superstitious forms of worship by trees and springs. When Christianity proved powerless to suppress the old beliefs, it simply followed in the footsteps of all previous religions and absorbed aspects of the existing paganism. For that reason, there are so many springs dedicated to saints or to the virgin and so many sanctuaries built on what had been sacred mounds. This is why we can still find so many mysterious (and sometimes even improper) practices that look, upon examination, as if they too belong to the very distant religious past of the western world.

One feature of the Gaulish religion is known as druidism, although that term is commonly thought to include all that we know of the Gaulish religion as well. Rather, the druids were the philosophers and divines of the Gauls. In view of that, MacBain cautions we should refrain from confusing their system with the ordinary Aryan religion of their ancestors. On the subject of the druids, MacBain quotes Professor Rhys:

> "At the time of Caesar's invasions, they were a powerful class of men, monopolizing the influence of soothsayers, magicians, and priests. But in Gaul, under the faint rays of the civilization of Marseilles and other Mediterranean centers, they seemed to have added to their other characters that of philosophers, discoursing to the youths, whose education was entrusted to them, on the stars and their movements, on the world and its regions, on the nature of things, and the power of the gods."

This differs from what we know of the druids of Irish history, where they were described as merely conjurors and magicians. (MacBain 1996, 83)

When Caesar wrote about the gods most commonly worshiped by the Gauls, he tried to correlate them with those of the Roman Pantheon: Mercury, Apollo, Mars, Minerva, and so forth. He states that the god most worshiped was Mercury; that is to say, the Gallic god was not named Mercury, but corresponded in his uniqueness to the Roman deity. He was regarded as the inventor of all the arts and the presiding deity over travel and commerce. Likewise, he fitted other Gallic deities into the framework of Roman gods: Apollo turned away diseases; Mars controlled warfare; and Minerva protected industry and the crafts.

Caesar further wrote that the most notable deity of the Gauls was (in Roman nomenclature) *Dis*, or Pluto, the god of the Underworld (a place inhabited by the dead). From him all Gauls claimed to be descended and, for this reason, they reckoned time by nights instead of days. Dis represents the powers of darkness, death, and evil, along with Aesus, Teutates, and Taranus. Hence, according to the Celtic historian, D'Arbois de Jubainville, Celtic mythology is interpreted as a variant of the universal solar myth, embodying the concept of the eternal conflict between day and night. (Rolleston 88, 1911) The God of Light appears in Gaul (as in Ireland) to be Lugh, or Lugas. He appears in Irish legend with distinctly solar attributes. When he meets his army before the great conflict with the Fomorians, he is beheld as if he were the rising sun god. Conversely, he is believed to have descended from his grandfather Balor, as a god of the Underworld with its connections to the Powers of Darkness.

However, Celtic historian Nora Chadwick maintains that frequent efforts to match the deities mentioned by Caesar with the names of Celtic gods from Romano-Celtic inscriptions or early Celtic literature have proved hopeless. (Chadwick 1997, 145)

Iberian Peninsula: Pagan Deities and Beliefs

We are not familiar in any detail with the religion of the Celtic people of Spain. Strabo, possibly following Poseidonius, says that they were *atheoi*, meaning they worshipped gods who by his standards were vaguely conceived and lacked anthropomorphic definition. They were not too distant from the Greeks in their beliefs that the gods looked kindly on those who were friendly towards strangers. There is no direct evidence of druids in the life of Celtic Spain, but the occurrence of place-names of the Nemet-type may well indicate the ceremonial groves associated with druidic religion. (Rankin 1996, 170)

Britons: Pagan Deities and Beliefs

From Caesar's account of the religion of the Gauls to the first native accounts of the histories of Britain and Ireland, there is practically a span of a thousand years. During the interval, Christianity had become established on both islands, and the practice of paganism had, for the most part, disappeared. The Christian chronicles make only passing references to the old beliefs. References taken from British inscriptions of the Roman period give us the names of one or two important gods and a host of minor and local deities. Otherwise, our information is mostly that acquired from heroic poems and tales, which do not date much earlier than the ninth century AD. Regarding the ritual of the old religion, we have local customs and superstitions as our only guides. (MacBain 1996, 86)

According to Alexander MacBain, the gods of Britain suffered from what appears to have been the "common lot" of gods elsewhere: they were "changed into the kings and heroes, the giants and enchanters of heroic tales and folklore." Geoffery of Monmouth describes the great deity "Belinus" as a mere mortal conqueror. With his brother, Brennus or "Bran," he laid siege to Rome when Gabius and Porsena were consuls. Gargantua appears twice as a British king under the title Gurgiunt. Camulus, the war-god who gave his name to Camulodunum (now Colchester), is presented as Coel Hen.

Inscriptions of Roman times show that the religious state of affairs in Britain was in no way different from that of Gaul. The local deities were assimilated into the corresponding deities of Rome, and in Britain we have combinations like those met with in Gaul: the Roman deity has the corresponding British name attached to him on the votive inscription by way of epithet. Thus, at Bath, altars are dedicated to Sul-Minerva, Sul being a goddess unknown elsewhere. On the Roman wall, between the Forth and Clyde, the name Mars-Camulus appears on the inscriptions. Among many others, there are spirits of "the mountain and the flood," "Sancta Britannia," and "Brigantia," the goddesses of Britain and the land of the Brigantes, respectively. The most interesting inscriptions are those found in the temple of a god discovered at Lydney Park, in Gloucestershire. One inscription appears to be to the "great god Nodon," indicating the temple would have been dedicated to the worship of Nodon, a god of the deep sea. This deity is identified with the legendary Nudd of Welsh fiction and the Irish King Nuada of the Silver Hand. He fought the two battles of Moytura, and fell in the second before "Balor of the Evil Eye," king of the Fomorians. (MacBain 1996, 90)

The information we have of British deities, as far as Wales is concerned, is derived mostly from the *Mabinogion*, a manuscript found in the fourteenth century but composed much earlier. Besides this, we have the triads, believed to have been of twelfth century origin. The *Taliesin* and other poems preserve echoes of the old myths. One of the Welsh Triads tells us that Britain, before it was inhabited, was called *Clas Myrddin* (Myrddin's Enclosure). Rolleston (referencing Professor Rhys) mentions Myrddin as the deity especially worshiped at Stonehenge which, Geoffrey of Monmouth asserts, was erected by "Merlin." Myrddin holds the place of the Sky—and Sun-god Nudd in Arthur's Mythological cycle. Some of the gods fight under Arthur's banner and perish on the battlefield of Camlan along with him. From the Welsh legends preserved in the *Ancient Books of Wales* as well as in *Mabinogion*, we have several deities with Irish equivalents both in name and position. Manannan the son of Lir is, in the Welsh myths, one of the seven who escaped from Ireland on the death of his brother, Bran the blessed, king of Britain. From Irish accounts of him, Manannan mac Lir appears to be a god of the sea and wind. (Rolleston 1911, 354)

Ireland: Pagan Deities and Beliefs

The Irish Celts were a religious people even before they embraced Christianity in the fifth century AD. They practiced an ancient pagan belief, akin to that practiced by Celts elsewhere. Their chief gods were those of the Iron Age Celts, deities from a pre-Iron Age matriarchal system that personified the forces of nature. It was a belief guided by its priests who were called druids. Patrick W. Joyce, in his book *A Social History of Ancient Ireland*, writes that the pagan Irish appear to have had no well-defined connected system of religion. There were many gods, but no supreme god, like that of Zeus or Jupiter among the Greeks and Romans. There was little or no prayer, and no settled general form of worship. There were no temples. There were altars of some kind erected to idols or to essential gods, which must have been in the open air. No information regarding the religion of the pagan Irish comes to us from outside; whatever knowledge we possess is derived exclusively from native literature. Moreover, all of this literature that has come down to us was written—mostly copied from older documents—in Christian times by Christians, chiefly monks.

Irish gods do not emerge as gods in the usual meaning of the term. They were neither worshiped nor sacrificed to. They are supernatural beings with magical powers. This portrayal, of course, is the result of Christian understanding. The greatest of all the gods is Dagda, "the good god," "lord of perfect knowledge," "father of all." (Chadwick 1997, 174) There are many different gods—some virtuous and some wicked. Some have been identified with ancient Gaul; not surprising, considering many of the Celtic tribes who colonized Ireland (and Britain) were from Gaul, and they naturally brought their traditions and beliefs with them.

Alexander MacBain writes there is no description of an Irish Olympus, but references to particular deities are not uncommon. The earliest reference to any Irish gods occurs in one of the oldest extant documents we possess of the Gaelic language: a manuscript in the Saint Gall Monastery, believed to be of the eighth century, containing incantations to the powers of Diancecht and Goibniu. Cormac's glossary, originally composed in the ninth century, mentions (as deities) Art, Ana, Buanann, Brigit, Neit, and Manannan. Keating quotes from the *Book of Invasions* a poem that makes Dagda "king of heaven," and he further names Badb, Macha, and Morrighan as the three goddesses of the Tuatha de Danann. (MacBain 1996, 104-105)

There was a belief in a land of everlasting youth and peace, beautiful beyond conception, always inhabited by fairies, and called by various names but commonly known as Tír-na-nÓg, the land of the ever youthful. Sometimes it is described as situated far out in the western ocean; sometimes it was deep down under the sea or under a lake or well; or sometimes it was in a hollow *shee* or fairy-hill. The inhabitants were the fairies who were immortal and lived in perfect peace in a perpetual round of sensuous, but harmless and sinless pleasures. In nearly all the old accounts of this happy land, the absence of wickedness is expressly mentioned. The man from Tir Tairngiri tells Cormac that it was "a land wherein there was naught save truth, and there is neither age, nor decay, nor gloom, nor sadness, nor envy, nor jealousy, nor hatred, nor haughtiness."

The absence of sin, and similar characteristics, are, Joyce writes, additions by Christian scribes. (Joyce 1997, 294)

The religious practices of pre-Christian Ireland were closely akin to those of the Continental Celts, but in the words of Katharine Scherman "diluted by distance and mutated in fusion with the religious practices of the earlier inhabitants." (Scherman 1981, 50) Historians describe how the Celts were a tolerant people in religious matters, easily adapting to the cults of those they subjugated, and fitting the resident deities into their own pantheon.

The chief gods of pagan Ireland were those the Iron Age Celts brought with them, representing their ideals of masculinity. They were the deities of society: the prototypes of the warrior, the magician, the craftsman, and the father-leader, all of these qualities now and then embodied in a single god. The goddesses were more universal and more primitive. They were legacies from a pre-Iron Age matriarchal system, and they personified the forces of nature: fertility and destruction. The tales of the Irish gods' and goddesses' activities are pretentiously dramatic, often to a grotesque degree. The theology appears to have no sense of balance. This may be due, in part, to Christian monks who wrote down the old stories. These scribes may have contributed to the ambiguities of our understanding of the ancient customs by their actions to block out heathen practices. In general, however, they seem to have respected the spirit of the old tales.

In describing the Gaelic gods, the writer must naturally begin with the Jupiter of the Gaels. This honor belongs most probably to Dagda. Though Dagda is very often mentioned, little information is given about him. He was one of the gods leading the Tuatha de Danann from Scythia to Ireland, and he brought with him from "Murias" a magical cauldron capable of satisfying the hunger of everyone. With Lug, he makes and carries out all the arrangements of the second battle of Moytura where he was wounded with a poisoned weapon by Cethlenn. The venom of that wound caused his death 120 years later. For eighty years previous to his death, he ruled the Tuatha de Danann as king. (MacBain 1996, 120-121)

Katherine Scherman writes that of the two gods, Dagda was the representative of an older, more generalized pantheon. In addition to being the patriarchal head of his people, his knowledge made him their chief magician. With his invincible club—so heavy that eight men had to carry it—he defended them against enemies. His magic cauldron fed them endlessly; his sexual unions with the goddesses of the earth ensured his people protection against the ancient, sometimes hostile deities. His activities are ritualistic manifestations of his all-embracing godliness. Lug, the younger chieftain, probably belongs to a later period of Celtic development. Where Dagda was good at everything in a non-specific way, Lug's skills (while also encompassing everything) were particularized. He could build chariots, work metal, cure the sick, compose poetry, work sorcerer's spells, and defeat an army single-handed. As the zenith of the Irish-Celtic hero, he was the favorite god of all mortal heroes, the ever-young Cú Chulainn. (Scherman 1981, 52-53)

As previously mentioned, another god of the Irish pantheon was Manannan, son of Lir (a sea-god of greater antiquity), who traveled over the oceans in his chariot. According to legend, the Isle of Man was named for Manannan; another legend sees him in parts of Leinster, rolling on three legs like a wheel through the mists. In *Cormac's Glossary*, a tenth-century work attributed to Bishop Cormac mac Cuilennain, Manannan was a merchant of the Isle of Man, an accomplished seaman who knew "through seeing the face of the heavens" when the weather would be fine and when stormy. The Irish call him god of the sea, an example of a god made mortal.

Some goddesses were mother and fertility figures, others were agents of death. In one case, three goddesses share the same dominion. Brigit, Anu, and Dana were generally deities of fertility and prosperity. Anu and Dana were the mothers of the gods, while Brigid watched over childbirth and brought plenty to the houses she visited, leaving her footprint in the ashes of the hearth. She was also the goddess of poetry. Other threefold goddesses presided in battle. Morrigan (great queen), Badb (carrion crow), and Macha (also a crow whose food was the heads of slain warriors) caused chaos in enemy ranks or appeared in animal form to harass a single fighter. While Cú Chulainn singly defended a ford against an army of challengers, Queen Meave sent the goddess Morrigan against him. Morrigan arrived as an eel to wind itself around his legs, then changed to a wolf, frightening herds of cattle to stampede against him. (Scherman 1981, 53)

Some goddesses embodied the functions of fertility and war in the same figure. One of these was Meave, namesake of the Connacht queen who initiated the war against Ulster in which Cú Chulainn was the hero-defender. The archaic Meave, believed to be the goddess of sovereignty, was worshiped in Ireland long before the Heroic Age in which Meave of Connacht flourished. It was the goddess Meave that every Tara king married symbolically. In another guise, she was the queen-wolf. She could outrun a horse, and when a warrior looked on her he lost two-thirds of his strength. (Scherman 1981, 53-54)

Like the Continental Celts, the Irish had no thought of an afterlife in which the good were rewarded in heaven and the sinful tortured in hell. There was a paradise, Katherine Scherman writes, but it was not a place you went after you died if you had been good on earth. It was a place of the heart's desire, a land of singing birds and gorgeous women, usually across the western sea, that frontier of mystery where no invaders had ever ventured and from which few returned. It had several names, the most familiar of which is Tír-na-nÓg (Land of Youth).

Pagan Religious Observances

Besides their beliefs and rituals of worship, pagan Celts had festivals to honor and pay tribute to the gods. Major religious observances focused on the solstices, equinoxes, and moon phases. The end of the old year and the beginning of the new was marked by the greatest of the ceremonies, *Samhain*, observed on November 1. It was a time when the spirits of the dead could roam freely. It was a time when all the important communal acts, meetings, and sacrifices took place. At Samhain, there was the elimination of boundaries between the dead and the living, between the sexes, between one man's property and another's, and, in divinations, between the present and the future—all of which symbolized return to chaos. Also, on this occasion, the male god Dagda and the female goddess Morrigan would come together and through their intercourse re-energize the tribe and all of its productiveness. It was also the day on which mortals made peace with the spirits. (Scherman 60, 1981)

Samhain has survived virtually unchanged in character and purpose since the earliest times. Not even its celebration date has changed. It predates Christianity by more than half a millennium. It is simply the oldest, continually celebrated festival in Western Europe. At Samhain, cattle were driven in from their pastures and stabled for the cold months ahead. Crops were brought up from the earth and bundled away in cellars to sustain the economy until the dawn of another spring. Yet Samhain was a creepy festival; the fairy-mounds opened and their inhabitants were abroad in a more real sense than on any other night. The souls of the dead returned and became visible. In Ireland, until more recent times, people did not leave the house on this night unless obliged to do so; if they did, they kept clear of graveyards. They were not to look behind when they heard footsteps. It was the dead that were following them.

In Wales, food (called *bwyd cennad y meirw*) was left out-of-doors to provide for the wandering dead, doors were left unbolted, and special care was taken before going to bed to prepare the hearth for the visit of dead relatives. In Scotland, it was a night of mischief and confusion, and its eeriness was intensified by the impersonation of spirits of the dead by young men who went about with masked, veiled, or blackened faces, and dressed in white or in disguises of straw. (Rees and Rees 1995, 90) The strong tradition behind the festival survives to the present day as Halloween and its Christianized version, the "Feast of All Souls." The Reformation almost killed it. Reformers like Calvin sought to suppress any customs that appeared even remotely of magic or paganism.

The next festival, *Imbolc*, observed on the first of February, celebrated the end of winter and the return of light. It was also thought to be associated with the goddess Brigid, a deity of fertility who, in Christian belief, became Saint Brigid and whose feast day of February 1 is still celebrated widely in Ireland. Beltaine, celebrated on May 1, was in honor of the Celtic god of fire, *Belenus*. Belenus is a very mysterious character who seems to have been just about everywhere in the ancient world. Some scholars link him with the horned Celtic deity Cernunnos; others place his origin as far afield as the ancient Middle East and see the famous Baal of the Old Testament as one of Bel's forerunners. May Day, like Halloween, was a period of division between one season and the next, and the divisions between the worlds grew exceedingly dim. On this night fairies enchanted unwary mortals, but their charms (given the joyful nature of the occasion) were little more than love spells or simple bewilderments. (Judge 2004, 143)

Lughnasa, observed on the first of August, was the feast of thanks to the god Lug for the harvest bounty. Lughnasa was an important Celtic festival that marked the advent of the autumn season. Although it had disappeared on the Continent by the late Middle Ages, the festival has survived in Ireland in many areas down to the present day. The Irish believed that on this day the god Lug married the beautiful goddess Eriu, supremacy of Ireland. Lugh was the hero-god of Irish mythology, a kind of Hercules character who saved colleens from monsters and shielded mortals from the ravages of malign gods. Most importantly, he also represented the sun. Ultimately, Lughnasa was Christianized into Lammas, a word derived from the Old English words for "loaf" and "mass." Even under the influence of the church, the festival retained most of its pagan elements, celebrating the gathering of the harvest and the coming of the fall. (Judge 2004, 173)

The Irish bards had a group of stories called "Caves," but few have survived in other than fragmentary form. However, in Ireland many legends surround one particular cave: the Cave of Cruachan at Rathcroghan in County Roscommon. Otherwise known as Ireland's Gate of Hell, it was looked upon as a passage between this world and the otherworld. It was greatly feared for people considered it to be the abode of evil spirits. According to legend, Cruachan was the source of plagues. One legend has it as "the fit abode" of the goddess Morrigan. Periodically on Samhain, the three-headed Ellen and other demonic beings would emerge from Cruachan to mingle among the ordinary folk. (Nigel 1996, l)

Transition from Pagan to Christian Beliefs

There is one final aspect of Celtic religion which should be mentioned, namely the transition to Christianity. Historian Miranda Green writes the conversion from polytheism to monotheism was made easy because the multiplicity of pagan deities could slip without difficulty into the characters of the Christian saints. The goddess Brigit became Saint Brigid, with her cult virtually unchanged. Saint Ann was probably originally the Irish goddess Anu. The Virgin Mary took over many functions of the Celtic Mother goddesses. In addition, pagan rituals were often adapted to Christian use: healing cults and holy wells exemplify this transformation. The pagan Celtic Otherworld corresponds very closely to the Christian Promised Land. Pagan tales such as the *Voyage of Bran* have a parallel in the *Voyage of Saint Brendan*. Thus, the religion of the pagan Celtic world not only survived, but many of its features were incorporated into the new Christian faith. (Green 1997, 22)

Chapter XIII—
Druids and Druidism

The long drawn-out struggle between Christianity and druidism [in Ireland] seems to have come to an end in the seventh century when the druids qua druids were finally displaced. Paganism outlived the druids, but not as a system, and the early Church seems on the whole to have taken the pragmatic view that people were free to believe what they liked so long as they accepted the ultimate authority of the Church.

—Proinsias MacCana, *Mythology in Early Irish Literature*

The Celts practiced an ancient pagan faith called druidism. It was a religion governed by its priests who were called druids. The druids wielded immense power over their communities; they were accorded special status and presided over religious ceremonies, which were for the most part held outdoors. In all matters of dispute, druids alone judged and decided, fixing punishments and rewards, as appropriate, when crimes were committed, or where boundary or inheritance disputes arose. A person or persons failing to abide by a druid's decision was excommunicated from public worship, and this was looked upon as a most demeaning punishment. All must avoid them and eschew any talk with them, lest the infection be passed on. Druids enjoyed a range of benefits: they were exempt from tax and were not required to serve in the military. (Hubert 1988, 230)

Notwithstanding the references to druids by classical scholars, and in spite of traditions recorded in native Celtic literature, chiefly that of Irish and Welsh, knowledge of druidism and its priest class is still far from being conclusive. It is true there are some valued Greek sources, but the bulk of the classical observations is from Roman writers, and much of it consists of anti-Celtic propaganda. By the time the Celts themselves came to commit their knowledge to writing, they had adopted Christianity and, not surprisingly, their explanation of their pagan ancestry might not have been altogether flattering.

The prime occupation of the druids was to manage, by means of magic, what they perceived as the supernatural powers of the natural world. This was seen as necessary in order to provide a positive outcome to any circumstance where the divine forces would act in favor of, rather than against, humankind. Miranda Green writes that all Celtic religious activity should be seen in this context. Moreover, the richness of Celtic spirituality is due in part to its adaptability and freedom of expression. The free Celtic traditions of open-air worship and metaphorical perceptions of the gods changed and developed in the Roman period. Roman cults were accepted and absorbed into the Celtic religious system, but Celtic perceptions of the divine world remained fundamentally the same. (Green 1997, 22)

According to Historian Rice Holmes, druidism existed in Britain, Ireland, Gaul, and (as far as it is known) wherever there were Celts amid a population of dolmen builders. There were Celts in Cisalpine Gaul, but there were no dolmens there, and therefore there were no druids. (Rolleston 1911, 82) This is an interesting observation. Another interesting observation is the druids formed an order in Celtic society, and that order was a brotherhood, a society of individuals collectively exercising a social function. The eminent Celtic historian, Henri Hubert, writes that their organization cut across the divisions of tribes and states. "The druids of Ireland were one single body, those of Britain turned their eyes to the sanctuary of Mona (Anglesey), and those of Gaul turned to the shrine among the Carnutes." Hubert further writes that all these groups communicated with one another. The druidical colleges obtained new members by training and cooption. There seemed to have been druidesses in Gaul and Ireland, but their role in the college of druids was not clear. (Hubert 1988, 232)

Much of the information on the religious beliefs and practices of druidism comes from Greek and Roman texts, much of it in reference to isolated facts with few references that provide a coherent account of druidism as a whole. We know of the druids from several Greek and Latin historians and writers, among them Caesar, Poseidonios, Tacitus, Diodoros, Strabo, Pliny the Elder, and Ammianus Marcellinus. The most detailed accounts, however, are those given by Caesar in his unflattering commentaries of Gaulish society. Diodorus of Sicily wrote in the first century BC that, "those men called by us *philosophoi* and *theologoi* are held in great honor by them (Celts); they call them druids . . . and no sacrifice may be performed without a druid present . . . for only they speak the language of the gods." Diodorus, in this instance, was writing about the Continental druids, primarily those of Gaul. (Rankin 1996, 272)

Posidonius and the Celts

As previously pointed out, we know of the Celts and their religious beliefs and practices through different kinds of evidence, such as Greek and Roman writers, archaeology, and the emerging study of early Celtic languages. But, by far, our best source for the more accurate story comes from a Greek philosopher of the first century BC named Posidonius. When Posidonius was a young man, he set out on an extraordinary journey through the yet unconquered Celtic lands of Western Europe. He wrote extensively of his journey and the people he met. Unfortunately, most of his work disappeared in early Christian times, but segments did survive. (Freeman 2006, 4) His trip turned out to be one of the great adventures of the ancient world. He wrote of what he saw and of the people he met. Posidonius carefully studied the druids and passed on important information concerning them. He wrote:

> "There are three groups among the Gauls who are given special honor—bards, vates and Druids. The bards are singers and poets, while the vates supervise sacrifices and study the ways of nature. The Druids also study nature but devote themselves to morality as well. The Gauls consider the Druids the most just of all their people, and so they are given the role of judge in all public and private disputes. In the past, they were even able to halt battles and bring an end to wars. Murder cases are especially given to the Druids for judgment. The Gauls believe that when condemned criminals are sacrificed, then the land will prosper. The Druids and other Gauls all say that the soul is immortal and the universe is indestructible, but at some time in the future, both fire and water will prevail." (Freeman 2006, 158)

As Posidonius continued to observe the druids, he discovered they were keen students of nature, and says their application of this knowledge was quite extensive. He tells how he was present when they sacrificed condemned criminals. He wrote, "The Gauls will keep a criminal under guard for five years, then impale him on a pole in honor of their gods. They will then burn his body on an enormous pyre along with first fruits of the land." Posidonius admits that the actual act of human sacrifice was rare in Gaul, but certainly gruesome. He squeamishly tells how such rituals could involve bizarre forms of divination, but points out that the druids only used it in the most crucial circumstances. He gives the following description:

> "The Gauls have an especially strange and unbelievable method of predicting the future for the most important affairs. They first anoint a human victim, then stab him with a small knife in the chest just above the diaphragm. They watch the man carefully and interpret future events

> by the way he falls, how his limbs shake, and the way that his blood spurts on the ground." (Freeman 2006, 160)

Julius Caesar on the Druids

The second great source of information on the druids is Julius Caesar. During his seven-year conquest of Gaul, Caesar had abundant opportunity to become familiar with Gaulish culture and religion. Caesar writes that the druids of Gaul formed a priesthood with a strong organization and well-defined hierarchy that spread across tribal boundaries. He further writes: "Among the druids there is one supreme leader who holds authority over the rest. When this chief druid dies, he is succeeded by whoever is most qualified. If there are several contenders for the position, the druids all take a vote—though they have been known to contend for the title with armed force." (Freeman 2006, 164) Caesar continues:

> "In most disputes, between communities or between individuals, the druids act as judges. If a crime is committed, if there is a murder, or if there is a dispute about an inheritance or a boundary, they are the ones who give a verdict and decide on the punishment or compensation appropriate in each case. Any individual or community not abiding by their verdict is banned from the sacrifices, and this is regarded among the Gauls as the most severe punishment. Those who are banned in this way are reckoned as sacrilegious criminals. Everyone shuns them; no one will go near or speak to them for fear of being contaminated in some way by contact with them. If they make any petitions there is no justice for them, and they are excluded from any position of importance."

Caesar also states that the Celts believed in an afterlife, which was not so very different from life on earth. Remarking on this tradition, he comments that although Gaul was not wealthy, funerals were splendid and costly. Lucan remarks that the Celts regarded death merely as an interruption in a long life—as a bridge between one life and another. He maintains that the Celts believed that human souls remained in control of their bodies in another world after death.

Caesar goes on to say that druidism had originally belonged to Britain before it came to Gaul and how, on a fixed day each year, the druids assembled in a sacred place in the territory of the Carnutes, considered to be the center of Gaul. Caesar writes of the rigorous training of the druids, mainly learning the oral tradition by heart, which could take as long as twenty years. He alludes to the druids' interest in the study of the natural world as well as religion, and how they taught that the souls of the dead underwent transmigration, apparently in order to prevent warriors from being afraid of death and thus make them more valorous in battle. (Green 1997, 86)

Pliny the Elder (AD 23-79) seems to be the first who commented on the reasons for the decline of the druids and certainly had no hesitation in attributing it to Roman repression. We have learned also from classical sources that the Romans made several attempts to suppress the druids. Augustus excluded them from Roman citizenship by forbidding Roman citizens to practice druidical rites. Tiberius banned them by a decree of the Roman Senate and Claudius attempted to "wholly abolish" them in AD 54. The Romans saw the druids as an intellectual class who could, and did, organize national revolt against Rome (Ellis 1994, 17) Much about druidism and its ancient practices and rituals remains shrouded in mystery because the druids wanted it that way, and, no wonder, since only they knew "the language of the gods."

Druidic Origins

There is no classical evidence of druids predating the second century BC, maybe a passing reference or two. The Greek philosopher Posidonius traveled through the heart of Gaul in the first century BC. His writings were copied by other classical authors, among them Cicero, Tacitus, Pliny the Elder, and especially Julius Caesar. Since these writers were not concerned with ethnology or comparative religion, our historical knowledge of druidism from classical sources is therefore scarce.

In more recent times, historians have committed much of their time speculating on the origins of druidism. Historian T.W. Rolleston (at the same time referencing Dr. Rice Holmes) conjectures that druidism was a religion of the aboriginal inhabitants of Western Europe from the Baltic to Gibraltar. He believes that when the Celts got to Western Europe, they found a people with a powerful priesthood, a ritual, and imposing religious monuments; that they were a people steeped in magic and mysticism and the cult of the Underworld. He adds, "We only know of druidism where Celts and dolmen-builders existed together." From this he speculates that, "druidism in its essential features was imposed upon the imaginative and sensitive nature of the Celts . . . by the earlier populations of Western Europe—the Megalithic People." (Rolleston 1911, 82)

Peter Berresford Ellis is, by and large, in agreement with Rolleston's view. He writes:

> "[T]he druids were an indigenous Celtic intelligentsia, evolving from the original wise men and women during the age of the 'hunter-gatherer' among the ancient ancestors of the Celts, losing their original functions but retaining the Celtic name of those with 'oak knowledge.'"

He goes on to underscore they were to be found in every part of Celtic society, but it was not until the second century that the Greeks realized these learned folk had a collective name of druids. Camille Jullian writing in *Histoire de la Gaule* (1908) claims druidism was a Celtic institution, but of comparatively late appearance in the development of Celtic society which, he believes, accounts for no Greek or Latin reference to druids before the second century. (Ellis 2002, 43-49) Historian Bertrand in his *L'Irlande Celtique* offers an interesting proposition. He postulates that soon after the conversion of Ireland to Christianity, the country is covered with monasteries whose entire organization seems to show that they were really druidic colleges transformed en masse.

Caesar writes that there were many similar druidic colleges in Gaul. They were very numerous, he tells us. They discussed and imparted to the youth many things respecting the stars and their motions, respecting the universe and our earth, respecting the nature of things, and respecting the power and the majesty of the immortal gods. He further adds that in spite of the severe study and discipline involved, crowds flocked to them for the sake of the power wielded by the druidic order, and the civil immunities, which its members of all grades enjoyed. Arts and sciences were studied there, and thousands of verses enshrining the teachings of druidism were committed to memory.

Some historians, Professor Rhys among them, go so far as to trace druidism to the Silurian people—an ancient tribe from the Valley of the Severn, so named by Tacitus and described by him as "Iberian" in appearance. There are similarities showing that druidism may have been an Indo-European institution with origins going back to the most distant past of Indo-European societies. One similar group was Hindu Brahminism. This society occupied the same place in the social hierarchy as the druids and served their social order in similar ways. As druidic doctrine was transmitted orally (from prehistoric times until comparatively recently), so were the texts of the Vedas. Brahminic students were taught, in schools set up deep in the forest, a corpus of doctrine whose tenets included the reincarnation of the soul, which many authorities claim the druids also promulgated. (MacBain 1996, 52)

Parallels are to be found elsewhere. Rutherford writes that recent studies, such as Mallory's, reveal numerous linguistic affinities between Proto-Indo-European and Celtic words. He gives as an example the word tuatha (folk or people) as being close to *teuta*, root for "teutonic" and "Deutsch," which have the same meaning. The

Sythians were among the earliest cultures having contact with the Celts. It was the Sythians who taught the Celts how to dye and weave wool in tartan patterns. What is certain is the extent of the Sythian effect on Celtic burial custom. The wagon or chariot burials found throughout the Celtic world were plainly the continuance of Sythian practice known from their burial sites. (Rutherford 1993, 34-36)

Places of Worship

More impressive and convincing among classical references to Celtic Druidism are those that relate not to the gods, but to their places of worship. Although the Celts sometimes built temples for the worship of their gods, they more often used natural landscape locations as the center of their religious observance. These are found frequently in sacred woods and near lakes and swamps. The most sacred grove in Britain was the one on Anglesey Island in northern Wales, which Tacitus says was "devoted to barbarous superstition." Suetonius Paulines and his Roman legions destroyed it in AD 61. Some of the sanctuaries, it is told, reflected a ritual preoccupation with the natural environment. The poet Lucan, in the first century AD, tells of a sacred grove near Marseilles:

> "A grove there was, untouched by men's hands from ancient times, whose interlacing boughs enclosed a space of darkness and cold shade, and banished the sunshine from above. No rural Pan dwelt there, nor Silvanus, ruler of the woods, nor Nymphs; but gods were worshiped there with savage rites, the altars were heaped with hideous offerings, and every tree was sprinkled with human gore. On these boughs, if antiquity, reverential of the gods, deserves any credit, birds feared to perch; in those coverts wild beasts would not lie down; no wind ever bore down upon that wood, nor thunderbolt hurled from black clouds; the trees, even when they spread their leaves to no breeze, rustled among themselves. Water also fell there in abundance from dark springs. The images of the gods, grim and rude, were

> uncouth blocks, formed and felled tree-trunks. Legend also told that often the subterranean hollows quaked and bellowed, that yew trees fell down and rose again, that the glare of conflagration came from trees that were not on fire, and that serpents twined and glided round the stems. The people never resorted thither to worship at close quarters, but left the place to the gods. When the sun is in the mid-heaven or dark night fills the sky, the priest himself dreads their approach and fears to surprise the lord of the grove." (Cunliffe 1997, 198; Pharsalia 3.400-25)

Trees were also regarded as a quintessence of the divine. In Gaul and Galatia, the oak, above all, was venerated; in Britain it was the yew; and in Ireland, the rowan. It was not until the Celts came under Etruscan influence at the end of the Hallstatt period that they gave their gods human shape. The wooden idols created by the wood-carvers prompted the poet Lucan to remark on them, "grim faced god images, coarsely hewn from rough tree trunks, bleached near shaded springs . . . ."

British Druidism

There is little mention of druidic influence in Britain before the revolt of Queen Boudicca, the heroine of British resistance against the Romans. It is true that Caesar regarded Britain as the home of druidism, and we cannot doubt the presence and influence of druids in Britain at the time of his expedition. Nor can it be imagined they were passive members of British society between that time and AD 61 when Suetonius Paulinus, the commander in chief of the Roman forces, "prepared to attack the island of Mona which was inhabited by courageous men and provided a refuge for all the exiles." (Markale 1993, 159; Tacitus, *Annals*, XIV, 29) Presumably, the reason for this Roman assault was that exiles were directing British resistance from Mona; these exiles, as Tacitus goes on to describe, were druids. Tacitus' description of the final terrible scenes at Mona is recounted next:

> "The densely packed armies of the Britons were on the opposite shore. All around them ran wild-haired women waving sticks looking like the Furies themselves. The druids were everywhere praying to their gods and calling down curses. These sights terrified our soldiers, who had never seen anything like them before. The legions stood there exposed to the enemy's weapons as if their limbs were paralyzed. But soon they pulled themselves together and listened to their commander who was yelling at them not to be scared of a mob of crazy women. Finally, the troops pressed forward, slaughtering everyone in their way. We left behind a garrison there that destroyed the sacred groves dedicated to their wicked superstitions. The Druids, after all, consider it their religious duty to cover their altars with human blood and practice divination by studying human entrails." (Freeman 2006, 170)

Irish Druidism

Ironically, our knowledge of Irish Druidism has come down to us by way of the ancient Irish monks who transcribed the oral accounts from earlier times. According to Irish tradition, the center of druidism in Ireland was in Uisneach in present-day county Meath. It was there that Mide, the first druid, lit the first fire in Ireland that blazed for seven years and could be seen across the length and breadth of the land. To the Irish, as to the Continental Druids, fire and water were the sacred elements, and early Irish law enshrines many traditions concerning the sanctity of both. The holy wells of Christian Ireland were holy wells to the druids in the pre-Christian era, and the festive bonfires lighted throughout Ireland on Midsummer Night (June 23) are of pre-Christian origin, when the people lit fires to commemorate their sun god.

According to P.W. Joyce, no reliable information regarding the religion of the pagan Irish comes to us from outside. Whatever knowledge we possess is derived exclusively from the native literature. Moreover, all of this literature that has come down to us was written—mostly copied from earlier documents—in Christian times by Christians, chiefly monks. No books, if any, penned in pre-Christian ages have been preserved. Christian copyists modified their originals in many ways, especially by introducing Christian allusions and, no doubt, by softening down many pagan features that were particularly repellent to them. Yet many passages, and some complete tales, remain thoroughly pagan in character. (Joyce 1997, 219)

Druids in Ireland were, according to Historian Joyce, the exclusive possessors of whatever learning was then known. They were not only druids in the precise interpretation of their role, but they were judges, prophets, historians, poets, and even physicians. There were druids throughout Ireland, but their chief seat was at Tara, also the seat of the high kings of Ireland. Irish druids had the reputation of being great magicians. We are told they could "raise druidical clouds and mists and bring down showers of fire and blood; they could drive a man insane or into idiocy by flinging a magic wisp of straw in his face." According to some of the old historical legends, the outcomes of battles were sometimes determined, not so much by the gallantry of the warriors, as by the magical powers of the druids. Joyce points out that the *Tripartite of St. Patrick* and Adamnan's *Life of St. Columba* refer to the druids and their magical powers, as do the historical tales. (Joyce 1997, 222-223)

Tigernach and other annalists relate how before the Battle of Cul-Dremne (AD 561)—fought between the northern and southern branches of the Ui Neill dynasty—Dermot (king of the southern Ui Neill and a Christian) called for the Druid Fraechan to make a protective magical *aire druad* (druid's fence) around the southern army. The druid's spell, however, collapsed when a warrior named Mag Laim from the northern side made a suicidal dash through the hexed line. The resulting effect was defeat and heavy casualties for Dermot's side, while Mag Laqim was the lone casualty on the other side.

Druids were held as the intermediaries with the spirit world and as such had the power to safeguard people from maliciousness of evil-disposed spirits; this, in fact, explains much of their sway over the people. Another important function was divination or the predicting of future events, practiced in connection with most important affairs and particularly with military expeditions. Queen Meave, before setting out on the *Tain* expedition, conferred with her druid to seek counsel and a foretelling of the future. He is said to have told her: "whosoever they be that will not return, thou thyself shalt certainly return."

King Laegaire's druids foretold the coming of Saint Patrick, and the Druid Dubdiad predicted the defeat and death of Congal in the battle of Moyrath. When Daithi was king of Ireland (AD 405-428), he ordered his druid to forecast events in his reign for the next year and was told (according to Joyce), "Art thou asleep, O King of Erin and Alban (Scotland)?" And the king replied, "Why the addition to my title? I am not king of Alban." To this the druid answered that he had consulted "the clouds of the men of Erin," by which he had found that the king would make a conquering expedition to Alban, Britain, and Gaul, which he did soon afterwards. (Joyce 1997, 229)

In the legends of the saints, there is mention of divination by the heavenly bodies. When Saint Columkille was a child, his foster-father went to a certain *fāith* (prophet) to ask him when the boy should begin his formal learning; the prophet, having first scanned the heavens, decided that he must start immediately. Finn mac Cumail, besides his other accomplishments, had the gift of divination, for which he used a rite peculiar to himself. A basin of clear water was brought to him, in which (having washed his hands, and having complied with some other formalities) he put his thumb in his mouth under his "tooth of knowledge," on which the future event he looked for was revealed to him. Thus, it is repeatedly mentioned in the tales from the Cycle of Finn. (Joyce 1997, 229-231)

The Druidic Tonsure

Male druids in Irish sources had a tonsure. It seems obvious that the druids of Britain also had a similar form of haircut although it is not specifically stated. The concept of a tonsure appears in many cultures and religions. Buddhists and Jaina monks, also Hindus, cut their hair as a form of religious initiation. Lucat Mael and Caplait, two druids who were the tutors of the High King Laoghaire's daughters, Ethne and Fidelma, are said to have cut their hair in a fashion know as *airbacc giunnae*. Joyce believes this meant "fence cut of the hair," implying the cut left a sort of eave or fence along the head, cut from ear to ear, leaving the front part of the head shaved. Saint Patrick considered the airbacc giunnae style as making them look like the devil and when these two druids were converted, he urged them to have their hair cut in a different style. When Christianity took hold among the Irish, this druidic tonsure was preserved and became the tonsure of the Christian monks. (Ellis 2002, 80)

Areas of Druidic Conformity and Dissimilarity

Irish and Gaulish druids were similar in several ways, yet dissimilar in others: in both countries, they were the only learned men of the time; their disciples underwent a long course of training. They were the king's chief advisers; they were very influential and held in great respect. Among both Irish and Gauls there were druidesses.

There were areas of dissimilarity as well. Gaulish druids were under a head druid with supreme authority and they held periodic councils or synods. There was no such institution in Ireland, though there were eminent druids in various districts, with influence accorded to eminence. The Gaulish druids held the doctrine of the immortality of the soul as applying to all mankind (the soul of every human being passing, after death, into other bodies of humans). There is no evidence that the Irish druids held the souls of all men to be immortal. Yet, tradition tells us there were a few distinct individuals who lived after death, some reappearing as other men, some as animals of various kinds, and a few lived on in fairyland without the intervention of death.

Another area of difference was that of human sacrifice. Human sacrifice was part of the rite of the Gaulish druids, sometimes an individual being sacrificed, sometimes great numbers together. There is no record of any human sacrifice in connection with the rites of the Irish druids. Another difference was that Gaulish druids prohibited their disciples from committing to writing any part of their lore, regarding this as an unhallowed practice. There is no mention of any such prohibition among Irish druids. The Gaulish druids revered the oak (and mistletoe when growing on it); Irish druids revered the yew, the hazel, and the rowan tree. The Gaulish druids were considered as priests while the Irish druids were merely wizards and learned men. Finally, Joyce tells us that the information we have relating to Gaulish and British druids is derived from Classical writers, there being few if any native accounts. Information about Irish druids comes from native Irish sources, none from foreign writers (Joyce 1997, 239-240)

Druid Women

Several Greek and Latin writers speak of *Dryades* or druidesses. And the existence of such female druids is confirmed by Celtic sources. (Ellis 2002, 91) At the outset, one must recognize the fascinating role of women in Celtic society. The rights and position of Celtic women far exceeded those of Greece or Rome. In Greece women had no political rights at all. They could take no part in the running of society and their social rights were severely limited. In Rome, women were generally allowed more rights than in Greece, but the *paterfamilias* still had complete control over his wife. Married women in Rome did not, as in Greece, live in seclusion but took their meals with their husbands, and were free to leave the house, provided they wore the *stola matronalis* to indicate their status.

In Celtic society, the position of women was vastly different. From history we find numerous female figures in supreme authority, for example Queen Boudicca, the ruler of the British Iceni. She is also described as a priestess of the goddess "Andrasta," which arguably makes her a druidess as well as a queen. The sagas support the idea of women as warriors. Female warrior-queens appear in many stories, notably Meave of Connacht who commanded an army and personally slew the hero-warrior Cethren in combat. Among Fionn mac Cumhail's elite Fianna warriors, there is the female champion Credne. Returning to historic personages, we find that contemporary with Boudicca was Cartimandua, ruler of the British Brigantes (circa AD 43-69). We hear of the earlier Gaulish chieftainess, Onomaris, who led the Celtic tribes in their wanderings into Iberia. The position of women, as it emerges in the Brehon Law system of Ireland (at a time when women were treated as mere chattels in most European societies) was incredibly progressive.

In Celtic tradition, the existence of female druids is quite obvious. References to *bandruaid* (druid women) occur repeatedly. The role of female druids is mentioned in the *Rennes Dinnsenchus* and many individual druidesses feature in Irish epics. In the most famous epic in Irish mythology, the *Táin Bó Cuailnge*, Queen Meave of Connacht consults a druidess named Fidelma from the *sidh* of Cruachan in County Roscommon. Asked if she possesses the *imbas forasnai* (the light of foresight), Fidelma says she does, and is then asked to predict how Meave's army will fare against the armies of Conchobhar mac Nessa of Ulster. Fidelma predicts its defeat at the hands of Cú Chulainn. Evidently, Saint Patrick was in fear of female druids. In the *Tripartite Life of Saint Patrick*, he cautions kings not to accept the advice of druids or druidesses and in his *Hymn* asks God especially to protect him from druidesses. (Ellis 2002, 92-102)

Christianity Absorbs Druidism?

The long drawn-out encounter between Christianity and druidism seems to have come to an end in the seventh century when the druids were finally displaced. Peter Berresford Ellis, in citing Father Joe McVeigh's polemic work, *Renewing the Irish Church: Towards an Irish Liberation Theology* (1993), describes how the first Christian missionaries to Ireland did not attempt a root and branch eradication of the Celtic Druidic tradition and beliefs. Instead, the new religion absorbed the holy mountains and the innumerable holy wells and gave them Christian names. It has been estimated that there were approximately three thousand holy wells (some of which, like Doon well in Donegal, remain in use). This popular or vernacular religion, separate and distinct from the institutional hierarchical Church, has, from the outset, been a vibrant characteristic of Irish Christianity. (Ellis 2002, 19-20)

From this time on, there was a workable *modus vivendi* which guaranteed the formal, as it were "constitutional" primacy of the Church without compelling people to choose between Christian teaching on the one hand and the vast body of inherited pagan tradition on the other. Once paganism had been dismantled, the druidic teaching on fundamental topics like cosmogony and eschatology weakened. The two systems were able to coexist without undue strain: they became complementary, rather than competing, and there is some evidence that they remained so for as long as the Gaelic order endured. (O'Driscoll ed., 1981, 149)

Druidism, in many ways, outlived the druids. Irish people gather together each year on the dates of ancient Celtic festivals to celebrate the rites once performed in honor of powerful pagan deities. Among the most important of these is Samhain (Halloween) which, according to tradition, was a time when Celtic gods were particularly hostile. It was a night when ancient gods walked among Celtic mortals. In the more modern rendition of this pagan rite, the spirits of Christian dead return to walk among the living every Halloween.

Chapter XIV—
Influence of Christianity

I am from Ireland
From the holy land of Ireland
I ask you, lord
Come dance with me in Ireland
For Christ's own sake

—Irish Anonymous, twelfth century

The arrival of Christianity to Western Europe was slow and gradual. There is little or no information as to how the conversion process began, but it is believed that the first Christian missionaries probably reached neighboring Gaul as early as the end of the first century. The earliest confirmed communities were those of Vienne and Lyons, which were established in the second century. The community of Lyons was presided over by a Bishop Pothinus. In AD 177, the modest Lyons community experienced severe persecution, and many of the Christians were subjected to imprisonment and, in many cases, torture and death. Among the martyrs was Bishop Pothinus. This information came from an Epistle from the Gallican Churches to the Churches of Asia and Phrygia revealed by Euesbius, bishop of Caesarea, circa AD 260-340. (Dillon 2003, 159)

Irenaeus, of whose personal history little is known, replaced Pothinus. Greek was still the principal language of the Church, but Lyons was a Latin city and on many occasions Irenaeus had to apologize "for what he regards as the deficiencies of his Greek style, on the ground that he is resident among the *Keltae* and for the most using 'a barbarous dialect.'" One well-known feature of his bishopric was his intervention (circa AD 190) in the controversial Easter dispute, which figured so prominently in the following centuries with the Celtic Church. There is no further information of a bishopric being established in Gaul in the second century. After the death of Irenaeus, the next Gaulish bishop mentioned is Saturninus of Toulouse whose episcopate began in AD 250. (Dillon 2003, 160-161)

Despite considerable persecution, Christianity continued to spread its influence. The solid foundations established by the church at Lyons made the town the metropolis of Gaul. Around AD 250, Saint Cyprian sent a group of missionaries from North Africa. Many of these men gave their names to places where they preached: Paul at Narbonne, Trophimus at Arles, Saturninus at Toulouse, and Gratianus at Tours. Some of these were victims of persecution by Decius in AD 251. Christian communities suffered further persecution at the hands of Aurelianus between AD 270 and AD 275, and still further prosecution at the hands of Diocletian. (Markale 1993, 138)

The fourth century brought a new Christian era to Gaul and to the West generally with the reign of Emperor Constantine the Great (AD 274-337). In AD 313, Constantine issued the famous Edict of Milan, which reversed Rome's policy of hostility to Christianity and accorded full legal recognition to Christians. By substituting Christianity for the official cult of the emperor as a state religion, "Constantine created a unifying principle of government, guided by the religious sanctions of a popular religion." As Christianity spread throughout the empire, it adapted to the existing administrative structure, which had provided a framework for Roman civic authority. Ecclesiastical administration was divided into provinces and dioceses. Even after the breakup of the empire, its administrative institution remained, but it was now in the hands of the Christians.

Early Christianity won its converts in the towns which, as capital of the old *civitates*, benefited from Roman administration in a way the *pagi* or country districts did not. This enabled the new religion to acquire a firm foundation and continuing support. (Johnson 1995, 138) It was not until Saint Martin was elected bishop of Tours in AD 372 that any real attempt was made to bring Christianity to the outlying country areas. Indeed, it was through Saint Martin that we arrive at the purely Celtic aspects of Christianity; his well-organized church at Tours played a major part in the spread of Christianity in Western Gaul, the least Romanized area of the country. Towards the close of the fourth century, almost every city had its bishop. The nobility joined the Church, not only in the cities, but also in the outer reaches, which evolved to form the nucleus of the "parish" endowed with a church and a priest. With the spread of the faith among the landed gentry, privately-owned churches sprang up, built at the expense of the landowners on their own estates. Despite it all, Gaul lacked an authoritative ecclesiastical center; there was as yet no central primacy to direct the role of the Church. (Dillon 2003, 163-164)

Glendalough Round Tower (County Wicklow, Ireland). The early medieval stone tower was built by the monks of St. Kevin's monastery in the sixth century. It likely served as a bell tower, landmark for approaching visitors, and place of refuge in times of attack.

Paganism and Druidism Decline

The reign of Emperor Flavius Gratianus (AD 375-383) marks a distinct era in the transition of the empire from paganism to Christianity. At the time of his accession, he declined the insignia of pontifex maximus, which even Constantine and the other Christian emperors before him had accepted. At the insistence of Saint Ambrose, who became his chief adviser, he decreed the statue of Victory be removed from the senate house in Rome (AD 382). In this same year, he abolished all grants for the support of pagan worship. Deprived of the assistance of the State, paganism rapidly lost influence. Gratianus did not go so far as to confer upon the Church the privileges he took from the pagans, but he gave proof of his zeal by undoing the effects of Valentinian's persecution, and by taking measures for the suppression of various forms of heresy. Though his policy was one of toleration in general, he made apostasy a crime punishable by the State (AD 383). In AD 388, Arcadius had the heathen temples destroyed in the East; in the West, Honorius confiscated temple revenues. In the fifth century, paganism was deprived of all its rights. Deprived of sanctuaries and resources, and finally of its clergy, paganism gradually gave way to Christianity. (Chadwick 1997, 194)

With the spread of Christianity in Gaul, the role of the druids in Celtic society was altered and diminished. According to Peter Berresford Ellis, the term "druid" (in pre-Christian Celtic society) referred to a social stratification depicting an intellectual class. This division of social groups, he points out, existed in all Indo-European societies and is seen at its most obvious in modern times in the Hindu caste system. When Christianity established itself, the generic term "druid" became corrupt because of its connection with pagan society and only applied to wizards, magicians, and bards. The real druid caste (like their Brahmin counterparts) did not disappear, but the generic term simply changed as the caste adapted to new religious and cultural values. The intelligentsia remained but, after the rise of Christianity, they were no longer called by the general term "druids." (Ellis 2002, 251)

The Rise of Monasticism

It was in the period of Christian organizational growth that monasticism arrived in Western Europe from the Eastern Mediterranean, imbuing the new religion with a more intense spiritual life. From the third century, asceticism had spread among Christians—from Egypt to Syria and as far as Mesopotania—persuading them to abandon all worldly cares and responsibilities, and to retreat into the desert where they could devote themselves to a life of solitude and spiritual contemplation.

One of the earliest communities organized was a monastery at Tabennesi on the River Nile. This Upper Egypt community was developed early in the fourth century under Saint Pachomius, whose military training in early life probably helped with the success of his organization at Tabennesi. Paul Johnson writes that sorting out fact from fiction about early monasticism is not easy. However, he believes the first community of *cenobites* (monks) living under a common rule was founded by Pachomius, who had a monastery of one hundred at Tabenna on the River Nile. Saint Jerome gives an anecdotal account of the activity engaged in the community: "Monks of the same trade are housed together under a superior, that is, weavers, mat-makers, tailors, carpenters, fullers and shoemakers . . . . Every week an account of their work is made to the abbot." Early in the fourth century, the monastic movement was introduced to Syria. Syrian monks were particularly ingenious in devising torments. One monk devised a cell that required him to live doubled-up. Another spent ten years in a cage like a wheel. Dendrite monks perched in trees. Grasier monks lived in the forests and ate like wild animals; some went completely naked, except for a loincloth of thorns. (Johnson 1995, 140)

Cenobitic monks were different from their *eremitic* (hermits) predecessors in their actual living arrangements. Whereas the eremitic monks lived alone in a *cell* (hut or cave), the cenobitic monks (cenobites) lived together in monasteries comprising one or a complex of several buildings. The eremitic form of solitary living did not suit everyone. Some monks found it to be too lonely and difficult; if one was not spiritually prepared, the life could lead to mental breakdowns. In the case of the cenobitics, each dwelling would house about twenty monks and within the house there were separate rooms or "cells" that would be inhabited by two or three monks.

From about AD 360, Bishop Basil of Caesarea placed monasticism on a more organized basis. His collection of written rules placed emphasis on commonsense and moderation; these rules were widely adopted and spread throughout the eastern empire. By the late eighth century, a hundred thousand monks were said to be living under Basil's rule. These monasteries ran schools in a number of cases; few of them farmed. (Johnson 1995, 141)

Gallarus Oratory, circa 700 AD (County Kerry, Ireland). A famous landmark on the Dingle Peninsula, this place of worship for early Christian farmers was made of local stones fitted carefully together without mortar in the shape of an upside-down boat.

Asceticism Spreads to Western Europe

Both cenobitic and eremitic forms of asceticism spread to Western Europe in the fourth century. They are believed to have traveled along the Mediterranean trading routes to Marseilles and then up the Rhone Valley into Gaul. The inspiration seems to have been Athanasius's popular *Life of St. Anthony*, which reached Gaul in AD 336 and was widely copied. Athanasius had lived for thirty-five years in solitude in a ruinous Roman fort in the mountain of Pispir between the Nile and the Dead Sea. (Dillon 2003, 164)

The earliest western monks were ascetics and eccentrics, like their eastern brethren; on the other hand, they tended to be more actively involved in the life of their communities. The most famous monk was Saint Martin of Tours, who died in AD 397. He followed the eastern type of cenobitic community: living with his eighty companions in caves in the river cliffs at Marmoutier. Though formally an army officer, he was described as plebeian in appearance—small, badly dressed, and uncombed. Yet, unlike the easterners, he seems to have been a rural missionary, preaching against paganism, working evangelical miracles, and attacking shrines with a pickaxe. (Johnson 1995, 142)

In his early life, Saint Martin had been an officer in the Roman army. After he converted to Christianity, he sought and obtained his release from military service. He then spent a brief period as a solitary in a cell at Milan. About this time, he developed a deep admiration for Bishop Hilary of Poitiers, a strong opponent of the Arian heresy that was threatening to overrun the Western Church. Saint Martin pursued Hillary to Rome and later joined him in Gaul where he settled under his auspices, first living ascetically with a few monks in caves and wooden cells at Ligugé. Later Saint Martin founded his "great monastery," Marmoutier (the first monastery in Gaul) near Tours. He was consecrated bishop of Tours in circa AD 370 (the earliest of the monastic bishops), an episcopate he held for twenty-six years. (Chadwick 1971, 190)

Although completely opposite to the essentially Episcopal form of Christianity establishing itself throughout Gaul, monasticism took root. Meanwhile, the Episcopal form took root among the elite classes and was playing an ever-increasing role as civic institutions disintegrated. At the same time, monasticism—supported by Bishop Hillary (the pillar of the Western Church)—was the focus of active disapproval by the Gaulish bishops. This growing hostility between the Episcopal and the monastic elements became more pronounced in the early years of the fifth century, and Episcopal disapproval was especially bitter against monastic appointments to vacant bishoprics. It was expressed explicitly in a prominent letter addressed in AD 428 by Pope Celestine to the bishops of Vienne and Narbonne on the occasion of the election of a bishop to the vacant see of Arles. In his letter, Celestine openly expresses his dislike of monastic bishops:

> "They who have not grown up in the Church act contrary to the Church's usages . . . coming from other customs they have brought their traditional ways with them . . . clad in a cloak and with a girdle round their loins . . . Such a practice may perhaps be followed . . . by those who dwell in remote places and pass their lives far from their fellow men. But why should they dress in this way in the churches of God, changing the usage of so many years, of such great prelates, for another habit?" (Dillon & Chadwick 2003, 166-167)

In Gaul in the fifth century, the Egyptian style of monasticism acquired a cultural purpose, and it was in this transformed state that it attracted the interest of Christian ascetics in areas of Celtic dominance: Ireland, northern England, Scotland, Wales, and Brittany. Ireland had been Christianized in the fifth century, at which time an ecclesiastical system of bishops and dioceses had been established in basic form. About AD 540, there is evidence of the first Irish monks. Southern Ireland had trading contacts with the Loire Valley, sending shoes and other goods in exchange for wine and oil; presumably, this was how the Irish first came into contact with the monastic idea. It took root very quickly for a number of economic and social reasons, becoming the dominant religious form rather than a marginal activity. There were no towns in Ireland; indeed it scarcely possessed villages. It was to a great extent still a nomadic and tribal society. (Johnson 1995, 143)

Sixth-century monasticism had a mobile element as well, tending to move between fixed points of reference, the sea providing the chief means of transportation. In each tribe, a leading family could establish an abbey, plus a series of dependent houses, and retain certain rights in them. Abbots were nearly always members of the ruling clan or tribal family; monastic holdings embraced lands, fishing rights, and other forms of subsistence-living.

The monastic quest for remoteness and solitude, exported from Egypt via Gaul, fit perfectly into the geography and life-style of a precarious economy on the rim of Europe. Irish monasticism was wholly integrated with local society; in fact it was, as Paul Johnson describes it, "the Church of Ireland." (Johnson 1995, 143)

Monasticism: A Revolt Against the Episcopal System?

Egyptian monasticism had been, to some extent, a revolt against ecclesiastical organization, and the Episcopal system in particular. Saint Martin and his followers showed the same disposition. Irish monks shared this belief, but the Irish Church was never consciously in rebellion against orthodoxy. It is remarkable that the Irish pagans were Christianized without a single case of martyrdom and without any recorded instance of heresy or internal prosecution.

Bishops were retained to carry out certain functions such as blessing the baptismal chrism and ordainations (which only they could perform), but they were functionaries, not leaders. They were expected to be humble and obey the abbot, who of course represented tribal leadership. Not that the abbot behaved like a grand personage.

One reason why the early monks disliked the Episcopal system was that it was identified with the external trappings of worldly society. It was wrong—even sinful—for a cleric, or even an abbot, to ride a horse. By doing so, he elevated himself above the common man. The abbot and his monks should live as close to subsistence level as possible, consistent with good health; they should preach the gospel on foot "after the manner of the apostles." (Johnson 1995, 144)

Gospel Spreads to Britain

Christianity is believed to have arrived in Britain at the same time, or somewhat later, than it arrived in Gaul. Tertullian (circa AD 200) writes that the Gospel had already reached some parts not under Roman control. Origen (circa AD 240) speaks of the Christian faith as a unifying force among the Britons, although he admits that many of the Britons had not yet heard the Gospel. Yet, there are indications that the British Church was already firmly established in certain areas of the island by the fourth century. Three British bishops attended the Council of Arles in AD 314: the bishops of London, York, and Colchester. Several bishops from Britain went to the council of Rimini in AD 359 and, towards the end of the fourth century, quarrels over doctrine and precedence between the island bishops had become so fierce that Victricius (bishop of Rouen) had to cross the Channel to restore order. Despite these references, it is acknowledged that the majority of Britons remained pagan, and only the upper classes adhered to the Christian faith. (Johnson 1995, 138)

In the post-Roman period, much of eastern Britain became (or remained) pagan following a continuing string of invasions and occupations by Angles, Jutes, and Saxons in the fifth century. Some of the conquered Britons fled to settle in Armorica, from then on called Brittany. However, it was not until the end of the sixth century that Pope Gregory sent Saint Augustine to Britain with a mission to undertake the conversion of the Anglo-Saxons of southeastern Britain. Conversion to Christianity had already begun among the

Picts and the Britons to the west and north a century and a half earlier when Irish missionaries with extraordinary zeal undertook converting pagans in foreign lands. Western and northern Scotland was evangelized by Saint Columba and his monks from Iona. Irish monks studied and taught at the monastery of Saint David in Wales. It is now generally acknowledged that Anglo-Saxons owe their conversion to Christianity, not so much to Saint Augustine and his monks, as to Irish missionaries.

Another Irish saint, Aiden, founded the monastic community at Lindisfarne, off the Northumberland coast in AD 634. Finan, who succeeded Aiden, is credited with converting Sigebert (king of East Anglia) and Panda (king of the interior provinces). Besides the monastery at Lindisfarne, Aidan also founded several monasteries and churches in northern England. (MacManus 1972, 214)

Throughout this period, the Celtic Church of northern Britain and Ireland—cut off from normal communication with Rome—embarked on its own path, while at the same time failing to keep pace with the many changes and reforms of the expanding Roman Church. Saint Augustine tried unsuccessfully to reconcile the older form practiced by the Celtic Church with the more up-to-date form that he brought with him from the Continent. The Britons were reluctant to change their time-honored ways, and it was not until the Council of Whitby in AD 664 that fundamental differences were ruled in favor of Rome, for the most part ending the struggle that had separated the Celtic and Roman Churches for so long.

Christianity Reaches Ireland

The first and most far-reaching outside influence on Ireland's Celtic culture was Christianity in the fifth century, and its influence was powerful. It brought to Ireland a new creed and, with it, its Latin culture in ethics and canon law. The first mission by Saint Palladius was less than successful in converting the polytheistic druids and their followers. Saint Patrick, arriving in AD 432, was more successful in persuading the Irish Celts to embrace the New Faith. While the teachings of the Christian Church had a powerful influence on Gaelic culture, they failed to make any substantial transformation to the framework of Celtic society itself. Nonetheless, a solution was found in reshaping these institutions along the lines of the country's own tradition of petty kings and overlords. Abbots and bishops were given a status equivalent to the tuath king; thus, many abbotships and bishoprics remained within the same extended kin-group, making it possible for those roles to be passed down from generation to generation.

Saint Patrick is generally considered to have organized his church in accordance with the Continental model of parishes: assembled into dioceses and presided over by bishops. Within a generation after his death, the Irish began embracing monasticism more fully and the Irish Church became organized on very different lines with monasteries, rather than parishes, as the key units. The consequence was that abbots generally had more power and influence than bishops.

Theories abound as to how this monastic takeover came about in Ireland. Paul Johnson, in *A History of Christianity*, proposes that trading links between Ireland and the Loire valley exposed the Irish to the monastic movement flourishing in Gaul at the time. The main stimuli, it is believed, may have resulted from an influx of Continental monks into Ireland, fleeing from the vast hordes of vandals spreading throughout Gaul following the collapse of the Roman Empire. Monks traveling to Ireland brought with them the principles of monasticism pioneered by Saint Martin of Tours in Gaul.

The Spread and Energy of the Irish Celtic Church

Irish monks, writes Paul Johnson, were an intimidating challenge to the early Dark Age Church and its hold on society. "Like the Montanist-type sects, they advocated a return to primitive Christian purity, but unlike them they could not be attacked on grounds of doctrinal error." Irish monks had a tremendous cultural dynamic. They were extremely learned in the scriptures and brilliantly gifted in the arts. They combined brilliant Latin scholarship with a native cultural tradition, which went back to the La Tène civilization of the first century. Monastic scribes and scholars adopted the Latin alphabet in the sixth century, setting in motion a cultural transformation, the outcome of which they themselves could not have imagined. "It was the adoption of the Latin alphabet that enabled the monastic *literati* to record and preserve a remarkable wealth of native pre-Christian beliefs and traditions." (O'Driscoll, ed. 1993 MacCana)

Irish monasteries were not just religious institutions in the narrow sense of the word. They opened their doors to students and scholars of all kinds; they became influential centers of learning and culture. In this respect, they took over the role previously fulfilled by the filidh in pre-Christian times. Several monasteries seem to have been founded on the sites of such druidic centers of learning. Monastic ideals quickly took root. Some eight hundred monasteries were founded by the end of the sixth century. Confederations emerged which gave abbots considerably more power than bishops. These centers were the closest equivalent to large-scale communities; Gaelic culture being rural, pastoral, and built around the *fine*. By the seventh century, Ireland had become one of the most advanced learning societies in Europe. Celtic monasteries were flourishing, opening their doors to men of learning from at home and abroad.

Over the next couple of centuries, the island experienced what became known as the "Golden Age of Celtic spirituality." At home and abroad, its great monastic schools were famed for their scholarships and their artistic manuscripts. Irish monks and scribes went abroad during Europe's Dark Ages and worked tirelessly at copying the West's treasure house of literature decimated by the barbarians that had descended on Europe following the fall of the Roman Empire. According to Thomas Cahill (*How the Irish*

Saved Civilization, 1995), "single-handedly, they saved European civilization."

Peregrinatio Pro Dei Amore

One of the most striking and original features of Irish Christianity was the love of wandering by the monks. One scribe described it as a spirit of restless energy. While it was given many names, most commonly they called it exile and regarded it as "white martyrdom." The monks left their homes and families in a spirit of penance to seek *peregrinatio pro Dei amore* (wandering for the love of God) and a state of grace through the pure and difficult life of the recluse or the lonely life of a stranger. In its most isolated form, it was the reason some monks literally cast themselves adrift at sea, happy to accept whatever the outcome might be. Many monks traveled with the intention of proselytizing, founding new churches, and seeking knowledge. Though some of the wandering monks made their travels in Ireland, others chose the more difficult road of leaving the homeland entirely, to return only in old age, or never again.

Saint Brendan

One of the first of the monks to go abroad was Saint Brendan. He was born in AD 484 in Fenit, County Kerry. After completing his religious training in Galway, he was ordained a priest. The local king at Ardfert gave him a grant of land and, with a small group of followers, Brendan founded a monastery there. As he slept one night, a voice told him of the "promised land" and he desired to go in search for it. The story of Brendan's voyage, *Navigatio Sancti Brendani*, was written in the tenth century. The *Navigatio*, in the words of Katherine Scherman, "takes the sailor monks in a dreamlike sequence from one fantastic island to another, each one exhibiting its special enchantment—some fearsome, some delightful." (Scherman 1981, 138) The ninth-century monk Dicuil (with others) settled in Iceland where he composed a respected geography, *Liber de Mensura Orbis Terrae*, which drew extensively on the reports of a fellow Irishman, Fidelis, who had journeyed as far as the Holy Land. (Moorehouse 1997, 123)

Saint Columbanus

Another Irishman, Saint Columbanus, landed in Brittany in AD 575 with a shipload of monks. They wore long white habits and carried crooked staffs and their liturgical books packed in waterproof leather bags. Paul Johnson writes that this was one of the most remarkable expeditions in history. Columbanus was disillusioned with the Europe he found in Gaul; virtue was more or less nonexistent. He found himself fighting loose morals, rather than ignorance, and teaching discipline instead of grammar. He established severe rules for his communities and instituted corporal punishment for those who infringed the rules. By the time he died at the age of ninety-three, he, his entourage, and their immediate followers had spread Celtic monasticism across a huge area of Gaul, Italy, and the Alps, and had founded about forty monasteries.

The success of Columbanus reflects the appeal of his mission. But his activities, for the first time, brought the nature of Celtic monasticism firmly to the attention of Church authorities—to western bishops in general and to the Bishop of Rome in particular. The Irish monks were not heretical, but they were plainly unorthodox. For a start, they did not look right in appearance. They had the wrong tonsure. Rome, as was normal, had the tonsure of Saint Peter, that is, a shaven crown. Easterners had the tonsure of Saint Paul, totally shaven; if they wished to make an appointment in the west, they had to wait until their tonsure rim grew before being invested. But the Celts looked like nothing on earth: they had their long hair at the back and (on the shaven front part) a half-circle of hair from one ear to the other, leaving a band across the forehead.

More serious, however, was their refusal to celebrate Easter according to the calendar calculations of Rome. There were a number of divergent calendar systems in the Mediterranean area;

the one used by the Celts corresponded with none of them. For Rome, the issue was a disturbing one. "Getting the right date for Easter was the most obvious instance of the problem of calculating time—man's effort to orient himself in relation to events." There had been liturgical rows about Easter going back to the second century and possibly earlier. In Western Europe, the newly Christianized barbarian societies (Franks, etc.) adjusted their sense of the annual routine, from the court downwards, to fit the Christian year. Divergence over the most important event in the yearly calendar was not merely inappropriate, but threatening. And how could the Church claim unity if it could not even agree on the date of the resurrection, the core of its belief? (Johnson 1995, 145-146)

Saint Columba

Saint Columba was an Irish tribal leader who traveled from his native Ulster to the Western Isles of Scotland, where he established the great monastery of Iona. He was the first Irish missionary to carry the Christian message out of Ireland. Born in Donegal, he studied at Moville under Saint Finian, a learned abbot trained in Saint Ninian's Candida Casa in Galloway. Columba arrived in Scotland in AD 563. At the time, it was called Alba and was ruled by the Picts who, according to Venerable Bede, were converted to Christianity by Saint Ninian, but had later slid back to paganism. Columba and his missionaries converted the Picts and Caledonians of the Scottish Highlands; after his death, his mission moved well beyond the border of Pictland into northern England.

King Oswald invited Saint Aidan, an Irish monk educated at Iona, to the English kingdom of Northumbria where he founded a monastery at Lindisfarne in AD 634. Like Iona, it adopted the spiritual traditions and the mannerisms of the Irish. In the words of one scribe, this set the stage for another great conflict between the Romans and the Celts, comparable to the one that had seen the latter driven to the western extremities of Europe by the imperial legions. This time, Rome was not hungry for territory so much as for religious authority. In AD 597, thirty-four years after Columba founded his monastery at Iona, Rome made its move. Pope Gregory I sent Augustine to Canterbury to bring the Gospel to the backsliding southeastern Britons.

Roman Versus Celtic Institutions

The Celtic Church's penetration of Europe by Irish monks was of great importance, culturally. Yet, in ecclesiastical terms, it threatened to undermine the Church's oldest and central institution, the episcopate. The response from Rome was to take over, to discipline, and so to contain the monastic movement. (Johnson 1995, 146)

Eventually, the two opposing currents of Christianity—Celtic and Roman—confronted each other. While the Augustinian missions were spreading north from Canterbury, eventually reaching York, the Irish influence of Columba and his successors was spreading the Gospel across northern Britain and southward through Northumbria. Katherine Scherman writes:

> "English Christianity, as practiced in Saint Augustine's territory was the direct child of Rome. By the seventh century the Roman Church, following the reforming dictates of Pope Gregory I, had become a centralized, strongly hierarchical institution demanding absolute conformity of thought and deed. Its ritual was rigid, its standards of obedience to a central organization exacting. No taint of heresy was tolerated and freedom of thought was discouraged. This tight-knit establishment was a necessity to the proper functioning of the ecclesiastical empire that had in a spiritual sense replaced the military and civil empire of the Roman Empire . . . .
>
> "In Ireland, untouched by Rome, Christianity had grown up outside these rigid boundaries, as had the Irish-Celts themselves; the island's creed harked back to an earlier

> Christianity, at once more austere and more tolerant . . . . In Ireland there was no attempt at centralization, no dictation of thought, no persecution for slight differences in ritual . . . . Irish Christianity was pure, spiritual, intensely personal, dedicated only to the absolute word of God . . . . Their country and their beliefs might have been out of the mainstream, but they themselves were very much in it, bearing their message of pure spirituality to barbarians and Roman Christians alike, ready to fight for it—indeed eager to fight, like their own heroes of pagan times.
>
> "And herein lay the conflict. Ireland owed allegiance to Rome only as the original source of her conversion; otherwise there was respect but no abject obedience. Subservience had never been a Celtic trait. The ancient ways of the Irish clergy—their asceticism, their love of nature, their instinct toward martyrdom, their complicated acceptance of the scriptures—were outmoded on the Continent and even considered suspect, particularly when coupled with observances of the rituals that were different from those practiced by decree from Rome. No one could accuse the Irish of heresy, as there were no truer Christians in all of Europe in their time. But the slight difference in observances became a focus for the vast basic vexation. It was not the people who objected: on the contrary, the generous and pure hearted Irish missionaries were loved everywhere by high and low alike. It was the establishment that was galled by these old-fashioned conservative, exasperatingly positive saints. Too outspokenly virtuous, they provoked feelings of guilt." (Scherman 1981, 166-176)

The conflict came to a head in AD 664, when the Synod of Whitby was convened to resolve the differences. At Whitby, Roman demands focused on two issues: abandoning the Irish tonsure and adopting instead the Roman style; and adhering to the Church's revised Easter date. Oswy (son of King Oswald of Northumbria) chaired the Synod. Irishman Colman of Lindisfarne (who was bishop of Northumbria) represented the Celtic side. His opposites were Wilfrid (the Roman-tonsured Abbot of Ripon) and Agilbert (Bishop of the West Saxons). By the time the Synod got underway, Colman had lost some of his support: the Celtic Church in Munster had decided to accept Rome's ruling following a directive from Pope Honorius. Colman's remaining allies outside Northumbria were the northern Irish and the men of Iona. When Oswy decreed in favor of Rome, Northumbria conceded and accepted the decision.

Iona hung on to the old ways even after the northern Irish monks had complied. Columba's old monastery at Iona did not celebrate Easter on the Roman date until AD 716, and clung to the Irish tonsure for a further two years. This was in spite of the fact that, as soon as the Synod of Whitby ended, Theodare (Archbishop of Canterbury) announced that "those who have been ordained by bishops of the Irish or Britons, who are not Catholic as regards Easter and the tonsure, are not deemed to be in communion with the Church . . . ." Not only did the outcome of Whitby bring the Celtic Britons into conformity with Rome, but ultimately the Christians of Ireland, Scotland, Brittany, and Wales followed suit. (Moorehouse 1997, 217-218)

Viking Invaders

By the time Ireland had fully assimilated into Roman Christianity, she encountered another and very different kind of invasion. The invaders were the Vikings—originally from Norway and later from Denmark—who came first to plunder and then to settle. They began their incursions at the end of the eighth century, and by the early tenth century had gained numerous footholds and had established many permanent settlements, mostly along the eastern seaboard. They founded the kingdom of Dublin, a separate Danish territory within the Irish polity, which had numerous overseas connections. They were inevitably drawn into the shifting alliances and warfare that occupied the Gaelic lords, which in the end may have worked to curb their expansion over the whole island. In 1014, a mighty army of Irish under King Brian Boru defeated the Vikings at Clontarf, north of Dublin, ending Viking dominance in much of Ireland. Thereafter, they settled down and became integrated into Irish society.

Elements of Norse culture endured to influence Irish culture: their artistic techniques and styles inspired Irish artisans, and words from their language became imbedded in the Gaelic tongue. However, the most enduring influence of the Viking invasion on Irish life was the expansion of Irish overlordship, which grew under conditions brought on by Viking attacks. Petty kings could do very little to combat Viking attacks, but overlords could provide larger armies. Nevertheless, the growth of military overlordships had little effect on the old tradition of political decentralized sovereignty. Sovereignty remained as fragmented as it had been before the Vikings arrived.

In the post-Viking period, cultural activity and the arts—which had experienced a setback during the Viking period—came into their own again, revealing new and exciting trends. Religious reform was undertaken and the organizational structure of the Irish Church was brought into conformity with that of the Roman model. During this time, an ambitious Connacht dynast, Turlough O'Conor, succeeded in seizing the high kingship after defeating the MacLoughlin dynasty. Shortly before, the MacLoughlins had replaced the O'Neills. The O'Conors held on to power for several centuries until they brought about their own destruction from internecine disputes and warfare with their kinfolk and neighbors.

Norman Invasion

After a period of relative quiet, Ireland was again invaded in the twelfth century. This time it was King Henry II and his Anglo-Norman barons from the neighboring island of Britain. The Ireland they found was still a regionalized patchwork of petty kingdoms. Henry set about consolidating this array of separate kingdoms into one kingdom under his kingship, setting up a governing administration and instituting laws of a feudal society which rested on a hierarchy of authority under his kingship. It was a governing system very different from that of the Irish, whose array of autonomous kingdoms embodied local custom rather than a unified application of rules and practices.

Despite their military prowess, Norman efforts to extend central administrative control over the whole of the island met with stubborn resistance and the struggle between the Gaels and the Normans dragged on for centuries. In essence, it was a challenge between the aristocratic leadership of both sides—the Gaelic nobility and the Norman lords. During the three hundred years following the invasion of the Anglo-Normans, the history of Ireland was a constant seesaw of Gaelic and Norman advance and retreat. The Anglo-Norman colonization effort had little more effect than the earlier Norse invasions in altering the general state of society. Matters remained very much as they were until the time of Queen Elizabeth in the second half of the sixteenth century, at which time the old system of tribal land tenure was replaced with the English system, and Brehon law was substituted for English administrative law. But even after this time, most of the ancient native customs remained and, indeed, many still remain.

Following the Anglo-Norman invasion of Ireland, the Irish artistic tradition began a gradual decline into a twilight zone where it reposed until the early nineteenth century. It then became popular again, fueled by nationalistic inspiration and a reawakening to the richness of the Celtic tradition.

Chapter XV—

Celtic Art and Literature

The Táin Bó Cúailnge (The Cattle-Raid of Cuailnge) is not only the longest, but also the most authoritative work of this tradition. Its position in Irish literature has been compared to that of the Iliad in Greek literature, and both works pose comparable scholarly problems.

—Doris Edel, *The Celtic West and Europe*

Historians credit the Celts as being a remarkable artistic people who were among the finest metal craftsmen of the ancient world. Barry Cunliffe characterizes them as more than just craftsmen, suggesting they carried with them a deep knowledge of mythology and used symbols and combinations that were a form of communication. He adds they were the repository and the performers of ancient skills and beliefs, and as such they were looked upon as extraordinary human beings. Most of what we know about the creative talent and technological skills of the Celtic craftsmen is from the countless objects of various sorts uncovered by archeologists, now preserved in museums throughout Ireland, Britain, and the Continent. (Conliffe 1997, 113)

Celtic art has been justly called the first great contribution by the Barbarians of European Art. Its origin is unknown, and the salient features are quite different from those of other national art—for instance, the arts of the Phoenicians, Iberians, Etruscans, and the Greeks. Yet, Celtic art is no isolated development, and its history is archetypical of many foreign contacts. Classical Mediterranean, Scythian, Persian, and native Hallstatt were some of the influences in its emergence. The term "Celtic art" is invariably used to mean the art of the La Tène culture (that of central Europe before the Roman conquest). However, Celtic art continued and flourished in Britain well into the first century AD and in Ireland (unaffected from outside influences) for several centuries later. (Dillon & Chadwick 2003, 288)

Celtic art is, as a rule, recognized as three separate traditions: the continental La Tène art style which flourished from the fifth century BC until the conquest of Gaul by the Romans in the first century BC; the insular (British and Irish) La Tène art style which also flourished from the fifth century BC, but continued until the Roman conquest of Britain in AD 43 (and somewhat later in areas beyond Roman control); and the Celtic insular art tradition that blossomed in Ireland, and to a lesser extent in Britain, between the fifth and twelfth centuries AD. There is also the art of the Hallstatt Celts (from the pre-La Tène period) which the experts characterize as more of a simple art form with little evidence of individual artistic expression.

Lloyd Laing refers to the Basse-Yutz flagons, now in the British Museum (London), as an example where one can see all the elements that went into creating Celtic art. The flagons, he describes, borrow elements from the Classical world, and also improves on them. The model the artist used was the type of bulbous wine jug that was being imported in the fifth century BC from Etruscan Italy to grace Celtic feasts. But the Celtic artist had not been content to loyally follow the original form:

> "From the carefully moulded foot the jugs blossom upwards, their sides concave, to reach the smooth angle of the shoulder. Drawn in, the necks carry the eye upwards and open out in the beaked spout. The handles are fabulous beasts, which grip the ornamental lids with their forepaws,

and are chained to them from their mouths. Where the 'handle' meets the shoulder of the vessel there stares out a moustachioed Celtic face, its eyebrows bushy and curling in arabesques which match the curls of its beard. The eyes were once set with coral, and coral once red, now white, is set in a pattern which seems a foretaste of the interlace so beloved of Celtic artists centuries later. On the spout a little duck swims towards the stream of wine and a pair of mythical creatures recline on either side of the neck." (Laing 1979, 66-67)

The Gundestrup Cauldron, circa 100 BC (National Museum of Denmark, Copenhagen). Discovered dismantled in a peat bog near Gundestrup in 1891, the imagery on the walls of this silver vessel is widely identified with Celtic deities and rituals, yet the workmanship suggests it was crafted by Thracians.

Continental La Tène Art Expression

La Tène art gets its name from the site in western Switzerland where the first Celtic artifacts of the pre-Roman period were unearthed.

In its early stages, its model and the stylistic stimulus came from the imported Mediterranean wine-drinking utensils. (Conliffe 1997, 116) It is generally acknowledged that this art form developed in the areas alongside the Saar and the Rhine rivers. It was imported from the south and the southeast in the first half of the fifth century BC; from there, it later spread throughout Celtic Europe. It drew on three main sources to create a variety of distinct but related styles: native (mainly metalworking that evolved from the Urnfield and Hallstatt cultures); classical from Greco-Etruscan influence; and imitated oriental sources.

The earliest examples from this period (acquired from archaeological excavations) show richly decorated ornamental objects that reveal the ingenuity and skills of the early Celtic craftsmen and artisans. Artists covered the surfaces of their metal work with elaborate carvings of arches and curving tendrils entwining human and animal masks of multiple dimensions of realism and fantasy. They mastered the art of enameling and the technique of producing quality stained glass. They devoted meticulous care to the fashioning of ornate weapons: bronze helmets, shields, swords, and chain-link armor. The fashioning combined a variety of techniques: casting combined with engraving, punching, tracing, and grooving the metal with an implement known as a "scorper." Bronze was the most common metal employed, but gold, silver, and iron were on occasion ornamented. Coral and glass were sometimes used to enhance the natural surface of the metal.

Not all La Tène art, however, was fashioned in metal; there was also some stone and wood sculpture. Celtic stone sculpturing was not all that common, and the two chief areas where they have been found to date are Provence and Germany. Another striking characteristic of La Tène culture is the elaborate decoration of pottery using motifs common to those of the metalworker. An example is from the region between Moselle and Transdanubia where, from the fifth to the third centuries BC, the prevalence and distribution of pottery with stamped decoration was widespread.

Ragstone Head, circa 200-100 BC (National Museum, Prague). Carved in La Tène style and wearing a torc, this Celtic deity was excavated from the sanctuary at Mšecké Žehrovice in Bohemia, Czech Republic.

British La Tène Art Tradition

British La Tène art tradition is an area of Celtic art which continued to evolve and flourish in Britain following the conquest of Celtic Europe by the Romans. It had its beginning about the middle of the third century BC when many Germanic tribes established themselves in southern Britain alongside the native population. The newcomers brought with them a fully developed La Tène art style from which developed, over time, what is termed the "native British tradition" with its distinctive creations and styles. British craftsmen showed a particular expertise for basket patterns.

Archaeology has furnished many tangible remains from this period which attest to the ingeniousness of British craftsmen. A bronze helmet found at Waterloo Bridge in London in 1868, dating from the first century BC, consists of a conical cap made of decorated sheet bronze from the top of which protrude two fearsome horns. A companion to this impressive object is a huge shield found in the River Thames at Battersea in 1857, believed to be from early in the first century AD. It, too, was made from thin sheets of bronze bound together and originally fastened to a leather or wooden backing. The front is covered with a rich array of ornaments arranged in elegant symmetry.

Many gold torques have been found in Britain including the biggest single find made at Snettisham in Norfolk where, between 1948 and 1950, some fifty-eight whole and fragmented torques (dating from the first century BC) were found in an impressive series of caches; and there were still other finds in 1964 and 1968. Lloyd Laing claims that the Snettisham collection comprises the richest array of Celtic treasures so far excavated from British soil.

A discovery of an Iron Age cemetery at Aylesford in Kent in 1886 by Sir Arthur Evans opened up an important chapter in the understanding of Iron Age Britain. The Aylesford interments belong to an extensive late-British cremation cemetery of a kind not hitherto described by English archaeologists. The Kentish finds spoke not only of Continental immigrations, but also of far-flung trade links with Mediterranean lands, which previously had been faintly hinted at in ancient sources. But more than this, they shed light on a well-developed warrior society. In one grave, which consisted of a circular pit cut into the chalk, was a "stave-built wooden bucket," covered in sheet bronze, which had once contained the cremation burial. According to archaeologists, the Aylesford bucket is distinctive given that on opposite sides of the bronze rim are two free-standing Celtic bronze heads, identical to each other and decorated with helmets and lobed headdresses. These heads are good examples of the severed-head image and have characteristics in common with earlier central European sculpture. (Green 1997, 37)

Basketry infilling is a feature of what had, arguably, been the pinnacle of British Celtic artistic achievements. Mirrors produced in the late first century BC and early first century AD for the Belgae aristocracy have an inspiration behind them that is Roman; it is apparent in the symmetrical arrangement of the pattern on the mirror backs. So distinctive is this decoration that it is known as the *Mirror style*, though it also appears on other objects.

Except for the Picts and the Scots, little Celtic art of distinction seems to have been produced in Britain after the seventh century AD. By the thirteenth century, it had disappeared altogether. Although elements of a Celtic tradition have been detected from time to time thereafter, it was not until the revival of Celtic art in the nineteenth century that it became popular again. (Laing 1979, 72)

Sketch of The Tara Brooch by William Frederick Wakeman (d. 1900) from *Wakeman's Handbook of Irish Antiquities.* An exquisite example of eighth century medieval Irish metalwork, the original brooch is located in the National Museum of Ireland, Dublin.

Irish Celtic Art Tradition

The third tradition of Celtic art, developed in Ireland between the fifth and twelfth centuries AD, flourished in four separate fields: ornamentation and illumination of manuscripts; metal-work; stone carving; and to a lesser degree, leatherwork. As in Britain, it had its beginnings in La Tène art, which arrived from the continent about 300 BC (superimposing on the earlier Bronze Age tradition). From this Irish La Tène art there evolved a tradition that can be traced to its golden era in the early Christian period, its temporary decline with the Viking invasions, and its remarkable renaissance in the eleventh and twelfth centuries AD.

Throughout its history, the Irish art tradition was closely akin to the European tradition. Although sources from which it drew its inspiration varied from one period to another, it was sufficiently dynamic to mold new styles and new ideas into something characteristically and unmistakably Irish.

Ancient Irish Celtic craftsmen and artisans practiced the art of working with bronze, silver, gold, and enamel and had become highly talented with their skills by the time Saint Patrick arrived in the fifth century. In the ancient tales and legends, gold and silver ornaments are everywhere mentioned as worn by the upper classes. These accounts are fully corroborated by the great number of objects of both metals that have been found, from time to time, in various parts of Ireland.

Joyce relates: how the monarch Tigernmas (circa 939 BC) first smelted gold in Ireland and was the first to introduce ornaments of gold and silver; how another king, Muinemon, first caused necklets of gold to be worn around the necks of kings and chiefs; and how a third king, *Fail-derg-doid*, was the first to cause rings of gold to be worn on the fingers of chiefs in Ireland. However true these ancient tales are, the fact remains there is a great collection of ancient ornamental objects—some of pure gold, some of silver, and some of mixed metals and precious stones—now preserved in the National

Museum of Ireland in Dublin. Those of the pre-Christian era have no interlaced work, but only spirals, circles, zigzags, parallel lines, etc. Those from the Christian era are decorated with the peculiar patterns known as *opus Hibernicum*: "interlaced work formed by hands, ribbons and cords which are curved and twisted and interwoven in the most intricate way, something like basketwork infinitely varied in pattern." (Joyce 1997, 545)

Among the articles recovered (and on display in the National Museum) are three of extraordinary craftsmanship and astonishing beauty: the Ardagh Chalice, the Tara Brooch, and the Cross of Cong—all made by Christian artists. The Ardagh Chalice, standing seven inches high and more than nine inches in diameter at its top, is elaborately ornamented with designs in metal and enamel. It was found in more recent times under a large rock at Ardagh, County Limerick. The Ardagh Chalice is believed to have been crafted sometime before the tenth century. Beyond this, nothing is known of its history. It has been described as combining "classic beauty of form with the most exquisite examples of almost every variety of Celtic ornamentation." Its decorative designs, of which there are about forty different varieties, all show "a freedom of inventive power and play of fancy only equaled by the work upon the so-called Tara brooch." (MacManus 1972, 307-310)

The Tara brooch—extensively ornamented with amber, glass, enamel, and distinctive Irish *filigree* (interlaced work of metal)—and its extraordinary delicacy and beauty make it, perhaps, the finest example of Celtic craftsmanship found anywhere. Found in AD 1850 near Drogheda, its crafting is thought to be contemporaneous with that of the Ardagh Chalice. There are many other handsome brooches, such as the Ardagh Brooch, the Roscrea Brooch, the Dál Riata Brooch—each with a particular beauty of its own. But for outstanding beauty, none of them equals the Tara Brooch. Both the face of the brooch and the back are overlaid with seventy-six different kinds of beautiful patterns, each designed in such diminutive precision that its perfection of detail can easily escape the naked eye.

The Cross of Cong, thirty inches in height, was a professionally crafted cross made to enshrine a piece of the true cross. Its surface is worked with painstaking adornment of clear Celtic design. A sequence of inscriptions in Gaelic describe how it was made in AD 1123 by order of Turlogh O' Conor, king of Connacht, for the church in Tuam then administered by Archbishop Muredach O'Duffy. The inscription also names the artist as Mailisa mac Braddan O'Hechan.

Some of the finest Irish metalwork is exhibited on shrines, called *cumdachs*, made to protect the valuable manuscripts of the time. These book shrines were mostly made from the eighth century to the twelfth century. Some of the finest are those of the *Book of Kells*, the *Book of Durrow*, and the *Book of Armagh*—several are preserved in the National Museum, Dublin. There were also belt shrines, such as the one from Moylurg consisting of leather strips richly ornamented with metal work, used to enclose relics. Other types were the cozier shrine used to cover the *bachall*, and the bell shrine to enclose a bell.

Ardagh Chalice, 8th century AD (National Museum of Ireland, Dublin). One of the greatest treasures of the early Irish Church, the gold and silver chalice was discovered in 1868 among a hoard of metalwork near Ardagh, County Limerick.

Artistic Stone Carving

Artistic stone carving (which developed quite apart from that of metalwork, although the motifs are often interchangeable) is chiefly exhibited in the great stone crosses—many of which are still standing in many parts of Ireland. Besides the elaborate ornamentation, most of the crosses display groups of figures representing various matters in religious history intended to impress upon those who were illiterate the messages of scripture and religious history by vivid illustration. One of the best examples of this artistry is the high cross of Monasterboice which stands twenty-seven feet in height.

One feature of the Irish Celtic cross is the circular ring around the intersection binding the arms together. This particular shape was developed in Ireland. A few high crosses of the Irish type are found in southern Scotland and northern England, but it is acknowledged they were crafted by Irish artists or under their influence. (Joyce 1997, 570)

The Illuminated Manuscript

Ireland's crowning artistic achievement was the creation of a new medium: illuminating manuscripts with a special style of pen adornment. This finely-wrought artistry on parchment was the product of successive generations of artists who brought it to astonishing perfection using Coptic motifs along with patterns from Celtic and Anglo-Saxon metalwork (pagan and Christian) to mold a characteristically Irish Celtic art. It was chiefly the work of monks and it is believed to have started at Columbanus' monastery at Bobbio, whose Irish monks had continuing contact with the homeland as well as with the East. (Scherman 1981, 330-331) Many of these manuscripts have survived, among them masterpieces such as the *Book of Durrow*, the *Lindisfarne Gospels*, and the *Book of Kells*.

The first of the surviving manuscripts with illustrations is the *Book of Durrow*, penned sometime between AD 670 and AD 680 and named for one of Saint Columba's earliest and most important monasteries in Ireland. It has elaborate "carpet" pages devoted to nothing but decoration in a style that is "anticlassical, abstract, and symbolic, unlike anything found in Continental medieval manuscripts." (Scherman 1981, 330) Stunningly intricate as it is, the *Book of Durrow* is said to lack the skill and scope manifest in later works. The *Lindisfarne Gospels*, penned in the eighth century, is another jewel. Its carpet pages are similar to those of the *Book of Durrow* but, according to the examiners, are more meticulously drawn: "clear and delicate, like finely-woven tapestries." The Lindisfarne manuscript was Irish in origin, but the work was mostly done by Irish-trained English clerics.

The *Book of Kells*, a vellum manuscript in Latin, is regarded as the greatest and most beautiful of the Gospel manuscripts. Its precise origin is unknown but, according to some experts, it was penned in Kells, County Meath; yet, others attribute the work to the Irish monks at Saint Columba's monastery at Iona (Scotland). The exact age is also unknown, but most agree that it was probably written in the seventh or early eighth century. Rich in imagery, beautiful in design and color, and laden with allusion and symbolism, the *Book of Kells* is nothing short of Celtic craftsmanship at its highest perfection. It is the last great manuscript of Ireland's golden age, consisting of 339 vellum leaves, or folios, but is believed to have originally contained more pages. When Archbishop Ussher bought the manuscript in AD 1621, he wrote there were 344 folios; another source suggests there may have been as many as 368 folios in the original document. It is surprising that so much of the book does survive.

The Abbey of Kells, from where the *Book of Kells* is first known, was plundered at least seven times before AD 1006. The book was then stolen and buried for three months. When it was recovered, its jewel-encrusted, golden cover was gone forever. On the dissolution of the Abbey, the book probably passed to the family of the last abbot, and may have had several owners before being collected by Archbishop Ussher. When he died, his daughter tried to sell it in Europe, but the sale was blocked and the book was sold to the army in Ireland instead. For five years, it lay in an open room in Dublin Castle until AD 1661 when

King Charles II presented it to Ussher's alma mater, Trinity College, Dublin. There it remains to this day. (Mackworth-Praed. 1994, 1-2)

The ninth and tenth centuries saw nothing of the dimension of earlier craftsmanship. Many of the great illuminators were killed in the Viking raids or escaped to the Continent. In the eleventh and twelfth centuries, there were some interesting creations, but these latter works are said to not have approached the brilliance and intricacy of the earlier masterpieces.

Following the Anglo-Norman invasion of Ireland at the end of the twelfth century, the Irish artistic tradition began a gradual decline into a twilight zone where it reposed until the early nineteenth century. It then became popular again, fueled by nationalistic inspiration and a reawakening to the richness of the ancient Celtic tradition.

Book of Kells—Portrait of Christ, circa 800 AD (Trinity College, Dublin).
Regarded as Ireland's finest national treasure, this illuminated manuscript Gospel book was created by Celtic monks.

Celtic Literary Tradition

Irish literature provides us with the earliest Celtic documents. The three cycles of Gaelic epic—the Mythological cycle, the Ulster or Red Branch cycle, and the Ossianic cycle of the Fenians—are stamped with a distinctive style and an archaism which remained virtually unaltered by the medieval copyists. There are some unauthentic insertions and interpretations, but the basic concerns of the Christian monks were to safeguard their national heritage as a font of culture for future generations. Markale writes that in the case of Welsh literature it suffered more from the effects of Romanization and Christianity, but certain passages of the oldest of those tales known as the *Mabinogion* (*Pwyll*, *Branwen*, *Manawyddan*, *Math*) as well as *Culhwch* and *Olwen* reflect extremely ancient traditions.

The most recent form of Celtic myths is the Round Table cycle which grew up around the mysterious King Arthur. As previously described, the Arthurian romances were first written at the direction of the Plantagenet dynasty which sought to glorify the English (and therefore British) monarchy in order to counterbalance the popularity given the Continental Capetian (and therefore Carolingian) dynasty by the chansons de geste. A figure had to be found who could match the stature of Charlemagne. When Arthur became that figure, the feelings of a conquered race found their way back to the surface and, through him, dominated Western Europe throughout the Middle Ages. Here, Celtic tradition was saved by the conquerors—in this instance, the Norman captors. (Markale 1993, 254-255)

The literature of Gaul was an oral literature, and there is no identifiable record of the existence of a written text. If such had existed in the native language of Gaul, none has come down to us; French, though based on Latin, did not reach the formality of a literary language until the Roman conquest had been over for centuries. In Spain, the earliest national literature was composed, not in the language of the most ancient inhabitants, but in a form of neo-Latin no older than the earliest literary compositions of the

French. In German territory, the beginnings of literature in the Germanic language did not appear until late in the eleventh century. (Hubert 1988, 262)

Both in age and in variety, the literature of ancient Ireland surpassed that of any other western European vernacular. It has been called the earliest voice from the dawn of western European civilization. Its labor included not only numerous religious and legal writings, but also a large body of lyric poetry and a long list of epic and other tales written in prose alternating with passages in verse. We have previously noted that early Irish epic and romantic literature comprises of, in addition to many outlying stories, three groups (or cycles) known respectively as: the Mythological cycle; the Ulster or Red Branch cycle; and the Ossianin or Finn cycle.

The debate continues as to whether the Irish had a pre-Christian written tradition. Joyce writes that many passages in the old native Irish tradition, both sacred and profane, state that the pagan Irish had books before the introduction of Christianity. In the memoir of Saint Patrick, written by Muirchu Maccu Machteni in the seventh century (now contained in the *Book of Armagh*), he relates how, during the contest of the saint with the druids at Tara, King Laegaire proposed that one of Patrick's books and one belonging to the druids should be thrown into water to see which would come out undamaged. The significance of the tale is that Muirchu's statement implies that the druids had books at that time. (Joyce 1997, 308)

The lay traditions, found in many old Irish manuscripts and documents, show that the pagan Irish used *Ogham* writing. Ogham was a species of writing, the letters of which were formed by combinations of short lines and points. But as far as is known from the specimens remaining, its use was mostly confined to stone inscriptions. Between two and three hundred Ogham monuments have been found in various parts of Ireland, but they are far more numerous in the south and southwest than elsewhere. Others have been found in Wales, England, Scotland, and the Isle of Man—but more in South Wales and Scotland than elsewhere.

Saint Patrick introduced Christianity in the fifth century AD and set up Latin schools run by the clergy. There were other schools in Ireland as well; schools of poets and lawyers had existed for a considerable time and remained completely separate from the learning introduced by the church. The education provided in the church schools (on the one hand) and the schools of poets and lawyers (on the other) were completely different, not only in subject matter but in its entire method of approach. By the seventh century, these two quite separate worlds—the Latin and the Irish—began to borrow ideas and techniques from each other. Some poets and lawyers were coming into close contact with the clergy of Latin education. As a result, the clergy began to record the memory method of learning into the new writing learning method. Ultimately, much of the memory tradition came to be recorded and preserved in monastic libraries.

Into the receptive atmosphere of a country already steeped in Celtic lore came the fresh impulse of Christianity to take the place of archaic pagan practices. It was a vital source of inspiration to the Celtic imagination. The new religion brought with it two incalculable benefits: a written language and the legacy of Greco-Roman classical culture. At the same time, every effort was made to preserve the existing native tradition. (Moody, Martin 1967, 76-79)

Chapter XVI—
Struggle for Change

Until traditions were crushed by Protestant Puritanism, Celtic people in Britain would visit shrines to worship the local spirit. In Ireland and Brittany, as well as in Wales and Scotland, the old gods and goddesses were often worshipped through the medium of Celtic saints—none officially canonized by the pope in Rome—and revered according to ancient tradition.

—Nigel Pennick, *Celtic Sacred Landscapes*

The Easter controversy may have seemed like a trivial disagreement between the Celtic and Roman Churches but, as Jean Markale wrote, it symbolized Celtic independence and steadfast resistance to the organizational structure of Roman Christianity. The Celtic Church established roots in Scotland in AD 536. In AD 565, Saint Columcille (Columba) established a monastery on the island of Iona in the west of Scotland. This became a flourishing settlement of the Irish Church which, in the following century under Saint Aiden, converted the residents of northern England. Aiden had arrived in Lindisfarne from Iona in AD 635 at the invitation of King Oswald of Northumbria. This marks the establishment of the Celtic Church in northern England.

Venerable Bede gives a major share of the credit to the Irish who, he claims, welcomed large numbers of students from England and eagerly entertained and taught them free of charge. Irish missionaries were prominent in England throughout the seventh century and beyond. Malmesbury and Glastonbury are Irish foundations. The former was founded by a recluse, Maeldubh, and became famous later under the great Aldhelm. Nora Chadwick draws attention to Sir Frank Stenton who wrote, "The strands of Irish and Continental influence were interwoven in every kingdom and at every stage of the process by which England became Christian." (Chadwick 1997, 202)

There are no extant records of the conversions of the Isle of Man, Wales, or Cornwall. Early records are entirely wanting, but archaeological finds suggest that the Manx church corresponded closely to the institutions of the Celtic Church elsewhere in the British Isles—being monastic in organization. It consisted of a principal monastic foundation corresponding to the Welsh *clas* churches and a number of subordinate churches, known in Wales as *llan*. In Wales, the Celtic form appears to have continued unchanged well into the seventh century. (Dillon 2003, 171)

Meanwhile, in southeastern England, Anglo-Saxons were being converted to the Roman form of Christianity. As the Augustinian mission spread north from Canterbury to York, the Celtic Church's influence was extending southward through Northumbria and beyond.

Some historians fault Saint Augustine of Canterbury, who died sometime between AD 604 and AD 609, for his lack of effort in reconciling the differences between the Roman and Celtic Churches. In AD 602, Augustine did in fact invite the British abbots and bishops to a special meeting at Saint Augustine's Oak to review the differences between both Churches. Historians tell us that instead of adopting a conciliatory tone, Augustine immediately delivered an ultimatum. He demanded the Britons join him in bringing the Romanized form of Christianity to the Saxons and to renounce their erroneous customs and their incorrect Easter cycle. The Britons asked for a delay before replying. When it became apparent that there might be some area of agreement, the Britons met again with Augustine in AD 605. It soon became clear that Augustine wanted nothing less than their total submission; the Britons refused to make any concessions and walked away. (Markale 1993, 148)

It was essential to Augustine's mission that he "bring together the older Church, which he found established in several areas in Britain, with the more up-to-date form which he brought with him from Rome." Evidently he failed, but was the failure altogether his? British Celts were averse to changing their time-honored ways. British Christianity had an honorable history and this was the sixth century, the age of saints. (Chadwick 1997, 199-200)

Resolving the Easter Cycle Controversy

Early in the seventh century, an effort to get Ireland to accept the Roman Easter cycle was, to some extent, successful. In AD 628, Easter was celebrated on March 27 in both Rome and Ireland. Pope Honorious I used this coincidence to make further pleas to the Irish to reconsider their stand. South of Ireland monasteries accepted before the end of the second quarter, but the monasteries of northern Ireland obstinately refused. In AD 661, Bishop Colman reopened the controversy at Lindisfarne. A conference took place at Whitby in AD 664 between Colman and Wilfrid, the Saxon king of Northumbria. The majority of the clergy attending the synod sided with Wilfrid who supported the pope. Colman left with his supporters (apparently displeased) to found the monastery of Galway. But Wilfrid's decision left much undone. The Britons kept many of the Celtic Church's customs, notably their form of tonsure and the particular office of abbot-bishop. (Markale 1993, 148-149)

Gradually, the Roman cycle came to be adopted by the remaining Irish communities, though Iona did not give way until AD 716. Finally, at the end of the eighth century, the Britons and Bretons yielded. In Devon and Cornwall, the change from Celtic practices to those of Rome did not come about until the tenth century when Athelstan's (the first king of all England, reigning AD

925-939) conquest of Cornwall influenced the outcome. (Markale 1993, 148)

The difference in organization and the principle of governance which originated in the early Celtic Churches of Gaul and Ireland were not confined to those countries. They prevailed throughout the Celtic countries, insular and continental. It gave rise to what was a long and serious struggle to bring the Churches of Ireland, Scotland, Brittany, and Wales into conformity with Rome's ecclesiastical structure. Spanish Galicia (where there was a Celtic diocese at Britonnia) had already accepted the reformed Easter at the Council of Toledo in AD 633. In many monastic foundations in central Europe, the change had largely come about by the eighth century. (Chadwick 1997, 204-214)

Medieval Church in Ireland

The Celtic Church from the sixth century onward was governed according to monastic rules. There was no central organization with authority over all the monasteries. Each large monastery was independent and governed by an abbot with full rights and responsibilities over its lands and finances, though in more or less close relationship with powerful secular authorities for patronage. (Dillon 2003, 176)

In the centuries leading up to the Viking invasion, monastic communities expanded at a rapid rate into important centers of commerce, learning, and wealth. They were also becoming politically powerful and, to a great extent, spiritually distressed. The great monasteries were increasingly falling into the hands of lay dynasties of *erenachs* and a growing secularization developed, reaching its peak in the tenth century. Abbots were irresponsible with their authority, the morals of the clergy were lax, and continued embroilment in secular affairs brought the Church into disgraceful behavior. This worldliness and laxity led to a powerful and puritanical movement that crept into the Irish Church in the eighth century. It was known as the *celi De* (also the "Culdees") and it continued through the ninth century.

One of the leaders of the celi De was Mael Ruain who founded a monastery at Tallagh near Dublin in AD 774. He adopted the rule of the Order of Canons founded on the Continent some twenty-five years earlier. It was a rule for the intermediate class of clergy between cloistered monks and secular priests who, though not fettered by monastic vows, nevertheless wished to live in common within the virtuous confines of severe discipline.

The Rule of the celi De was harsh. Discipline was severe. In reaction to the lax monastic morals of the day, Mael Ruain decreed absolute chastity for all who had taken vows. Women were shunned. The sanctity of Sunday was absolute. Tallagh and its sister communities were established along the lines of the old monasteries, collecting tithes from the surrounding farmers and each following its own rule under the absolute direction of its abbot. (Scherman 1981, 207)

Over time, the celi De became enmeshed in secular affairs, even to the extent of taking military action. Feidlimid, king of Cashel in the mid-ninth century, besides being one of Ireland's powerful kings, was also a bishop and a reformer. He used the celi De to enforce his convictions on monasteries he believed were not in conformity with the strict rules of the organization. Enraged when Clonmacnoise refused to accept his candidature for abbot, he laid siege to the monastery, killing many of its members. The excesses of Feidlimid, and those like him, destroyed whatever basis of credulity the celi De had; in a matter of time, the movement lost its support. The constitutional structure of the Irish Church remained unchanged, at least for the time being, and responsible to no central authority. Each monastic community continued to be self-ruling and subject only to the tenets and temperament of its individual leader. (Scherman 1981, 227)

Vikings, Not Rome, Initiate Organizational Reform

It was the Vikings in the end, not Rome, who brought about reform to the Irish Celtic Church, and it was the Vikings themselves who initiated the first movement of change. In the early eleventh century, Sitric (Norse king of Dublin) became a Christian, after which event he went on a pilgrimage to Rome. Upon his return, he established a Continental-style, Episcopal model bishopric in Dublin. Its first bishop, Dunan, died in AD 1074. A bishop by the name of Patrick followed him; the archbishop of Canterbury consecrated him.

The Viking reform movement continued its propagation to other Norse towns, establishing dioceses and consecrating bishops. Gilbert (first bishop of Limerick) and Malthus (first bishop of Waterford) were Irish monks trained in England under the aegis of Saint Anselm, the great reforming archbishop of Canterbury. While Canterbury was initially successful in lining up the Dublin diocese under its auspices, the same was not true of Limerick and Waterford. Both rejected any attempts by Canterbury to bring them under its primacy, arguing that their Church should instead preserve her historic independence.

Synod of Cashel AD 1101

Efforts at reforming the Irish Church continued. A synod was called at Cashel in AD 1101 to consider reforming measures. It failed to undertake any organizational changes. Instead, it enacted decrees within the framework of the existing monastic system, such as: the liberation of monastic leaders from paying secular tribute; the prohibition of simony (the crime of buying or selling ecclesiastical preferments, beneficies, etc); and the regulation of ecclesiastical appointments. It demanded, in particular, that: erenachs and abbots be in religious orders and unmarried; those guilty of the most serious of crimes be excluded from sanctuary; and marriage with very near kindred be barred. (Otway-Ruthven 1993, 38)

At the time, Irish secular law (Brehon law) recognized some ten different kinds of marriage; while safeguarding to some extent the rights of wives, it permitted divorce and remarriage for a variety of reasons. It has been described that in no field of life was Ireland's apartness from the mainstream of Christian European society as obvious as in that of marriage. Throughout the Medieval period, and down to the end of the old order in the seventeenth century, what could be called Celtic secular marriage remained the norm in Ireland, and Christian matrimony was no more than the rare exception appended to this system. Even after the downfall of the aristocratic order in the seventeenth century, the constraints and regulations associated with modern Catholic teaching on love and marriage were very slow to take root. The "country marriage," a marriage pact engaged in privately without benefit of clergy, was quite valid and possible in Ireland down to the end of the eighteenth century. (Tuama 1981, 299)

Synod of Rathbresil AD 1111

The Synod of Rathbresil, ten years after Cashel, set forth radical changes for the Irish Church. Bishop Gilbert of Limerick (who by then was papal legate and as such regarded himself as the leading churchman in Ireland) proposed what amounted to a new constitution for the Irish Church. Two provinces were created: Armagh and Cashel, with the primacy being given to Armagh. There were to be twelve sees under Armagh and eleven under Cashel. The existing territorial dioceses of Waterford and Limerick were fit into the general framework, but not Dublin, which was still subject to Canterbury. This set the Church in Ireland on the road to organization in the standard Continental pattern. The Synod of Kells followed Rathbresil in AD 1152, presided over by Cardinal John Paparo as papal legate. *Pallia* were given to the four archbishops of Armagh, Cashel, Dublin, and Tuam; the Irish diocesan system, as it was to endure, was fully in place. (Otway-Ruthven 39)

Monastic Tradition Plummets

It should not be supposed that this transformation, set forth for the Irish Church, was achieved without difficulty. The old monastic dynasties did not always take to the changes calmly. Implementing the proposals brought about the collapse of the monastic tradition that had been in existence for six centuries. The Church had to replace lay abbots, whose families had virtually owned the monasteries from the beginning, with suitable men in holy orders. Furthermore, the Church had to get rid of the surplus old-style subordinate bishops who had always performed their holy offices at the bidding of the abbots.

Armagh had notable difficulties, and even when these were overcome, there remained the immensely complicated task of reorganizing property rights. As late as AD 1210, the clergy in Connacht assembled before the archbishop of Tuam to arrange for transfer of the *termon* or *coarb* lands to the bishoprics in which they lay. These were the lands of Celtic monasteries, and the solution generally was to leave the erenach families in possession as hereditary tenants of the church. Then, cathedral chapters were to be organized, a process not completed until after the Norman invasion in AD 1169. (Otway-Ruthven 1993, 39) The Synod of Rathbreasil, however unworkable, laid the groundwork for bringing the Irish Church finally into line with the Church of Rome. It also prescribed revisions for many abuses that had crept into the Church during the preceding centuries.

By the early thirteenth century, the Irish Church was no longer an independent entity. It was now organized much as it was elsewhere in western Europe. There were, of course, some survivals from the older order: there were still coarbs and erenachs in parts of Connacht and Ulster but, on the whole, these survivors were unimportant. (Otway-Ruthven 1993, 129) For better or worse, Ireland was now fully in the Roman Catholic Church fold. For some, this meant a loss of the freedom, tolerance, and imagination that had set the

Irish clerics apart for centuries. But, the reformation brought with it a makeover of the Irish Church: standards were established to remedy abuses; and rules were enacted to correct lax morality and to establish uniform ethical standards.

Side-by-side with all this, and an essential part of the process, was the introduction of continental monastic orders—the Cistercians and the Arroasian canons regular—at some date before the middle of the twelfth century. By the AD 1160s, a number of houses of both orders had been founded in many parts of the country, superseding the older Celtic foundations. (Otway-Ruthven 1993, 40)

Meanwhile, there was a remarkable cultural regeneration in Ireland. Irish scholars of the eleventh and twelfth centuries began gathering the country's pagan lore from the oral tradition and placing it in written form. We owe our knowledge of the pre-Christian Irish Celts to this period of collected works. There were also challenging developments in art and architecture. Ireland's conservative, almost primitive style of church building evolved into a stylish blend of Continental and traditional that became known as Irish Romanesque. (Scherman 1981, 231)

Progress in the Political Sphere

The accession of Brian Boru to the high-kingship near the end of the tenth century marked a break with the past. It paved the way for a strong central monarchy, and in spite of considerable strife among the various dynasties Ireland seemed to be moving in that direction. Then, an army of Normans, Flemings, and Welsh landed in Ireland near the end of the twelfth century, changing the course of Irish history. Oddly enough, it was Pope Adrian IV (an Englishman) who gave permission to the English king Henry II "to enter the island of Ireland in order to subject its people to law and to root out from them weeds of vice." They were "to enlarge the boundaries of the church, and to proclaim the truths of the Christian religion to a 'rude and ignorant people.'" (Moody and Martin 1967, 107-108)

When the Anglo-Normans arrived in Ireland, they found an island that was (as it had been for centuries) a regionalized patchwork of petty kingdoms. Rory O'Connor, the high king, lacked the authority to enforce law and order. There was no concept of national community, and societal unity existed only as far as a common language and cultural traditions were concerned. There were countless wars and clashes between belligerent chieftains. Henry set in motion a system of governing that eventually led to a centralized government in Ireland. Its basis was the occupation of the land set forth in accordance with the design of Norman feudalism. As in England, the king would enjoy the right of prerogative wardship: that is, he had the wardship of all the lands as a tenant-in-chief, even though some were the domain of other lords.

With this arrangement, a second sphere of influence—that of the Anglo-Normans—began to emerge in Ireland. The Anglo-Norman king had two particular advantages denied to his Irish counterpart: first, in the centralized monarchical authority; and, second, in the active support of the ecclesiastical hierarchy. Reverend F.X. Martin maintains "the tragedy of the Norman invasion was not the conquest of Ireland—for that never took place—but the half-conquest." This, he argues, came about because the Normans never settled Ireland in sufficient numbers to fully complete the conquest. Moreover, the English kings were too preoccupied with threats at home and wars on the Continent to focus on their barons in Ireland. Martin believes that if the conquest had been completed as was the case in Normandy, England, or Sicily, a new nation would have emerged, combining the qualities of both the Irish and the Normans.

When Henry Plantagenet left Ireland, his loyal followers (who had accompanied him) stayed behind, intent on settling there. The Anglo-Normans seized the wealthiest estates and formed a new aristocracy. The FitzGeralds, Birminghams, Butlers, and Burkes came to replace the O'Briens, O'Rourkes, McCarthys, and O'Neills. Strangely enough, after AD 1255, there came about a series of setbacks for the conquerors lasting until Tudor times. The Anglo-Norman nobles who controlled the Irish lush countryside and rural economy gradually became more Gaelic than the Gaels themselves. But this did not lessen English supremacy. All decisions were still made in London. As Jean Markale writes, from then on unhappiness descended on the island. There were endless wars, rebellions, famines, and religious conflicts.

Near the middle of the AD 1500s, the Tudor monarchy under Henry VIII began to flex its muscle in Ireland. In vain, the Irish fought back as Henry moved to dismantle native rule and impose some meaningful semblance of English government throughout Ireland. It was at this crucial juncture of political events that a new religious question entered into Anglo-Irish relations. Henry, breaking with Rome—not out of doctrinal differences, but over his desire to divorce his first wife, Catherine of Aragon—authorized the English Parliament to recognize him as "supreme head of the English Church," thus, substituting his own authority for that of the papacy. Henry moved quickly to overthrow "native rule" in Ireland and to replace papal power with royal authority in the Irish Church. Arriving in Dublin in AD 1536, he summoned the Irish Parliament to enact reformation statutes bringing the Church in Ireland into conformity with the Church of England.

Onward from AD 1603, Ireland began a slow and extended descent into total subjugation. Recurring outbreaks of rebellion led to liquidation of the Old Catholic Irish aristocracy and to repeated planting of English and Scottish settlers. Under foreign domination, the Celtic dream faded. Large numbers of the population emigrated. Despite all this, the Gaels of Ireland kept their Celtic traditions alive. After eight centuries of struggle to maintain its identity, Celtic Ireland survived. In AD 1921, twenty-six of its thirty-two counties formed an independent nation, the first and only truly Celtic state in the modern world.

Chapter XVII—

Flowering of Celtic Literary Artistry

Ireland has in her written Gaelic literature, in her old love tales and battle tales the forms in which the imagination of Europe uttered itself before Greece shaped a tumult of legend into the music of her arts . . . . The legends of other European countries are less numerous, and not so full of the energies from which the arts and our understanding of their sanctity arose, and the best of them have already been shaped into plays and poems

—Lady Gregory, *Ideals of Ireland*

The historical Celtic world—with its primary social, religious, and political backgrounds—has been addressed in the preceding chapters. The Celtic people struggled in vain to retain a foothold on the periphery of Western Europe when the Romans and later the Anglo-Saxons pushed them further and further west. In the final conquest, Scotland and Wales were integrated into Saxon England; Brittany united with France; and Ireland (the oldest and most Celtic of the kingdoms) remained a collection of autonomous tuaths (petty kingdoms) until it, too, was finally conquered by its neighbor England in the seventeenth century. Yet, the Celtic spirit, so dynamic and distinctive, continued to exert a powerful influence in the intellectual and artistic world, even though the early realms, identified with its beginning, have long disappeared.

From the early nineteenth century AD, there was a renewed awakening of the Celtic consciousness, mostly in communities along the Atlantic peripheral, but particularly in Ireland. Interest in Celtic art and literature, and the reappearance of mystics and visionaries, established the continuum of the Celtic spirit. This was particularly true of Ireland.

Kingdoms of Ireland, circa 900 AD.

Medieval Irish Literature

Ireland, more than any other Celtic land, has produced an incredible quantity of literature—prose tales, epics, saints' lives, mythological stories, and historical memoirs. The oldest stories belong to the Mythological cycle, and they form the basis for the medieval account of ancient Irish history known as *Lebor Gabala*, or Book of Invasions. The next set of tales is from the Ulster cycle, which is of the Heroic Age and of Cú Chulainn who was the greatest figure in ancient Irish heroic literature. He has been appropriately compared to Achilles in Greek mythology and to Siegfried in German tradition. The third cycle, the Ossianic cycle of the Fenians, did not gain universal appeal until the eleventh century when the old stories were translated into a new art form—the narrative poem or ballad with dramatic overtones. The cycle includes one superb prose narrative, *The Pursuit of Diarmait and Grainne*, a pleasant love story with a "back-to-nature charm." The recording of Ireland's oral tradition was historically important to the ancient Irish, and the painstaking copying of Christian and classical works preserved much of what would otherwise have been lost. (Scherman 1981, 260-262)

Irish Early Modern Literary Period

In AD 1169, Ireland was invaded by the Anglo-Normans. The invasion began as an action of Norman lords acting more or less independently of the crown. Once successful, their invasion was embraced by their king, Henry II, who set foot on Irish soil on October 17, 1171, at the head of a large army. He established his court in Dublin, proclaiming himself "Lord of Ireland." With this proclamation, Ireland was one more sovereign claim in Henry's consortium of realms that included England and Wales, Normandy, Anjuv, Maine, Poitou, and Aquitaina as well. According to Irish tradition, Henry had the blessing of the papacy for his incursion into Ireland

Henry II set in motion a system of governing that eventually lead to centralized government in Ireland. Its basis was the occupation of the land set forth in accordance with the design of Norman feudalism. As in Britain, the king would enjoy the right of prerogative guardianship; that is, he had charge of all the lands as a tenant-in-chief, even though some land was the Domain of other lords. Government, the direct and personal affair of the king, was modeled on that of England, evolving along the same lines throughout the Middle Ages and beyond.

The Early Modern period in Irish language and literature began following the social and political changes brought about by the invasion of the Anglo-Normans in AD 1169. It lasted until the seventeenth century and it is characterized by a restructured literary standard. This standard was cultivated principally by the secular literary schools, which were maintained by professional poets and literary scholars known as the filidh (bards). Verse compositions by these professional poets formed a substantial part of the literature, which is extant from this period. Much of the professional poets' verse consists of eulogies to their aristocratic patrons, but there is also a substantial body of extant religious and personal poetry. Among the more eminent professional poets of this period were: **Donnchadh Mór Ó Dálaigh** (1175-1244), **Muireadhach Albanach O'Dálaigh** (1180-1250), **Gofraidh Fionn Ó Dálaigh** (1320-87), **Tadgh Óg Ó Huiginn** (?-1448), **Tadgh Dall Ó Huiginn** (1550-91), **EochaidhÓhEodhusa** (1567-1617), and one of the last in the tradition, **Flatha Ó Gnímh Fear** (1602-40). As can be recognized from this abbreviated list, the profession was largely hereditary.

The Early Modern Literary period came rapidly to an end following the overthrow of the Gaelic order in the seventeenth century. The transition from the Gaelic tradition to Anglo Irish is evident in a literary prose intended to preserve the documentation of Gaelic tradition, such as the great synthesis *Annála Rioghochta Éireann* (Annals of the Kingdom of Ireland) written in 1632-36 under the supervision of **Michael Ó Cléirigh**. There was also **Geoffrey Keating**'s comprehensive history *Forsa Feasa ar Eirinn* (Foundations of Knowledge About Ireland), which was completed around 1634. As for verse, its transition was manifest by a sudden decline in patronage for poets. The most prominent poets of the period were **Pádraigín Haicéad** (1600-54), **Dáibhí Ó Bruadair** (1625-98), and **Aogán Ó Rathaille** (1670-1728), regarded as one of the greatest poets in the Irish tradition. He was also one of the last to receive some patronage for his work. Even after aristocratic literary patronage had totally ceased by the eighteenth century, literature in Gaelic continued to be cultivated by members of the Catholic clergy, farmers, artisans, and schoolmasters (McCoole and Briggs 166).

Anglo-Irish Literary Tradition Period

The *Treaty of Limerick*, ending the Jacobite struggle in AD 1691, was the final act in the collapse of Celtic Ireland where, for more than two millennia, its unique insular Celtic civilization had flourished—untouched by Roman society, enhanced by Christianity, assaulted but not crushed by the Norsemen, and invaded but not conquered by the Anglo-Normans. The Irish Parliament, now entirely Protestant, began work on bolstering the Protestant grip on all walks of Irish life. Catholics were forced into a state of powerless subordination. The great confiscations of land under Queen Elizabeth I in the previous century had finally resulted in making the landlord class of Ireland almost exclusively Anglo and Protestant and the tenant class almost exclusively Irish and Catholic.

Ireland's Catholic Gaelic tradition was severely crushed in the eighteenth century. Nevertheless, there was a great literary advance; it was almost totally Protestant, yet its frame of mind was classical and its perspectives were cosmopolitan. Writers identified with this period wrote only in the English language. It has been said, "the only sign of 'Irishness' in these writers was their affection for that comic personage—bibulous, irascible, generous, eloquent and sentimental—who came to be known as the 'stage Irishman.'" (McCoole and Briggs 166)

George Farquhar (1677-1707), **William Congreve** (1670-1729), **Richard Steele** (1672-1729), **Oliver Goldsmith** (1728-1774), **Edmund Burke** (1729-1797), **George Berkeley** (1685-1753), **Richard Brinsley Sheridan** (1751-1816), and

Jonathan Swift (1667-1745) were the most notable writers. They were typically educated at Protestant grammar schools and Dublin's Trinity College.

Swift became dean of Saint Patrick's Cathedral in 1713. When his hopes for a bishopric failed to materialize, he turned his caustic pen to Irish problems. Among his body of early writing was *A Modest Proposal* (1729), suggesting that Ireland's governing class, during a time of famine, sell the country's starving babies to feed the rich. His well-known *Gulliver's Travels*, a satire on contemporary society, takes a gloomy view of mankind.

Berkeley made major contributions to philosophy, which brought him a reputation throughout Europe. His first work, *An Essay towards a New Theory of Vision* (1709), was concerned with the manner in which objects were perceived by sight. His masterpiece, *A Treatise concerning the Principles of Human Knowledge*, was published in 1710 and its arguments were expanded in a more popular form in *Three Dialogues between Hylas and Philonous* (1713).

Goldsmith's first popular success was *Letters of a Citizen of the World* (1762), a compilation of his "Chinese Letters" in the *Public Register* which purported to be the reflections of a Chinese philosopher living in London. His poem, *The Traveler* (1764), was considered by Samuel Johnson to be the best English language poem since the death of Alexander Pope. In 1770, Goldsmith's poem, *The Deserted Village*, went quickly into five editions. It deals with rural depopulation in Ireland, contrasting the needy poor with opulent and indolent landlords: "*Ill fare the land, to hastening ills a prey, where wealth accumulates, and men decay.*" Goldsmith's reputation as a playwright was established with *She Stoops to Conquer* (1773).

Burke wrote about the miseries of Ireland in terms of a global responsibility that took in the French and American revolutions. He had a distinguished parliamentary career, raising the standard of debate and fostering the party system.

Advent of the Irish-Celtic Literary Renaissance

The union of Ireland with Britain took effect on January 1, 1801. Ireland now lost its parliament, and the ascendancy class could no longer legislate independently on its own affairs. The "protestant nation" of the eighteenth century ceased to be. The Union made little difference to many people at the time. Dublin society was immediately affected with the end of the assembly of Lords and Commons in the parliament buildings in College Green. The protestant ascendancy, which had been opposed to the union, because it would deprived them of the control of affairs they had enjoyed through the Irish Legislature, soon found they were deprived merely of responsibility. Control remained through the separate Irish executive, which the Union retained. Catholic Emancipation, which Prime Minister Pitt had promised with the Act of Union, had failed to materialize. Opponents, both in Britain and Ireland, succeeded in blocking it. George III believed that signing an emancipation bill was a breach of his coronation oath. With the failure of the emancipation bill, Ireland's majority Catholic population continued to be represented exclusively by Protestants at Westminster, as it had been the previous century in Dublin. But the religious question stubbornly persisted, fueled by vocal representatives of the newly Catholic middle class that was rapidly expanding in Ireland. The leader of this group was a talented lawyer named Daniel O'Connell. He founded the Catholic Association whose object was to further Catholic interests in all areas of life.

A new medium, from the standpoint of the growing Irish Catholic middle class, made its way into Anglo-Irish literature early in the nineteenth century. Introduced by native Irish writers, using English instead of Gaelic, it personified sentiments that differed in many ways from those of their Anglo-Irish contemporaries. This breed of Catholic writers included such names as **Charles Kickham** (1830-1882), **Gerald Griffin** (1803-1840), and **John** and **Michael Banim**. **William Carleton** (1794-1896), in his *Traits and Stories of the Irish Peasantry*, offered a vivid account of life among Ireland's rural poor.

Throughout the early nineteenth century, there was much activity relating to Gaelic manuscript study and translation by scholars of early Irish works. The nationalist tradition, fusing a revived Celtic-Irish literature with the existing Anglo-Irish literature, is generally thought to have begun with writers of the early nineteenth century: **John O'Donovan** (1806-1861), **Eugene O'Curry** (1796-1862), **Sir Samuel Ferguson** (1810-1886), **Thomas Moore** (1779-1852), **Sir Charles Petrie** (1790-1866), and their contemporaries.

Ferguson can be credited with paving the way into Ireland's literary past. His first great work, *The Tain Quest*, presents, in modern English poetry, the characters and events of the ancient Red Branch cycle. He was also a noted antiquarian, his most important work being *Ogham Inscriptions in Ireland, Wales and Scotland.* **O'Curry**, one of the great translators of his time, was an important pioneer in recovering and translating materials on ancient Irish history. **O'Donovan** edited, amplified, and translated into English many of the works of the Masters, including the *Annals of the Four Masters* by three **O'Cleary**s and **O'Mulconroy**. **Petrie** established the National Museum, assisted in founding the National Library, and promoted the collection and conservation of old Irish manuscripts and documents.

These individuals and their contemporaries set in motion the Irish-Celtic literary renaissance of the post Anglo-Irish Ascendancy era, from which emerged the great Irish writers of the late nineteenth and twentieth centuries.

Ireland's Continuing Literary Contribution

Among Ireland's internationally acclaimed writers of the late nineteenth and twentieth centuries were:

Bram Stoker (1847-1912) started out as an unpaid drama critic for the *Dublin Evening Mail* before embarking on a writing career. His first novel, *The Snake's Pass* (1890), concerns a search for legendary treasure in the west of Ireland, and he went on to write several other novels including his famous novel, *Dracula*, in 1897.

Oscar Wilde (1854-1900) had his first success with *The Happy Prince and Other Tales* (1888), a collection of fairy stories with a satirical edge. Wilde's only novel, *The Picture of Dorian Gray* (1891), shocked the Victorian public, who found it immoral. With its scintillating conversations, *The Picture of Dorian Gray* hinted at Wilde's potential as a playwright. His *Lady Windermere's Fan* confirmed it.

George Bernard Shaw (1856-1950) started out reviewing books for the *Pall Mall Gazette* and as art critic of *The World*. He also became an entertaining music critic for *The Star* under the penname Corno di Bassetto and wrote on the theatre for the *Saturday Review*. Over time, Shaw became a prolific playwright. His play, *John Bull's Other Island*, had a run of successes at the Royal Court Theatre in London, establishing Shaw as a major playwright. Shaw's next great success was *Pygmalion* (1914) which, after his death, was made into the musical comedy *My Fair Lady*. Shaw received the Nobel Prize for literature in 1925.

William Butler Yeats (1865-1939) acquired a reputation of a folklorist and poet when his *Folk and Fairy Tales of the Irish Peasantry* was published in 1888. With Lady Gregory and others, he founded the Abbey Theatre in 1904. He was the leader of the Irish literary revival and worked incessantly for the furtherance of Irish literature. However, it is in his poems that Yeat's reputation principally rests. They are among the greatest in the English language. With Shaw and Russell, he founded the Irish Academy of Letters in 1932. In 1923, Yeats received the Nobel Prize for literature.

James Joyce's (1882-1941) reputation as a great writer began with the release of *A Portrait of the Artist as a Young Man* in 1916. *Ulysses* (published in 1934) is, of course, his most important work, and its "stream of consciousness" technique has been widely adopted by other novelists. **Lady Gregory** (Augusta Persse) (1852-1932) made a lasting contribution with her writings, which drew inspiration from Gaelic literature and folklore. With William Butler Yeats and others, she founded the National Theater Society.

Post Independence Era

Following Ireland's separation from Britain in 1922, a new era of writers, poets, and dramatists emerged ushering in the modern era of the Celtic-Irish literary movement. Among them: **Flann O'Brien** (1911-1966) who wrote under the penname for Brian O'Nolan. His writing included his comic novel, *At Swim-Two-Birds*, which author Graham Greene praised as being in the line of James Joyce's *Ulysses*. **Samuel Beckett** (1906-1989) has been described as the greatest experimenter in fiction since Joyce, a playwright more radical in innovation than Pirandello, and a writer of imaginative power comparable to Kafka. The success of his play *Godot* brought him international fame. He received the Nobel prize for literature in 1969. **Kate O'Brien** (1897-1974) is regarded as one of Ireland's great twentieth century novelists. Her most successful novel, *That Lady* (1946), was set in sixteenth-century Spain. **Sean O'Faolain** (1900-1991) is often referred to as the Irish Chekhof for his accomplishments as a short story writer. **Seamus Heaney** (1939-) is Ireland's best-known poet of the second half of the twentieth century. He was awarded the Nobel Prize for Literature in 1998. **Brendan Behan**'s (1923-1964) prison life experience for IRA activities was the focus for his autobiographical *Borstal Boy*. **Sean O'Casey** (1880-1964) was a successful dramatist who had several of his plays rejected by the Abbey before heeding the advice of Lady Gregory that his writing gift lay in characterization. The outcome was *The Shadow of a Gunman*, an unexpected success in 1923. He went on to write a number of other successful plays, among them *The Plough and the Stars*, *Juno and the Paycock*, *The Bishop's Bonfire*, *The Drums of Father Ned*, and *Red Roses for Me*.

The short story continued to be a favorite medium for Irish writers. Among the short story writers whose collections have contributed to the genre are: **Elizabeth Bowen** (1899-1973) who published several collections of short stories, including *Encounters*, *The Death of the Heart*, and *The Heat of the Day*; **Frank O'Connor** (1903-1966) wrote two novels *The Saint and Mary Kate* and *Dutch Interior*, but his international reputation rested on the short stories collected under such titles as *Bones of Contention* and *Crab Apple Jelly*; **Liam O'Flaherty** (1896-1984) wrote several short stories, including *The Informer* (made into a successful movie by John Ford), *Mr. Gilhooley*, *The Assassin*, and the stories in *Two Lovely Beasts*.

John M. Synge's (1871-1909) one-act play, *The Shadow of the Glen*, staged in Dublin in 1903, was a portrayal of a loveless rural marriage. It was criticized as an insult to Irish womanhood. He wrote several additional plays of which the best known is *Playboy of the Western World* (1907), which caused uproar on opening night when the puritanical Dublin audience took offence at a reference to "females standing in their shifts." **George Moore** (1852-1933), having recognized his shortcoming as a painter, turned to writing, publishing two early volumes of poetry, *Flowers of Passion* (1878) and *Pagan Poems* (1881). His short story collection in *Celibrates* (1895) was followed by two more novels, *Evelyn Innes* (1898) and *Sister Teresa* (1901). Moore was an inexhaustible writer who wrote with increasing elegance. Of his later novels, *The Brook Kerith* (1916) and *Heloise and Abelard* (1921) are the most notable. There were other writers, of course. *The Barracks and the Dark* marked the appearance of **John McGahern** as a remarkable novelist. *Paddy Clarke Ha Ha Ha* earned **Roddy Doyle** the Brooker Prize.

Scottish Literary Artistry

The Gaelic form of the Celtic language was brought to Scotland about AD 500 by colonists from Ireland. At the time, Scotland was referred to as Caladonia. By the ninth century, however, the name Scotia had replaced most of the region north of the Firth of Clyde. A Gaelic king ruled this Scoto-Pictish kingdom, but his authority over a large portion of his newly-acquired realm was nominal. The Hebrides, for instance, and sizable tracts of North and West Scotland were under Norse domination. Nevertheless, there existed a Gaelic-speaking court, with its attendant patronage, which was of great importance in preserving Gaelic culture.

When the court became Anglicized at the end of the eleventh century, it was a significant setback for Gaelic in the Scottish realm. As the distinguished Scottish scholar John MacInnes describes it:

> "No longer the *sermo regius* of Scotland. Gaelic was now fated never to fulfill what had seemed to be its destiny: to become the language of cultured society throughout the Kingdom and the medium of expression in its leading institutions. Instead there began the process which ultimately banished it to the remote and inaccessible parts of the land and although development did not by any means cease, Gaelic literature became largely cut off from the influence of the great innovating movements of post-medieval Europe."

Yet, a special relationship with Ireland remained intact until the seventeenth century. In spite of differences, political and religious, Ireland and Gaelic Scotland continued to be one cultural area. As the vernacular dialects of the two countries began to diverge, the mandarin class who cultivated the arts standardized a common language—a flexible, classical form of Gaelic. These learned men moved freely throughout the lands of a "sea-divided Gael," enjoying a kind of diplomatic immunity. Inevitably, they promoted a sense of cultural solidarity within Scotland as well as between Scotland and Ireland. (O'Driscoll, ed. 1993, 271)

Late Medieval Anglo-Scottish Literature

Scotland's literature offers a rich and varied blend of creativity and heritage, enhanced by a mixture of languages—English, Scottish Gaelic, Scots, Brythonic, French, and Latin. **John Barbour** is often referred to as the father of Scots poetry. His epic work, *Brus* (1375), describing the Scottish wars of independence against England and the rise of Robert the Bruce, is believed to be the earliest major work in Early Scots literature.

Scotland fought a series of battles in the late thirteenth and early fourteenth centuries to establish its independence from England. Under Edward I, England was intent on expanding its influence over Scotland. Then the young queen of Scotland, the Maid of Norway, died and there was no direct heir to take her place. Edward quickly moved to promote Jon Balliol as king, believing he would accept Edward as his overlord. When Edward demanded Scottish support for his invasion of France, the Scots refused and instead signed a mutual aid treaty with France. Edward then invaded Scotland.

The invasion of Scotland in 1296 was the beginning of the wars of independence. Balliol abdicated in 1296, leaving Scotland without a monarch for next ten years. In the interim, Edward ruled and (out of England's interference in Scottish affairs) there grew a national resistance. Along came Robert the Bruce in 1298 who took over the title of Guardian of Scotland. He next claimed to be heir to Scotland's throne through his great-great grandfather, David I; in 1306, he crowned himself King Robert I at Scone. He then set out to claim Scotland back from the English. By early 1314, he had succeeded in taking back all of Scotland's castles that were in English hands. One of his great successes was at Bannockburn in June 1314 where Scottish forces routed a much larger English army. Six years later in 1320, Bruce and the Scottish nobles issued the Declaration of Arbroath asserting Scottish Independence. The Treaty of Edinburgh between Robert I and Edward III in 1328 brought the Wars of Independence to an end.

Classical French and Chaucerian literary language had an increasing influence on Scots poetry in the fifteenth century, along with the use of a wide range of genres. Scottish versions of popular continental romances were also produced in the same period, for example: *Launcelot o the Laik* and *The Buik of Alexander*. This was the era of the makars, a group of writers (poets with links to the royal Court) who significantly advanced the status of Scots as a literary language. Much Middle Scots literature was produced by makars. Chief among them: **Gavin Douglas** (circa 1414 to circa 1522) whose work *Eneados*, a Scot's version of Virgil's *Aeneid*, is one of the earliest translations of a major classical text into a European vernacular. **Robert Henryson** (circa 1425 to circa 1500) is known primarily for his reworking of Aesop's fables and his *Testament of Cresseid*. He is regarded as the most important Scottish writer of the fifteenth century. **William Dunbar** (circa 1460 circa 1520) is noted for his colloquial virtuosity in such poems as the *Tretis of the Tua Mariit Wemen and the Wedo* (Treatise of the Two Married Women and the Widow), and **David Lyndsay** (circa 1490 to circa 1550) whose political play *Ane Satyre of the Thrie Estaitis* is regarded as the flagship of Scottish drama.

Gaelic was still a significant language in Scotland and **Walter Kennedy** (circa 1455-1518), one of the makars associated with the court of James IV, is believed to have written poetry in the language, although only scattered examples of his work survive. His most impressive surviving poem, *The Passioun of Crist*, is a depiction of the story of Christ from nativity to the ascension. One of the earliest extant original prose pieces of the late fifteenth century is **John Ireland**'s *The Meroure of Wyssdome* (1490), a philosophical manual for the young James IV. Another of his surviving works is the *Asloan Manuscript* (circa 1515), an anthology of short prose compositions incorporating history, geography, mortality, translation, and scripture. Earlier fragments of his work, *Auchinleck Chronicle*, have also survived.

Beside Kennedy and Ireland, there were other writers at the forefront of the golden age of Scottish literature in the fifteenth and sixteenth centuries; many of their works have been lost. Those that managed to survive are due, in part, to manuscript collectors such as **George Bannatyne** (Bellenden) (1545-1608) who collected Scottish poems. Bannatyne was also a translator. Among his literary translations are Hector Boece's *Historia Gentis Scotorum* as *Chroniklis of Scotland* (1536) and the first five books of *Livy's History of Rome*. Bannatyne's manuscript, along with the Asloam and Maitland Folio manuscripts, are the chief repositories of Middle Scots poetry.

From the seventeenth to the early nineteenth centuries, Scottish literature became quite popular. **Allan Ramsay** (1686-1758), poet and literary antiquary, pioneered the use of Scots in contemporary poetry at a time when most Scottish writers had been Anglicized. In 1760, **James Macpherson** (1736-1796) claimed he had found poetry written by Ossian (*Tales of the Ossianic Cycle* from early Irish literature). He published translations which acquired international popularity, being proclaimed as a Celtic equivalent of the Classical epics. *Fingal*, written in 1762, was translated into several European languages. It inspired many Scottish writers, including the young Walter Scott, but it eventually became clear that the poems were not direct translations from the original Gaelic, but pretended translations made to suit the aesthetic expectations of Macpherson's audience. **Walter Scott** (1771-1832) was initially more inclined to poetry and even collected Scottish ballads before launching into a novel-writing career in 1814. A novel by Scott, which contributed to the image of him as a Scottish patriot, was *Rob Roy*. He also wrote a *History of Scotland*.

James Hogg (1770-1835), a writer encouraged by Scott, made creative use of his Scottish religious background in producing his distinctive *The Private Memoirs and Confessions of a Justified Sinner*. It introduces the "doppelgänger" (a tangible double of a living person that typically represents evil in fiction, folklore, and popular culture) theme, which would be taken up later in the century by another Scotsman (Robert Lewis Stevenson) in *The Strange Case of Dr. Jekyll and Mr. Hyde*. Hogg is believed to have borrowed his literary motif from the concept of the "co-choisiche" in Gaelic folk tradition.

Walter Scott and **Robert Burns** are the best-known Scottish writers who were strongly associated with the Romantic Era. While Scott's work is not exclusively connected with Scotland, his popularity in England and abroad did much to form the modern understanding of Scottish culture. Burns is considered Scotland's national bard; his works have recently been edited to reflect the full breadth of their subject matter. Strange as it may seem, his work was censored during the Victorian era.

Nineteenth and Twentieth Century Writers

A Scottish intellectual tradition is reflected in the *Sherlock Holmes* books of **Sir Arthur Conan Doyle** (1859-1930). Doyle was Edinburgh-born and his creation of a doctor-character and a scientist-turned-detective with impressive deductive faculties cannot avoid the association in the reader's minds with the Edinburgh of the long tradition of medical studies.

Robert Louis Stevenson (1850-1894), another son of Edinburgh, wrote many famous books that are still popular and feature in many plays and films. His books rank among the best known in the world. The short novel, *Strange Case of Dr Jekyll and Mr Hyde* (1886), depicts the dual personality of a kind and intelligent physician who turns into a psychopathic monster after imbibing a drug intended to separate good from evil in a personality. Two other classic books by Stevenson are *Kidnapped*, a fast-paced historical novel set in the aftermath of the 1745 Jacobite Rising, and *Treasure Island*, a classic pirate adventure.

The arrival of the twentieth century witnessed a renaissance of Gaelic poetry in Scotland. Its most supportive figure was **Hugh**

MacDiarmid (1892-1978) who formed a type of "Synthetic Scots" that combined different regional Scottish dialects and archaic terms. **Sorley MacLean** (1911-1996), regarded as one of the greatest writers in Gaelic work in the twentieth century, was to many the father of the Gaelic Renaissance. His poetry took an ancient vanishing language and showed the world what a powerful medium it was for expressing very contemporary thoughts and emotions. He gave Gaelic a twentieth century voice, a voice blazing with passion and raging with anger against past injustices endured by the Gaels.

In his 1978 article on "The Gaelic Continuum in Scotland," John MacInnes writes:

> "Within that community in Scotland there is still a vast reservoir of Gaelic: immense resources of vocabulary and idiom; repertoires of traditional songs and stories; the poetry of the present day as well as that which has been handed down by the oral tradition for many centuries to the native community." (O'Driscoll, ed. 1993, 270)

Welsh Literary Artistry

Welsh literature suffered from the effects of Romanization and Christianity, but certain passages of the oldest of the tales known as the *Mabinogion* and *Culhwch* ac *Olwen* reflect particularly ancient traditions. The extant version of *Culhwch* ac *Olwen* has been dated to the second half of the eleventh century, but its orthography, vocabulary, syntax, and, moreover, certain stylistic features suggest that a written version of parts of it may have existed a century earlier. The tale deserves the attention of the student of Arthurian literature as it represents Arthurian tradition before the changes which can be seen in the *De Excidio et Conquestu Britanniae* by Geoffrey of Monmouth and in the continental Arthurian literature. (Edel 2001, 239)

The earliest reference to verse composed in the Welsh language is found in the *De Excidio et Conquestu Britanniae* by **Gildas**, written not later than circa AD 547. This work contains an uncompromising denunciation of the evil way of life of five British kings of the period, the most infamous of whom was Maelgwn Gwynedd, king of northwest Wales. In addition, poets composing in Welsh are mentioned by name in the *Historia Brittonum*, a collection of historico-legendary material put together during the first half of the ninth century by British historian Nennius, but using earlier sources. His work includes a list of five early poets, two of whom, **Taliesin** and **Adeirin**, were considered in the Middle Ages to be the authors of the poems contained in two thirteenth-century manuscripts known as the *Books* of Taliesin and Adeirin. (O'Driscoll 2003, 161) In the early part of the twelfth century, Geoffrey of Monmouth wrote his *Historia Regum Britaniae* expressly to commemorate the exploits of King Arthur. In the view of some historical sources, his history lacks factual responsibility and is not worth mentioning as a record of fact, but does however provide many names of poets and chroniclers of the period. (Rolleston 1911, 338)

The great period of Welsh poetry came into existence in the twelfth century with the rise of the Court poets (*Gogynfeirdd*). Significantly, its start coincided with the rise of the bardic schools in Ireland, and follows the reign of Gruffyd ap Cynan (King of Gwynedd) whose mother was the daughter of a Norse king of Dublin. Gruffyd had spent his youth in Ireland where, it is believed, he developed a keen interest in the Irish literary and musical tradition. Factual or not, it is nonetheless historically true that from the twelfth century the craft of poetry studied and practiced in North Wales had a more skilled structure than before. It brought about a new era in the growth of Welsh literature.

Yet the myths and legends, which have come down to us in the Welsh language, in many respects are different from those in Gaelic. For one thing, Welsh material lacks the extensiveness of the Gaelic body of writings, and is of a later date. The Welsh tales of the *Mabinogion* are mainly drawn from the fourteenth century manuscript, *The Red Book of Hergest*. One of them, the romance of

Taliesin, came from another source, a manuscript of the seventeenth century. The four oldest tales in the *Mabinogion* may have been written in the tenth or eleventh century while many Irish tales reach back to the seventh or eighth century. (Rolleston 1911, 344)

Prophecy was an artistic literary form in Wales between the twelfth and fifteenth centuries. But it was prophecy born of defeat, foretelling a hero—Arthur, Cadwaladr, Owain—who would rise again to deliver his people. Many of these prophetic poems are attributed to Taliesin or to the legendry Myrddin. (Dillon 2003, 272) Perhaps the most striking poem in the period of the Gogynfeirdd is the famous lament for Llywelyn ap Gruffudd (last of the Welsh princes) by Gruffudd ap yr Ynad Coch. Llywelyn was killed in an attack on the castle of Builth in 1282, and his death put an end to any hope of freedom in Wales.

From the middle of the sixteenth century onwards, the Courtly praise tradition of the poets went into decline. This came about when the monasteries, a major source of patronage for the poets, were dissolved by Henry VIII. It was also a period when Welsh nobility was identifying more with their English rulers and, consequently, there were fewer patrons willing or able to support the poets. Finally, the conservatism of the poetic Welsh style was not yet ready to lend itself to the new world of renaissance learning, or the use of the printing press.

Between 1900 and the First World War, Wales experienced a new awakening in Welsh literature. Welsh scholarship received its first major boost with the publication of two influential histories: *The Welsh People* by **John Rhys** and **Brynmor Jones**, and *Wales* by **Owen Edwards** (1858-1920). These were followed in 1911 by the monumental and inspiring work of **J.E. Lloyd**, *A History of Wales from the Earliest Times to the Edwardian Conquest.* In 1913, the Welsh people were introduced to another important publication, *A Welsh Grammar, Historical and Comparative* by **John Morris-Jones** (1864-1929). An influential poet of the early part of the twentieth century was **R. Williams Parry** (1884-1956) from the quarry region of North Wales. His 1910 Eisteddfod prize-winning poem, "Yr Haf," is a paean to the joys of love and nature. Another prolific author of the period was **Thomas Gwynn Jones** (1871-1949).

After a relatively quiet period between 1950 and 1970, several Welsh language novels were written by such authors of influence as **Aled Islwyn**, **W. Leslie Richards** (1916-1989), and **Marion Eames** (1921-?). Richards wrote several novels and four volumes of verse, as well as editing the works of other Welsh writers. Eames produced four first-class historical novels, two of which deal with Quaker Rowland Ellis who founded the Welsh community in Pennsylvania.

Unlike Ireland, which had a thousand years of uninterrupted interference from foreign intervention before the Viking invasions, Wales had to deal with successive waves of invasions, interaction, and direct rule. Despite all these influences, she retained a strong sense of her national, Celtic identity. The Welsh language has survived, and even flourished in some respects, in the face of intense competition from the pressures of English. So, too, has the National Eisteddfod of Wales, an annual event recreating many Welsh traditions.

As for the Bretons, they were reoriented away from their Celtic kin towards France and Latin civilization. The Gauls, on the other hand, wrote nothing down in the pre-Roman period, and therefore have left behind no works of Celtic literature.

Chapter XVIII—
Conclusion

According to the distinguished historian, Jean Markale, Celtic civilization was paradoxical. It spread its influence from Ireland to Galatia at the same time adhering to regional variations and, furthermore, preserving a remarkable unity of language, religion, and customs. Still, the Celtic realm was fragmented into countless smaller divisions; it was impracticable to talk of a Celtic kingdom, much less an empire. The territories in which the Celts lived had no real frontiers and no central governing body. Present-day political terminology had no place in their impracticable realm, eroded as it was by its own internal contradictions and by the external pressure of other civilizations with their own conceptions of the order of things. The Arthurian epic is a reflection of this paradox.

Arthur appears to live in a unified society. The classic, if artificial, image of the Round Table with its lack of precedence among the seated knights is significant. Replaced in its original context of a gathering round the central hearth in the chieftain's house, the assembly of knights takes on a distinctly symbolic character. It becomes the organization of the universe around the fire, whether it be a real fire, a sacred flame, a cosmic star, or the kind of feminine sun represented by Guinevere, the nucleus and guardian of society. But around this central axis, everything diverges, disperses. The knights leave on their individual adventures and quarrel among themselves. Arthur is not a king, but a convener of kings, a chief above other chiefs, but with no legal authority. His society is composed of members of different clans and nations who join temporarily together. And, because he has no one in residence, his court moves with him around the country, from the North to the Southwest. (Markale 1994, 221-222)

King Arthur's court reflects the same paradox as does Celtic civilization as a whole. It is this paradox which is believed to have dealt the deathblow to Celtic civilization. In reality, Celtic civilization never died; it was only overshadowed by the restrictive occupation of foreign rulers. Gaul may have changed under the Roman occupation, but the Celts of Gaul never became Roman. Britain under the Roman Empire may have enjoyed a new unity of purpose, but once the empire had withdrawn, all Celtic propensities to decentralization surfaced again. Nonetheless, as if to compensate for the apparent lack of national unity, historians write that the Celtic spirit of the Britons reasserted itself more explicitly than ever before. (Markale 1977, 222)

By the end of the first century AD, most Celtic lands southwest of the Rhine-Danube line were under Roman occupation. North of the Danube, the Celtic territories of Bohemia and Moravia remained in the hands of German tribes. In the Great Hungarian Plain and Transylvania, Celtic enclaves had been absorbed either within the land inhabited by the Dacians and Getae, or by the incoming Sarmatian tribes. Only along the extreme northwestern periphery, in Ireland and in north and west Scotland, Celtic-speaking communities continued to exist outside the Roman system. (Cunliffe 1997, 258) Engulfed by Roman civilization, Celtic society nevertheless began a steady decline all over Western Europe. Throughout the Middle Ages, however, while the post-Roman empires of Britain and France were imposing their principles and rule of law on their Celtic subjects, they were inadvertently shaping a new spirit of Celtic revivalism. Enhanced by new advances in research and the sorting out of relevant information, the Celtic past, in all its manifestation, took on a renewed consciousness.

Celtic culture and language have steadfastly prevailed throughout history despite many setbacks. In spite of the setbacks, the Celts never looked back; they fed on the past solely to build the future. They turned their eyes ever outward, above the real, towards the Land of Eternal Youth. Like the cauldron of their mythology, the resurgence of the Celtic spirit in the nineteenth and twentieth centuries originates from the fact the Celts themselves are boundless. Addressing a major Symposium on the Celtic Consciousness in Toronto in 1978, Professor Robert O'Driscoll, used the cauldron metaphor to illustrate the ever-renewing spirit of the Celts:

> "[T]he vessel is a symbol of the inexhaustible resources of the spirit, forever renewing itself, whether it be the hidden spirit that animates all matter, or, in modern psychological terms, an energy in the depths of the mind that, if developed, can free man from dependence on the body and the tyranny of historical fact. On a more literal level, the cauldron seems an appropriate image to represent the fate of the Celts in the Western World. They seemed to have emerged from the east; then, for almost a thousand years, they dominated the center of Europe, stretching from the Black Sea to Iberia and from the Mediterranean to the North Sea and Ireland. Two thousand years later they survive on the western periphery of Europe, having been pushed to the extreme edge of the cauldron."

About the Author

Patrick Lavin is a Celtic history enthusiast who spends his retirement years doing research and writing about the ancient Celts. He has seven published books to his credit, including *The Celtic World: An Illustrated History* and *Celtic Ireland West of the River Shannon*. Originally from County Roscommon, he immigrated to North America in the 1950s, graduated from California State University Northridge, and retired from a career with the United States government—most of which was spent in Washington, D.C. A member of the Society of Southwest Authors, Patrick currently resides with his wife in Tucson, Arizona. Visit his Web site at www.patricklavin.com.

Chronology

The following is a chronology of dates relevant to historical occurrences referred to in this book:

7000 BC	Start of Mesolithic period
4500 BC	Start of Neolithic period
1500 BC	Onset of Early Bronze Age
1200 BC	Beginning of Urnfield cultural stage
900 BC	Etruscans settle in Italy
814 BC	Phoenicians establish Carthage on Tunisian coast
753 BC	Traditional founding date of Rome
700 BC	Beginning of Hallstatt cultural period
600 BC	First Celtic-speaking people arrive in Ireland
600 BC	Founding of Greek trading center at Massilia
500 BC	Celtic military expansion begins
500 BC	Hallstatt cultural phase ends; La Tène era begins
474 BC	Celts defeat Etruscans near Ticino
400 BC	Celtic drive Etruscans from Po Valley
390 BC	Battle of Clusium: Celts sack Rome
387 BC	Celts defeat Roman army at Allia
355 BC	Celts pay visit to Alexander the Great
320 BC	Greek explorer Pytheas visits Pretanic Islands
300 BC	Beginning of Irish La Tène cultural period
279 BC	Celtic incursions into Greece
279 BC	Celts attack the Temple of Delphi
270 BC	Celts settle in Phrygia, thereafter named Galatia
244 BC	Celts are defeated at Macedonia and Pergamon
264 BC	Beginning of First Punic War
225 BC	Romans defeat Celts at Telamon

218 BC	Beginning of Second Punic War
206 BC	Carthaginians driven out of Iberian peninsula
192 BC	Celtic domination of northern Italy ends
150 BC	Posidonius journeys through Celtic lands
121 BC	Romans annex Gallia Narbonensis (southern Gaul)
78 BC	Julius Caesar appointed governor of "Further Spain"
55 BC	Julius Caesar undertakes invasion of Britain
52 BC	Romans conquer Gaul
44 BC	Caesar is assassinated
29 BC	Romans begin reigning in the Celtic tribes of Iberia
AD 47	Romans conquer the Celts of Britain
AD 61	Roman legions destroy druidic sanctuary at Mona
AD 61	Boadicea leads Iceni revolt against the Romans
AD 78	Julius Agricola appointed governor of Britain
AD 117	Emperor Hadrian abandons Caledonia
AD 122	Romans build Hadrian's Wall
AD 313	Emperor Constantine issues Edict of Milan
AD 337	Emperor Constantine dies
AD 432	Pope Celestine sends Saint Patrick to Ireland
AD 436	Romans leave Britain for good
AD 576	Scotti are granted autonomy in Caledonia
AD 563	Saint Columba begins conversion of the Picts
AD 579	Saint Augustine sent to convert the Anglo-Saxons
AD 590	Saint Columban departs for the Continent
AD 664	Council of Whitby convenes
AD 927	A unified Anglo-Saxon England emerges
AD 1014	King Brian Boru defeats Vikings at Clontarf
AD 1169	Anglo-Normans invades Ireland
AD 1284	Wales surrenders her sovereignty to English crown
AD 1603	Scotland surrenders her authority to the English crown
AD 1800	Act of Union unites Ireland and Britain
AD 1922	Ireland becomes the first independent Celtic nation

Bibliography

The following material was consulted in the preparation of this book:

Armstrong, Karen. *A History of God: The 4,000-Year Quest of Judaism, Christianity and Islam*. New York, NY: Ballantine Books, 1993.

Bartlett, Thomas and Jeffery, Keith (editors). *A Military History of Ireland*. Cambridge, UK: Cambridge University Press, 1996.

Beckett, J.C. *The Anglo-Irish Tradition*. London, UK: Faber and Faber, 1976.

Berleth, Richard. *The Twilight Lords: The Fierce, Doomed Struggle of the Last Great Feudal Lords of Ireland Against the England of Elizabeth I*. New York, NY: Barnes & Noble Books, 1978.

Bonwick, James. *Irish Druids and Old Irish Religions*. New York, NY: Barnes & Noble Books, 1986.

Bradley, Ian. *The Celtic Way*. London, UK: Darton, Longman and Todd, 1994.

Bulloch, James. *The Life of the Celtic Church*. Edinburgh, UK: Saint Andrew Press, 1963.

Cahill, Thomas. *How the Irish Saved Civilization*. New York, NY: Nan A. Talese, 1995.

Chadwick, Nora. *The Celts*. London, UK: Penguin Group, 1997.

Clancy, Padraigin (editor). *Celtic Threads*. Dublin, Ireland: Veritas Publications, 1999.

Colum, Padraic. *A Treasury of Irish Folklore*. New York, NY: Kilkenny Press, 1989.

Cotterell, Maurice. *The Celtic Chronicles*. West Cork, Ireland: Celtic Press, 2006.

Cross, Tom Peete and Slover, Clark Harris (editors). *Ancient Irish Tales*. New York, NY: Barnes & Noble Books, 1996.

Cunliffe, Barry. *The Ancient Celts*. New York, NY: Oxford University Press, 1997.

Curtis, E. and McDowell, R. *Irish Historical Documents 1172-1922*. London, UK: Methuen & Co. Ltd., 1943.

Cusack, Mary Frances. *An Illustrated History of Ireland from* AD *400 to 1800*. Guernsey, UK: Guernsey Press, 1995.

D'Alton, John. *King James' Irish Army List: 1689* AD. Kansas City, MO: Irish Genealogical Foundation, 1997.

Dames, Michael. *Mythic Ireland*. New York, NY: Thames & Hudson, 1992.

De Paor, Liam. *The Peoples of Ireland: From Prehistory to Modern Times*. South Bend, IN: University of Notre Dame Press, 1986.

Dillon, Myles and Chadwick, Nora. *The Celtic Realms: The History and the Culture of the Celtic Peoples from Pre-History to the Norman Invasion*. Edison, NJ: Castle Books, 2003.

Edel, Doris. *The Celtic West and Europe*. Portland, OR: Four Courts Press, Ltd., 2001.

Edwards, Ruth D. *An Atlas of Irish History*. New York, NY: Routledge, 1998.

Ellis, Peter Berresford. *Erin's Blood Royal.* New York, NY: Palgrave Publishing, 2002.

Ellis, Peter Berresford. *The Celtic Empire*. New York, NY: Carroll & Graf Publishers, 2001.

Ellis, Peter Berresford. *The Druids*. London, UK: Constable & Robinson, Ltd., 2002.

Eluere, Christiane. *The Celts—Conquerors of Ancient Europe*. New York, NY: Harry N. Abrams, 1993.

Finlay, Ian. *Celtic Art, An Introduction*. London, UK: Noyes Press, 1973.

Fitzgerald, Robert (translator). *The Odyssey Homer*. New York, NY: Anchor Books, Doubleday & Company, Inc., 1963.

Flanagan, Laurence. *Ancient Ireland—Life Before the Celts*. New York, NY: St. Martin's Press, 1998.

Freeman, Martin (editor). *Annala Connachta, 1224-1544*. Dublin, Ireland: Dublin Institute for Advanced Studies, 1996.

Freeman, Philip. *The Philosopher and the Druids*. New York, NY: Simon & Schuster, 2006.

Ginnell, Laurence. *The Brehon Laws*. London, UK: T. Fisher Unwin, 1894.

Green, Miranda J. *Celtic Myth and Legend*. London, UK: Thames & Hudson, 1997.

Green, Miranda J. *Exploring the World of the Druids*. London, UK: Thames & Hudson, 2010.

Gregory, Lady. *Irish Mythology*. London, UK: Chancellor Press, 2000.

Hamilton, Edith. *Mythology*. New York, NY: The New American Library, Inc., 1942.

Harbison, Peter. *Pre-Christian Ireland*. New York, NY: Thames & Hudson, 1988.

Hayes-McCoy, G.A. *Irish Battles*. New York, NY: Barnes & Noble Books, 1969.

Herm, Gerhard. *The Celts*. New York, NY: St. Martin's Press, 1977.

hÓgáin, Dàithi Ó. *The Lore of Ireland*. Cork, Ireland: The Boydell Press, 2006.

Hollister, C. Warren. *The Making of England 55 BC to 1399*. Lexington, MA: D.C. Heath and Company, 1996.

Hubert, Henri. *The Greatness and Decline of the Celts*. New York, NY: Dorset Press, 1988.

James, Francis G. *Ireland and the Empire, 1688-1770*. Cambridge, MA: Harvard University Press, 1973.

James, Simon. *The Atlantic Celts*. London, UK: British Museum Press, 1999.

Jeffares, A. Norman (editor). *Yeats' Poems*. Dublin, Ireland: Gill & Macmillan, 1989.

Jiménez, Ramon. *Caesar Against the Celts*. Edison, NJ: Castle Books, 2001.

Johnson, Paul. *A History of Christianity*. New York, NY: Simon & Schuster, 1995.

Jones, Gwyn. *A History of the Vikings*. New York, NY: Oxford University Press, 1984.

Joyce, P.W. *A Social History of Ancient Ireland*. Kansas City, MO: The Irish Genealogical Foundation, 1997.

Judge, Michael. *The Dance of Time*. New York, NY: Arcade Publishing, 2004.

King, John. *Kingdoms of the Celts*. London, UK: Blandford Publishing, Ltd., 1997.

King, John. *The Celtic Druids' Year*. London, UK: Blandford Publishing, Ltd., 1995.

Laing, Lloyd. *Celtic Britain*. New York, NY: Charles Scribner's Sons, 1979.

Laing, Lloyd and Jennifer. *Celtic Britain and Ireland*. New York, NY: St. Martin's Press, 1995.

Lavin, Patrick. *The Celtic World: An Illustrated History*. New York, NY: Hippocrene Books, Inc., 1999.

Le Goff, Jacques. *Medieval Civilization 400-1500*. New York, NY: Barnes & Noble Books, 2000.

Lehane, Brendan. *Early Celtic Christianity*. London, UK: Continuum International Publishing Group, 1994.

Lucas, A.T. *Treasures of Ireland.* New York, NY: Viking Press, 1973.

Lyndon, James. *Ireland in the Later Middle Ages.* Dublin, Ireland: Gill & Macmillan, 1973.

MacBain, Alexander. *Celtic Mythology and Religion.* Royston, Herts., UK: Oracle Publishing Company, 1996.

MacCulloch, J.A. *The Religion of the Ancient Celts.* New York, NY: Dover Publications, 2003.

Mackworth-Praed, Ben. *The Book of Kells.* London, UK: Random House, 1994.

MacManus, Seamus. *The Story of the Irish Race.* New York, NY: The Devin-Adair Company, 1972.

MacRitchie, David. *Ancient and Modern Britons.* Freeman, SD: Pine Hill Press, Inc., 1991.

Markale, Jean. *King of the Celts.* Rochester, VT: Inner Traditions International, Ltd., 1994.

Markale, Jean. *The Celts.* Rochester, VT: Inner Traditions International, Ltd., 1993.

Matthews, John (editor). *The Celtic Seers' Sourse Book.* London, UK: Blandford Publishing, Ltd., 1999.

McCullough, David W. *Wars of the Irish Kings.* New York, NY: Crown Publishers, 2000.

McDowell, R.B. *Ireland in the Age of Imperialism and Revolution 1760-1801.* New York, NY: Oxford University Press, 1979.

Mongan, Norman. *The Menapia Quest.* Dublin, Ireland: The Herodotus Press, 1995.

Moody and Martin (editors). *The Course of Irish History.* New York, NY: Weybright and Talley, Inc., 1967.

Moorhouse, Geoffrey. *Sun Dancing.* New York, NY: Harcourt Brace & Company, 1997.

Morris, John. *Londinium, London in the Roman Empire.* London, UK: Weidenfeld & Nicolson, 1998.

Nichols, Ross. *The Book of Druidry.* New York, NY: Castle Books, 1990.

O'Cróinín, Dáibhí. *Early Medieval Ireland 400-1200.* New York, NY: Longman Group, Ltd., 1999.

O'Driscoll, Robert (editor). *The Celtic Consciousness.* New York, NY: George Braziller, Inc., 1981.

O'Faolain, Eileen. *Irish Sagas and Folk Tales.* London, UK: Oxford University Press, 1966.

O'Keeffe, Tadhg. *Medieval Ireland.* Charleston, SC: Tempus Publishing, Inc., 2001.

O'Rahilly, Thomas F. *Early Irish History and Mythology.* Dublin, Ireland: Dublin Institute of Advance Studies, 1946.

Otway-Ruthven, A.J. *A History of Medieval Ireland.* New York, NY: Barnes & Noble Books, 1993.

Pennick, Nigel. *Celtic Sacred Landscapes.* New York, NY: Thames & Hudson, 1996.

Powell, T.G.E. *The Celts*. New York, NY: Thames & Hudson, 1989.

Rankin, David. *Celts and the Classical World*. London, UK: Routledge Publishing, 1996.

Rees, Alwyn and Brinley. *Celtic Heritage*. New York, NY: Thames & Hudson, 1995.

Rolleston, T.W. *Myths and Legends of the Celtic Race*. London, UK: Constable and Company, Ltd., 1911.

Rouse, W.H.D. (translator). *Great Dialogues of Plato*. New York, NY: The New American Library, 1956.

Rutherford, Ward. *Celtic Lore*. San Francisco, CA: The Aquarian Press, 1993.

Scherman, Katherine. *The Flowering of Ireland*. Toronto, Canada: Little, Brown and Company, 1981.

Squire, Charles. *Celtic Myths and Legends*. Bath, UK: Parragon Books, 2000.

Tanner, Marcus. *The Last of the Celts*. New Haven, CT: Yale University Press, 2004.

Wacher, John. *Roman Britain*. Stroud, Gloucestershire, UK: Wrens Park Publishing, 1998.

Wallace, Martin. *Famous Irish Writers*. Belfast, Northern Ireland: Appletree Press, Ltd., 1992.

Webster, Richard. *Omens, Oghams & Oracles*. St. Paul, MN: Llewellyn Publications, 1995.

Wells, H.G. *The Outline of History*. London, UK: Cassell & Company, Ltd., 1966.

Wentz, Wyevans. *The Fairy-Faith in Celtic Countries*. Glastonbury, UK: Lost Libraries, 1981.

Index

C

D

E

F

G

H

I

J

K

L

M

Mediterranean 11, 12, 25, 26,	Northumbria 104, 209, 210, 211, 231, 232, 233 Nova Scotia 7 O OBrien, Flann 251 OBrien, Kate 251 OCasey, Sean 251 OConnell, Daniel 248 OConnor, Frank 252 OConnor, Rory 240 OCurry, Eugene 249 ODonovan, John 249 OFaolain, Sean 251 OFlaherty, Liam 252 Ogham 229, 249 Olwen 228, 258 OMulconroy 249 Ordovices 85, 89, 91 Otherworld 161, 162, 164, 165, 176 P
Mesolithic 11, 24, 25, 112, 113,	
Mil 119, 141, 142, 143, 144,	
145, 163	
Minoan 26	
Mongon 161	
Moore, George 252	
Moore, Thomas 249	
Moravia 4, 46, 263	•
Morbihan Bay 73	•
Morini 72	
Morrigan 173, 174, 176	
Morris-Jones, John 260	
Mount Badon 101, 156	
Moytura 143, 158, 168, 171	_ los fire longs of in a
Munster 108, 118, 119, 120,	P
129, 130, 132, 134, 145,	Paris 2, 74
150, 212	Parisi 85
Mycenaean 26	Parry, R. Williams 261
N	P-Celtic 15, 116
N	P-Celts 119
Narbonenis 76	Petrie, Sir Charles 249
Nennius 98, 101, 103, 156, 259	Phoenicians 27, 29, 39, 40, 61,
Neolithic 3, 11, 25, 30, 31, 82,	215
111, 113, 114, 117, 140	Picti 85, 91, 117, 123
Nervii 72, 73, 74	Plato 17, 22
New Zealand 7	Pliny the Elder 179, 182
Niall of the Nine Hostages 92,	Poland 11, 28, 32
108, 130, 133, 135	Posidonius 17, 21, 30, 31, 69,
Noreia 67	137, 179, 180, 182